THE S‾ EY IN
MA‾ ‾ER‾ ‾ AND IDENTI‾ ‾S

Masquerade, both literal and metaphorical, is now a central concept in
many disciplines. This timely volume explores and revisits the role of disguise in constructing, expressing and representing marginalised identities,
and in undermining easy distinctions between 'true' identity and artifice.

The book is interdisciplinary in approach, spanning a diverse range of
cultures and narrative voices. It provides provocative and nuanced ways
of thinking about masquerade as a tool for construction, and a tool for
critique. The essays interrogate such themes as:

- mask and carnival
- fetish fashion
- stigma of illegitimacy
- femininity as masquerade
- lesbian masks
- cross-dressing in Jewish folk theatre
- the mask in seventeenth- and eighteenth-century London
- the mask in nineteenth-century France
- the voice as mask.

Efrat Tseëlon teaches Media and Social Psychology at University
College Dublin.

MASQUERADE AND IDENTITIES

Essays on gender, sexuality and marginality

Edited by Efrat Tseëlon

London and New York

First published 2001
by Routledge
11 New Fetter Lane, London EC4P 4EE

Simultaneously published in the USA and Canada
by Routledge
29 West 35th Street, New York, NY 10001

Routledge is an imprint of the Taylor & Francis Group

© 2001 Efrat Tseëlon

Typeset in Baskerville by
M Rules
Printed and bound in Great Britain by
TJ International Ltd, Padstow, Cornwall

305. 3/TSE

British Library Cataloguing in Publication Data
A catalogue record for this book is available from the British Library

Library of Congress Cataloging in Publication Data
Tseëlon, Efrat.
Masquerade and identities: essays on gender, sexuality, and
marginality/Efrat Tseëlon.
p. cm.
Includes bibliographical references and index.
1. Masks–Symbolic aspects. 2. Masks–Psychological aspects.
3. Masquerades. 4. Disguises. 5. Sex role. 6. Marginality, Social. I. Title.
GN419.5 .T74 2001
306.4–dc21
00-065309
ISBN 0 415 25106 0 (pbk)
ISBN 0 415 25105 2 (hbk)

336289

To Søren,
in memory of Venezia

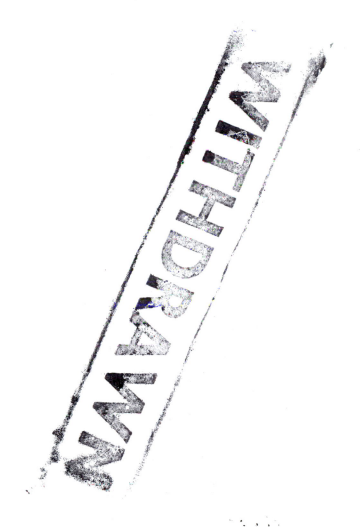

CONTENTS

CONTENTS

PLATES

CONTRIBUTORS

Ahuva Belkin is Professor of Theatre and Art History, at the Department of Theatre Studies at Tel Aviv University. She has published extensively on the history of the theatre and art, recently specialising in Jewish theatre. Her recent publications include an edited collection on Leone de Sommi and the Performing arts and *Between Two Cities – the Hebrew Play Simchat Purim*. Her next book, *The Jewish Folk Theatre: The Purimspiel* is forthcoming.

Halla Beloff is a social psychologist who taught at Edinburgh University for many years and is now Visiting Professor in Photographic Culture at the University of Derby. Her publications include the book *Camera Culture* and writings on Julia Margaret Cameron, Cindy Sherman and Rembrandt's self-portraits. She is currently studying the visual and social context of Virginia Woolf's portrait photographs.

Christie Davies got his Doctorate in Social and Political Sciences from Cambridge University and is Professor of Sociology at the University of Reading. He is the author of *Jokes and their Relation to Society* and *The Mirth of Nations* (in press). He is currently preparing a new book about bastards. He has also published extensively about deviance and the ideas of Erving Goffman. He has been a visiting lecturer in India, Poland and the United States and his work has been translated into Bulgarian, German, Hebrew, Italian, Polish and Japanese.

Christoph Heyl is a lecturer in the Department of English Studies at Johann Wolfgang Goethe-Universität, Frankfurt. His main fields of research are the social/cultural history and literature of seventeenth- and eighteenth-century England. He has written a comprehensive study of privacy in eighteenth-century London (*A Passion for Privacy*, forthcoming) and is now working on the history of early modern collections and related phenomena.

Ann Ilan-Alter is a cultural historian with a Ph.D. in European and French Cultural History from Rutgers University. She has taught at Sarah Lawrence College, Rutgers University, New York University and Adelphi University. Currently she teaches in the Bard College Clemente Program in New York City and works as the Director of Grants for Pamphlet Architecture, Ltd./Princeton Architectural Press. She has organised exhibitions, including one at the New York Public Library, 'Censorship: 500 years of' (1984). She has also lectured and written about masked balls and other popular entertainments in nineteenth-century Paris. Her chapter in this volume is part of a longer work on the masked balls at the Paris Opera between 1830 and 1852.

Wendy Leeks is Associate Dean at the Faculty of Media, Arts & Society at Southampton Institute. She has published articles on Ingres and French art, and on psychoanalysis and queer theory. Her special interest is in psychoanalytic approaches to spectatorship.

Saskia Maas studied Language and Culture at the University of Tilburg. Her focus was on film and after her studies she published articles related to Film and Gender Studies. She is currently working in theatre as the business director of a theatre company in Amsterdam.

Valerie Steele is acting director of the Museum at the Fashion Institute of Technology and editor of *Fashion Theory: The Journal of Dress, Body & Culture*. She received her Ph.D. from Yale University, and is the author of nine books, including *Fetish: Fashion, Sex and Power*, and *Paris Fashion: A Cultural History*.

Efrat Tseëlon teaches Media and Social Psychology at University College Dublin. Since receiving her Ph.D. in Social Psychology from the University of Oxford she has engaged in transdisciplinary pursuits with a cultural, reflexive agenda. She has published widely in her areas of research: identity, difference and personal appearance. Her book, *The Masque of Femininity*, explores the social construction of Western woman through fashion, beauty, body and personal appearance.

Alkeline van Lenning is Assistant Professor in the Department of Gender Studies, Faculty of Social Sciences in Tilburg, The Netherlands. She writes especially on gender and the body.

FOREWORD

Susan B. Kaiser

By what seemed to be an amazing coincidence, as I was beginning to work on this foreword I happened to hear that Oprah Winfrey's show that day dealt with the theme of 'taking it off' or 'shedding your disguise'. In this show, a series of individuals described as hiding who they really are behind their 'masks' or 'disguises' parade through the show and are persuaded to 'help themselves by simplifying their looks':

> A man who has been 'working the strip' of remaining hair on his head, trying to disguise his baldness, loses the strip; the audience cheers his baldness.

> A woman in the audience reveals that she has been stuffing her bra with toilet paper; as she strategically removes it, Oprah cheers 'Free at last!' And, 'We have some bras for you – just your size.'

Oprah describes how it is 'time to liberate these brave women' who have been 'hiding' behind their very long (waist-length) hair. When these women return later with new, professional 'bobs' and suits with turtleneck sweaters, the audience applauds and family members cry. The women are now described as 'beautiful, and so modern!' Their former hairstyles are characterized as 'security blankets'.

> A man with a ponytail gets it clipped off.

> Mothers who have been 'hiding behind' their sweats during the day at home are 'made over' with the latest loungewear styles.

> Oprah herself is wearing designer silk pajamas and laughs at how she 'used to wear suits every day'.

Perhaps the overriding, unstated assumption underlying the show is that the 'simplified truths' about personal identity can be revealed if masks are removed. These masks, as it turns out, happen to be outdated, working-class or related to 'insecure' self-feelings about attractiveness and sexuality. The 'real me' makeovers transform the individuals into looks that are more refined, contemporary and middle class. The show is a potent reminder of how immersed Western culture (or mainstream US society, at least) is in a modernist appearance–reality binary. Although the show deals with everyday masks, there is a certain carnivalesque quality to the initial self-presentations. They appear to hold a simultaneous attraction and repulsion for the audience. As Efrat Tseëlon points out in this volume, the carnivalesque characterizes what is 'abjected from the bourgeois social order'. In Oprah's 'take it off' show, the 'before' or 'masked' images become the carnivalesque, the otherness abjected from the bourgeois social order. The made over, 'after' or 'true, liberated' images serve to reinforce the dominance of that order.

Reading *Masquerade and Identities* has provided me with a theoretical lens, not only for interpreting an Oprah Winfrey show but also for thinking more critically about masks in relation to modern discourses of difference and fantasies about identity. As this volume reveals, a mask is not just a cover or a disguise; it can reveal a moment of reflexivity about the otherness within and beyond ourselves.

Tseëlon describes the goal of *Masquerade and Identities* 'as an attempt to rethink masquerade as an analytical and critical category'. It clearly fulfills this goal in a way that fills a void in fields ranging from cultural studies to gender studies, fashion studies, history, dramatic art and social psychology. Tseëlon and her colleagues offer a fresh, thought-provoking perspective on masquerade as an epistemology for interrogating identity and power.

What does it mean when we cannot easily classify appearances? How has masquerade historically challenged the everyday, bourgeois isolation imposed by the public–private binary opposition? How does dressing, or not dressing, the part belie gender hierarchies? How have masks been used historically to transgress or to reinforce gender and class boundaries? In what ways have they been used to release social tension? Can 'passing' enable a deeper understanding of self–other relations? What is the relationship between masquerade and personal, sexualized identities? Do masks provide a sense of freedom in, and consciousness about, self-representation? Can they be used to enhance self-reflexivity?

Masquerade and Identities explores these and other questions in a way that opens theoretical discourse, raising new questions and suggesting new approaches for interdisciplinary inquiry on the relationship between identity and culture.

Collectively the contributions to this volume, combined with the conceptual framework offered by Tseëlon, move toward more provocative and nuanced ways of thinking about masking and masquerade. This volume reveals how one cannot think simply from a 'real me'. Nor is masking just about gender, sexuality, class, race or religion. Rather, it explores the boundaries and intersections among these identities; the process of masking belies that there is no single or no 'true' master status in identity. Masking enables the interrogation of identities, partial identities, potential identities and non-identities. It can be used to establish a sense of modern order, while simultaneously disintegrating such order. It provides a means for both delineating self from other and interrogating the other within the self.

Masquerade and Identities reveals how experimentation with difference has been undermined by the modern conflation between mask and disguise. The concept of disguise suggests the essentialness of identity, whereas a more critical analysis of masking reveals attempts to undermine such essentialness by wearing otherness on our bodies. Masquerade challenges the hegemonic containment of others and unpicks the concept of authentic identity by suggesting the possibility of becoming, rather than merely delineating, the other.

Returning to the Oprah show, there are intriguing parallels between the carnivalesque and the masks we wear every day. Who decides, particularly in the latter context, what is a mask? And who uses masks to release social tensions associated with everyday life? Why and how does this occur? In the context of the Oprah show on masking, the everyday becomes carnivalesque as the participants become the objects of the audience's gaze. And there is an intriguing connection among temporality, bourgeois order and perceptions of masks. Looks perceived as disruptive of contemporary bourgeois order are constructed as masks in the context of the show. But which is the mask: the 'before' or the 'after' (more contemporary, bourgeois) image?

Masquerade and Identities reveals the arbitrariness of such binary ordering. Yet it does much more. It moves the theoretical discourse on masking forward in such a way that enables a more complex understanding of the dynamic interplay among masking, identity, difference and the very processes of constructing and deconstructing order, if not power itself.

PREFACE

It starts as all good stories begin: Once upon a time . . . by chance I saw a travel column with details of that year's carnival in Venice. The Venetian carnival, which up to that point existed in the realm of fantasy in my mind, was about to become a reality. When I descended on this breathtaking spectacle – whose exquisite masks and ornate costumes are framed against the backdrop of Venice's canals, bridges, palaces and narrow alleyways – I felt a sense of homecoming. I have been fascinated by masks and marionettes as far back as I can remember. Their dual quality of real and fantastic, doll-like and human, familiar and other, dynamic and static (as well as their sheer artistic beauty) were leitmotivs in my life. And so enchanting was the carnival experience that I was to come back twice to lead two groups of masking enthusiasts through the corridors of my dream.

Highlights from those experiences woven into another narrative cloth featuring marginalised identities are presented in this volume. The themes of otherness and difference hovered above the collection from its inception. In an uncanny repetition of the substance of the papers, and the staple experiences of those who are hard to categorise, the trajectory of the collection resonated with my other life experiences. It echoed the struggles to get heard and get acknowledged in a world accustomed to seeing only what lies within conventional boundaries.

And so it was as in many a folktale, after the heroes jumped through hoops and over hurdles, and overcame the proverbial monsters and dragons, they found refuge in the receptive comfort of the editors who believed in their project. And they all lived happily ever after. For a while.

ACKNOWLEDGEMENTS

I would like to acknowledge the helpful editorial comments and suggestions of Susan Kaiser from the University of California at Davis, Richard Harvey Brown from the University of Maryland, Ian Burkitt from the University of Bradford, Ronit Lentin from Trinity College Dublin, and Smadar Tirosh from *Mishkafaim: The Israel Museum Art Quarterly*. I would particularly like to thank Wendy Leeks from Southampton Institute, whose keen eye and editorial gifts provided us with an invaluable resource.

A special acknowledgement is due to all the participants in the conferences *Mask, Masquerade and carnival* (Venice 1994) and *Masquerade and Gendered Identities* (Venice 1996) for their enthusiasm and inspiration. With fond memories I also thank our Italian colleagues who provided the enchanted setting for these very special conferences. Dr Grazia Casolo Contarini from *Venezia Congressi* arranged an excellent choice of excursions and restaurants. These allowed us to absorb the ambiance, savour the views and indulge in the flavours of 'the real Venezia' and the surrounding islands. Daniela Vedaldi and Giuseppe Ursotti of the world-famous eighteenth-century Café Florian on the Piazza San Marco hosted our welcome receptions with elegance and refined quality. Finally, across the Piazza in Hotel Bel Sito & Berlino at Santa Maria del Giglio GR. UFF. Luigi Gino Serafini and his staff so willingly accommodated the conference and generously made available to us their 'hall of mirrors' for our exclusive use. This proved a suitably reflective environment for our purely reflexive pursuits.

Both conferences benefited from the reliable backing of the faculty of Cultural and Education Studies at Leeds Metropolitan University, for which I am grateful.

Last, but not least, I want to extend a very special gratitude to Caroline Wintersgill, then at UCL Press (now at Cassell), and to Talia Rodgers and

Rosie Waters, both from Routledge, who could tell a gem from lookalike stones. Without their vision, encouragement and support this collection would not have seen the light of day.

INTRODUCTION*
Masquerade and identities

Efrat Tseëlon

At the beginning of Pedro Almodóvar's film *High Heels* (1991), Manuel is murdered. Rebecca (his wife) and her singer mother Becky (his ex-lover) are both among the murder suspects. In a characteristic Almodóvarian move, Judge Dominguez who conducts the investigation is gradually revealed to embody several incompatible, astereotypical masquerades all at once. He is Letal – the drag artist (who impersonates Becky in a night club, and courts Rebecca); he is also Hugo – the drug dealer (who befriends women and abandons them). Both of these roles he assumes as part of his undercover operations. He is a maternal kind of a police investigator (uncharacteristically sensitive and compassionate) who impersonates (qua Letal) an unmaternal 'driven' kind of mother; an effeminate drag artist as well as a womanising drug dealer; and a representative of law and order alongside its deviant (drug dealer) and marginalised (drag artist) Others. Even as a private person Eduardo (Dominguez) cuts an ambiguous figure. He allows the viewer neither the comfort of a stable viewing position nor the closure of knowing who 'the real' persona is. In his own home (which he shares with his mother) he still wears a false beard. And when he proposes to Rebecca she asks, confused, which of the personae is asking her to marry him: Letal, Hugo or the Judge – to which he answers 'all three of them' (2001a, 2001b).

This film, in a manner somewhat reminiscent of that discussed by van Lenning, Maas and Leeks (this volume), more than others in the genre of cross-dressing films surveyed by Garber (1992), touches on two themes at the core of masquerade. These themes are ambiguity and the status of masquerade as a challenge to categories of identity. In his classic *Masks, Transformation, and Paradox* (1986) Napier argues that masks share an ability

---

* An earlier version of sections of this paper has been delivered as keynote address on April 10, 1999 in Cheltenham at an interdisciplinary forum – *Anatomy, Identity, Hegemony* – on power, resistance and representations of the body.

1

to address ambiguities and to articulate the paradoxes of appearance. 'Masks' he says,

> testify to an awareness of the ambiguities of appearance and to a tendency toward paradox characteristic of transitional states. They provide a medium for exploring formal boundaries and a means of investigating the problems that appearances pose in the experience of change.
>
> (*ibid.*, p. xxiii)

Referring to a cross-dressing type of masquerade in her *Vested Interests: Cross-dressing and Cultural Anxiety*, Garber notes that it constitutes 'a challenge to easy notions of binarity, putting into question the categories of "female" and "male" whether they are considered essential or constructed, biological or cultural' (1992, p. 10).

There is a wider issue beyond gender categories that is addressed by cross-dressing, indeed any masquerade or the carnivalesque (Bakhtin, 1965). This is the issue of problematising categories of essential identity in general, not just gender identity. Masking is the tool for deconstructing those categories of identity. The Oxford English Dictionary makes fine distinctions between mask, disguise and masquerade in terms of totality and intention. It refers to masking as concealing in the sense of 'protecting, hiding from view'. It defines disguise as concealing in the sense of 'misrepresenting' (employing false elements), and masquerade as 'assuming false appearance'. Attempting to distil some distinguishing features from a range of anthropological, historical, literary and feminist literature that address masking, I could suggest that while the mask represents (it can be symbolic, minimal, token or elaborate), disguise is meant to hide, conceal, pass as something one is not. Masquerade, however, is a statement about the wearer. It is pleasurable, excessive, sometime subversive. The mask is partial covering; disguise is full covering; masquerade is deliberate covering. The mask hints; disguise erases from view; masquerade overstates. The mask is an accessory; disguise is a portrait; masquerade is a caricature. But these distinctions are tenuous, as each also shares the attributes of the other, at least in some uses or historical contexts. Indeed, even in the dictionary definitions, the word 'disguise' appears in all three. For that reason, within the framework of this collection the terms are used interchangeably. We eschew engagement in unhelpful semantic distinctions between mask, masquerade and disguise which collapse upon detailed examination. Instead, the book dwells on the dynamic similarities between mask, masquerade and disguise.

Thus, whatever shade of meaning of masquerade one chooses to employ, it is obvious that through a dialectic of concealing and revealing masquerade serves a critical function. It calls attention to such fundamental issues as the nature of identity, the truth of identity, the stability of identity categories and the relationship between the supposed identity and its outward manifestations (or essence and appearance).

The notion of identity I am using here is of an organising structure around which notions of 'self' (as a legal, moral and motivational category) and 'other' are constructed. Embedded as it is in contemporary theoretical and political debates, it is, to use Woodward's (1997) definition, a way of understanding the interplay between our subjective experience and the cultural historical settings in which it is formed. The notion of identity alerts us to the inevitability of difference. It provides the basis for understanding what holds us together, but also what sets us apart. It also highlights the intimate connection between inclusion and exclusion.

The preoccupation with masquerade and identity is informed, in part, by wider cross-cultural insights. But at its core it remains, particularly in this volume, rooted in a European context (cf., Mauss, 1979). In what follows I would like to sketch the route from essentialist approaches to identity which are based on the cultivation of fictive differences, to masquerade. Masquerade unsettles and disrupts the fantasy of coherent, unitary, stable, mutually exclusive divisions. It replaces clarity with ambiguity, certainty with reflexivity, and phantasmic constructions of containment and closure with constructions that in reality are more messy, diverse, impure and imperfect. The masquerade, in short, provides a paradigmatic challenge not only to dualistic differences between essence and appearance. It also challenges the whole discourse of difference that emerged with modernity.

But before I turn to the story of 'from identity to masquerade' I would like to clarify some issues regarding the format of the contributions. The volume is not intended to provide a comprehensive and exhaustive account of either the issues of masquerade or, indeed, of any of the theories that are invoked along the route. Rather, it aims to signpost relevant landmarks en route to highlighting a specific facet, making an argument or offering reflective observations.

Some reviewers of this collection expressed expectations of homogeneity of presentation of the 'normative academic prose writing' kind. The model of prose underlying such expectations is a 'textbook style' of a narrative flow (logical, rational, methodical). It also involves a linear progression of a systematic exposition from a definition of concepts, through a particular style of explicating 'canonical' theoretical positions (such as Goffman's or Foucault's), to well-defined conclusions. Those reviewers' reactions touch the core of the very enterprise that this collection is about. The collection introduces issues of masquerade as identity construction and as identity critique through a range of styles and narrative forms. All contributors (some of whom are not native English speakers) mask their original voice with an English performance that is currently an integral part of an accomplished academic identity. While some others adhere more closely to the masquerade of 'proper academic style', others masquerade in unorthodox forms of presentation, offering more idiosyncratic, associative, reflective, implicit voices. Coming from ten disciplines and five cultures, some use expansive and others dense style, some expositions are skin-tight and others are more loose; finally, some narratives are open-ended, while others lead towards a clear closure.

Identity and masks: a brief history

Already its earliest sources in Western civilisation mark the mask as closely connected to the notion of the person. In the classical theatrical tradition of Greek and Rome the mask was used as identification of character, not as a deception or disguise. Indeed, mask in the ancient world should be taken at face value (Jenkins, 1994). The Roman 'person' was a legal entity: masks and names conferred individual rights to rites and privileges. The Stoics added a moral dimension (obligations) to the judicial category of the person (rights). The idea of the individual as a locus of personal accountability and moral obligation has always been of the very essence of Judaism (Johnson, 1987). But it was Protestant Christianity which made the soul, as divorced from social and bodily life, a metaphysical category (Hollis, 1985).

At the beginning of the Middle Ages Augustine (who is credited with introducing the Christian notion of the person) posed theatre and its personae as antithetical to true identity. From medieval times onwards, the mask acquired evil and sinister connotations. It has come to connote disingenuity, artifice and pretence in contrast to original identity, which connotes truth and authenticity (Napier, 1986).

Thus, the philosophy of the mask represents two approaches to identity. One assumes the existence of an authentic self. This approach views the mask – real or metaphoric – as covering, on certain occasions, and even deceiving by pretending to be the real self. The other approach maintains that every manifestation is authentic, that the mask reveals the multiplicity of our identity. The fundamental questions are: Is there an

4

essence to cover? Is a mask a real or an ideal self? Does it hide or liberate the real self?

This dualistic model of personhood is evident in a long tradition of importation of dramatic vocabulary into social life. Human life as a puppet show staged by the gods was an image voiced by Plato in the Laws, Petronius in Satyricon, and later by Shakespeare and Balzac. In that theatre of life people who engage in situation-appropriate behaviour are playing 'roles' or wearing masks. For Nietzsche roles are masks expressing the duality of private agency and social control. Thus, the distinction between self and role is not between a deeper truth and a surface appearance but between two masks, two ways of speaking, two modalities (Kaplan and Weiglus, 1979). But it was Goffman's dramaturgy that ruled out a simplistic one-to-one correspondence between actors in the dramatic theatre and the theatre of life. In *The Presentation of Self in Everyday Life* (1959) Goffman proposes a detailed analysis of social life as some form of performance on stage. However, as I have argued elsewhere (Tseëlon, 1992, 1995), Goffman's actor is not a manipulative 'impression manager': he or she plays on different stages, none more 'real' than the other.

The paradox of the masquerade appears to be that it presents truth in the shape of deception. Like a neurotic symptom it reveals in the process of concealing.

'Discourse of difference' and the fantasy of coherent identity

As we have seen, the view of the mask as antithesis to the authentic person is a phenomenon of the Middle Ages. However, concern with difference as a basis for personhood (or identity) is a quintessentially modern preoccupation. According to Bauman (1990, 1991, 1998) loose, anecdotal and trivial stereotyping of strangers and equanimity towards difference were features of the ancient world. During the Enlightenment typologies developed that produced categories of essence. Modernity's obsession with order and ordering, epitomised by the nation-state, created a myth of cultural homogeneity. This was achieved by suppressing all that was defined as Other. The Other is that which cannot be classified, the residue of a normative taxonomy. Its existence poses both a constant threat and a necessary corollary to the classification system itself. Thus, the nation-state became a source of identity that was intertwined with exclusion. By setting boundaries around the self one is also defining the non-self (insiders/outsiders, established/strangers). It is the Other (or the stranger) and not the enemy who is the real problem for the nation-state. The enemy is

5

clearly marked and external to the system, whereas the Other is the enemy within. Often lacking an observable sign of difference, the Other becomes a source of ambiguity, hence a threat. Sander Gilman, for example, documented a vocabulary of differences developed to represent a whole range of such others (the Jew, the gay, the mentally ill) in Western texts (e.g. 1986, 1991).

Masks, says Eliade (1990) are a means of dealing with otherness. Indeed, they represent not simply the quintessential Other but also its inversion and the possibility of transcending it. The mask shares some basic troubling features with the stranger in modernity: both defy order, introduce ambiguity and suggest lack of commitment and the questionability of belonging and not belonging. In the ancient world or in tribal societies, the mask had a fixed role – transformative, protective, empowering; its modern and postmodern usages are multiple and shifting, metaphorical and real, expressing danger and relief. To place oneself as Other or as masked is already to position oneself in a resistive position, whereby difference is threatening to (the logical explanations, habitual practices and unquestioned assumptions of) the established order and its defined categories.

That ambiguity was threatening to modernity is evident in the work of natural scientists of the eighteenth century. Their taxonomies and typologies of differences between peoples, animals and plants privileged the physical and observable as the bases for their classifications. Grounding claims to authoritative knowledge in biology was to become a persistent trend. Historian Nancy Stephan (1982) maintains that this shift brought about a change from an emphasis on fundamental physical and moral homogeneity to an emphasis on essential differences. Thus, around 1800 the pre-Enlightenment model of male and female bodies as hierarchically ordered versions of one sex gave way to a picture of distinct sexes (Laqueur, 1990). Yet there was no scientific development to justify this shift – quite the contrary. Advances in developmental anatomy in the nineteenth century pointed to the common origins of the sexes in a morphologically androgynous embryo, not to intrinsic differences. 'At stake,' Laqueur says, 'are not biological questions about the effects of organs or hormones but cultural political questions regarding the nature of woman' (*ibid.*, p. 22).

Foucault has shown that categories of sexuality were similarly constructed. In *The History of Sexuality* (1980) he took issue with the conception of sexuality as a singular and all-important human attribute, involving members of one sex being oriented towards members of the opposite sex as their object. This conception, he argued, is the product of a process of policing desire that dates back to the seventeenth century.

The practice of manufacturing a fantasy of difference (corporeal, moral, spiritual) where no secure measurable or visible distinguishing difference exists in practice was not limited to sex and sexuality. The idea of race, for example, which emerged in the nineteenth century to ground ethnic differences in biology was initially invoked, as Kenan Malik (1996) reminds us, to explain essential class differences within European society. It reflected a backlash against Enlightenment ideas of equality and progress, and signalled the elite's fear of social changes which that same elite had previously welcomed.

The discourses of science and empiricism were mobilised to legitimise all these presumed categorical differences (which were, in fact, differences of social power) along biological lines and ground them in the body. A major ideological tool in this process was the idea of degeneration. It involved a notion of 'natural' predisposition to certain traits, weaknesses, flaws or kinds of disease, attributed to various categories of social otherness. In Victorian social evolutionism this notion was applied to the lower classes, women and blacks; in the racial theories of the Third Reich to Jews, gypsies, the mentally ill and homosexuals. In the psychiatric literature and practices of the early twentieth century it was applied to various behaviours labelled as sexual perversions, several involving clothing obsessions and rituals (such as fetishism and transvestism). These were coded as signs of male degeneracy, homosexuality and criminality (Matlock, 1993).

Alternatives to an essentialist epistemology and a dualistic model of personhood

The cracks in the wall of supposedly solid categories is manifested, for example, in the history of deviance in both popular and high culture. In *The Politics and Poetics of Transgression* (1986) Stallybrass and White observed that this history is a reworking of 'scientific' categories of difference that overlie fantasies of difference. Stallybrass and White located the source of these fantasies in the repression and exclusion of the carnivalesque by Europe's middle classes in the modern period. The abjection of those forbidden carnivalesque contents is what consolidated the cultural identity of the bourgeoisie. The carnivalesque represented all that was abjected from the bourgeois social order: the lower strata of body (the grotesque body), of society (the poor and prostitutes), of culture (the vulgar and contaminated) and of matter (sewage, refuse, dirt). In the course of the 'civilising process' (as elaborated by Elias (1978, 1982)) from the Renaissance onwards legislative effort was invested in ridding European life of the rowdy spirit and transgressive potential of carnival and popular festivity. Its feasting, drinking, violence and spectacles (such as processions and fairs) were marginalised and subjected to surveillance and social control. Yet the carnivalesque was not entirely eliminated from European cultural life. It was displaced into such areas of bourgeois discourse as art and psychoanalysis (in the form of the unconscious). To use the terms of the discourse of psychoanalysis itself, the repressed carnivalesque has returned in the ambivalent mixture of attraction and repulsion exhibited towards the objects and subjects of these cultural forms. What has been expelled as other returns as the object of horror and fascination, nostalgia and longing (cf., Tseëlon, 1998).

Further challenges to the essentialist thesis (the notion of originary identity categories) – have been meted out by many feminist, psychoanalytic, post-colonial and queer interrogations. These have exposed the idea of a unitary representation superimposed over fragmented identity as a fiction, a fabrication whose construction compels belief in its necessity and 'naturalness'. 'An experience of wholeness and coherence', contends Ewing is actually 'a semiotic process that highlights and organizes certain fragments of experiences' (1990, p. 263). A recent wave of deconstruction of narratives of national identity sparked by Andersen's notion of 'imagined communities' amply demonstrates that an image, especially a coherent, neat and unidimensional one, is always erected on the ruins of more complex ones – at the cost of displacing, repressing, excluding dissenting voices. Along similar lines, 'depth models' of subjectivity (contrasting essence with appearance) have been demystified by 'surface models', such as the discursive and the performative. The surface models share a preoccupation with social aspects of phenomenon 'that are there for all to see' not buried in some psychic or intentional depth. Language or performance become the objects of investigation in their own right, not as signifiers of some underlying structure.

Language

The first surface model, the discursive Wittgensteinian thesis elaborated by Billig (1997), Edwards and Potter (1992), Harré and Stearns (1995) and Potter (1996) among others argues that social and psychic parameters (from emotions and cognitions to notions of self and identity) do not represent 'real' structures deep inside us. These 'structures' are produced through discourse. The second surface model, the semiotic thesis, is manifest, for example, in Barthes' idea that we are most blind in the face of the obvious (1979). It is also fundamental to Lacan's (1992) 'object' of desire which masks not a more substantial order of things but emptiness or void: a fantasy construction. Felman (1987) describes his rejection of the traditional psychoanalytic search for hidden meanings as a shift from

analysing the signified to an analysis of the signifier. Žižek puts it suc-
cinctly in *The Plague of Fantasies* (1997) when he talks about the
relationship between apparently innocent pure utility (e.g. functional,
material objects revealed, for example, in architectural design) and ideology:

> external materiality reveals inherent antagonisms which the
> explicit formulation of ideology cannot afford to acknowl-
> edge . . . As Pascal put it, if you do not believe, kneel down, act
> as if you believe, and belief will come by itself . . . This 'purely
> material sincerity' of the external ideological ritual, not the
> depth of the subject's inner convictions and desires, is the true
> locus of the fantasy which sustains an ideological edifice.
>
> (*ibid.*, p. 4,6)

Performance

The performative thesis originates in the work of Austin (see, for example,
1962), who regarded certain utterances, or speech acts, not as merely
descriptive statements of fact but as expressions which constitute an act.
Victor Turner introduced the notion of the performative to refer to a feature of ritual. Ritual, he contended, is essentially a performance, an
enactment, and not rules or rubrics; hence, 'living ritual may be better
likened to artwork than neurosis' (1982, p. 81). He emphasised the proces-
sual sense of performance over the more mechanistic structuralist
implication of 'manifesting form', and stated: 'Even if a rubrical book
exists prescribing the order and character of the performance of the rites,
this should be seen as a source of channelings rather than of dictates' (*ibid.*,
p. 80). The relationship between the performance and subjectivity has been
elaborated by Butler (1990a, 1990b), who proposed that identity is constituted in time through what she terms 'corporeal styles' consisting of
repeated and rehearsed sedimented public acts (bodily gestures, movements, enactments).

The mask shares elements with these models: like the discursive it is
ambivalent and contextual, and like the performative it signals transformation not fixity.

From performance to masking

Masking is an extension of the notion of a performance. Like performance it evokes an idea of an authentic identity ('behind the mask' or

'behind the performance') only to dismantle the illusion of such identity. It is often used in the Bakhtinian carnivalesque sense of a possibility of being something other than what one is; as a dissimulation of authentic identities or a disarray of accepted roles.

The link between performance, subjectivity and masking was nicely captured in a recent exhibition at the National Portrait Gallery in London (*Performances*, 5 March–23 May 1999). Performing artists were asked to select and enact a 'signature' in the form of a piece of text. These choices were then photographed and completed with computer-generated imagery by David Buckland, an artist photographer and theatre designer. 'Do they have the perceptiveness of portraits', asks Buckland, 'or are they "performances": simply photographs of actors in role?' (Rose Aidin, 'Caught in the act', *The Sunday Times*, 21 February 1999).

Anthony Minghella (director of *The English Patient* and *Truly, Madly, Deeply*) reflected:

> These pictures are not portraits in the conventional sense. Each photograph is a narrative. They are story photographs. With bits of clues scattered around the edges, the viewer is encouraged to deconstruct the image . . . Contrary to the unadorned and neutral representational aura that they seem to possess, they are actually highly worked long after the performer has left the studio. Nevertheless, by our choices you will know us. Most of us hide in photographs, avoid surrender . . . Ironically, the use of costumes and disguises, or role-playing, has acted in these pictures in the same way as they can for an actor . . . by being . . . absolutely revealing.
>
> (in *ibid.*)

Indeed, the performative model obliterates the distance between the 'person' and the 'act'. The act becomes part of the stylistic device that produces the substance: performance is identity.

The most notable attempt in contemporary cultural debates to relate notions of masking to identity comes from psychoanalytic and feminist elaborations of masquerade in the context of gender subjectivity. In this context masquerade is viewed as a feminine strategy of disarmament. Riviere introduced it first in 1929 in her analysis of the behaviour of some professional women who flash their femininity as a disarming signal that their power is just a charade. Thus, she suggested, femininity is assumed, like masquerade, to deflect attention from the woman's desire for power through its opposite: constructing a very feminine, non-threatening image of herself – a fetish of the castrated woman.

For Riviere the display of femininity hides an unconscious masculinity. Through her masculine success, the masquerading woman appears to be in possession of the phallus. In order to ward off expected masculine anxiety, she is renouncing the wish to appropriate masculinity through active reversal: a display of receptivity and passivity. Her mask of womanliness is a representation of her subjection to the male order (Heath, 1989, pp. 48–9). As Fletcher (1988) correctly noted, Riviere's notion of femininity is 'not the Lacanian conception of a lack or a non-identity. Behind Riviere's mask there is always something else' (p. 55). For Lacan the display of femininity, like any 'object' of desire, is masking a lack, pretending to hide what is in fact not there.

> Paradoxical as this formulation might seem, I would say that it is in order to be the phallus, that is to say that the desire of the other, that the woman will reject an essential part of her femininity, notably all its attributes through masquerade. It is for what she is not that she expects to be desired as well as loved.
>
> (Lacan, 1982, p. 84)

But the psychoanalytic notion of masquerade of femininity is limited. Modleski (1989) pointed out that it is limiting because it is deployed for a critique of gender in a generic way that disavows difference. For de Lauretis (1986) masquerade is preferable to mask. She sees the latter as constraining the expression of one's identity, and the former as giving some pleasure to the wearer, even when required.

In contrast, the conception of masking underlying this volume reveals a broader and more paradigmatic notion of disguise. It encompasses both suggestive and substantive forms of disguise, both conscious and unconscious masking, as well as literal and metaphorical forms of covering. Fundamentally dialectical, masking is used here as both a 'technology of identity' and as means of interrogating it; the tool for self-definition and deconstruction. As a means of self-definition, it constructs, represents, conceals, reveals, protests, protects, highlights, transforms, defends, gives licence to, empowers, suppresses and liberates. It provides a hiding place for the enactment of desired scripts, dreamed of scripts, feared scripts, forbidden scripts. It provides different stages to enact other possibilities – those that escape the narrow, rigidly defined roles we conventionally inhabit. As a means of deconstruction, the mask is a moment of reflexivity. It is the quintessential postmodern device for destabilising categories, questioning, defying overdetermined images, problematising certainties, subverting established meanings, exposing the seams of crafted facades and the rules of narrative, the practices of ritual, the mechanics of the act, the stylised elements of the performance.

In terms of substance, the essays collected here sample ways of exploring the role of disguise in constructing, expressing or representing marginalised identities; identities of otherness. They make no assumption about the ontological status of 'the unmasked identity'. Rather, they share a common premise that identity is an embodied rhetorical strategy, and that such strategies are embedded in power relations. The masks assembled here share a concrete reference point; they are linked to clothing items or general appearance features. As such, they inhabit the space between the material and the symbolic (between fashion theory and social theory). Based on a range of thematic contributions to symposia conducted in 1994 and 1996 in conjunction with the Venice carnival, the volume provides a gallery of contributions. The articles, however, do not offer a comprehensive account of all the theoretical, disciplinary, chronological or cultural contexts in which masquerade and disguise can be explored. Nor are they intended to offer an authoritative, exhaustive, definitive account of all the issues that might be addressed. The main emphasis is not on the mask as an artefact (for such an account cf. Mack, 1994a) but on the event or the process of masking, for, as Mack puts it :' It is not the fact that the mask is an identifiable type of object which is common, but the fact that masking is a continuing and commonly-employed technique, a technique of transformation' (Mack, 1994b, p. 16).

The chapters in this collection are arranged along two themes of otherness: gender and sexuality. They appear in a narrative structure which is only one of the possible narratives that could have been produced. And they contain elements of such other issues as ethnicity, legitimacy and deviance.

The collection starts with a chapter by Efrat Tseëlon that situates the mask historically and anthropologically within the European context which is the focus of this book. It also raises a number of relevant theoretical issues.

Next, three chapters look at an intersection of sexuality and marginality. Following Foucault's *History of Sexuality*, categories of sexuality have become ideologically suspect. Compulsory heterosexuality, 'legitimate' and 'normal' sexuality have been exposed as socially constructed and as ideological devices of social control. Christie Davies proposes a thesis of a symbolic masquerade (false identity) which he identifies as paradigmatic among those born outside the boundaries of legitimate (married) sexuality. Davies discusses the stigma of illegitimate birth as a formative experience 'a training for disguise'.

Foucault has documented the history of policing desire by the state through surveillance since the seventeenth century. Matlock (1993) argues that two centuries later psychiatry was mobilised to socially control sexuality by pathologising what it defined as inappropriate. He notes a shift in the 1880s in the psychiatric focus (in Europe) from madness (which was a medieval preoccupation) to perversion. In the 1882 essay that was the first to articulate sexual perversion, Jean Martin Charcot and Valentin Meagnan (quoted in Matlock, 1993) argued that women hide their perversions better than men. In his 1887 essay on love and fetishism Alfred Binet (in *ibid.*) tried to locate a dividing line between the normal and the perverse. He then located perverse desire with excessive ornamentation and artifice, with masquerade (which is feminine) as opposed to normal love (which is a 'symphony'). At the turn of the century (in France) clothing and costume obsessions were coded as signs of homosexuality, masturbation, criminality and degeneracy, and as such played a pivotal role in the understanding of sexual difference. The main perversions were inappropriate gender dressing (transvestism) and inappropriate modes of sexual arousal (fetishism). Both are addressed by two contributions to this volume.

When women tried to be men, psychiatry debated whether they were lesbians. When the woman deviated from male fantasies and rejected the masquerade of femininity she marked herself as perverse. Thus, feminine struggle against fashion is not merely a case of resisting social dictates. It is about claiming the woman's right to own her subjectivity (Silverman, 1986). This issue is illustrated by Halla Beloff's chapter on the mask of lesbian fashion as a source of identity.

The clothes obsessions of male fetishists emerged as being closely related to the masquerades psychiatrists attributed to women. 'We are all more or less fetishists', admitted Emile Lauret in 1896. 'Every woman whom a man loves in his heart is forcibly a little bit of a fetish.' Illusion plays a pivotal role in 'normal' as well as 'pathological' fetishism. Valerie Steele's chapter provides a close-up of the masquerade of fetishism amidst reflection on the nature of the categories of normal and perverse sexuality.

In the next section masquerade and gender construction and deconstruction are examined. This section opens with Alkeline van Lenning, Saskia Maas and Wendy Leeks who present an emblematic piece. They provide a paradigmatic illustration of the psychoanalytic notion of femininity as masquerade (a performance of femininity). Examining the construction of gender which displays both hegemonic and subversive features, their analysis of the cross-dressing motif in the film *The Crying Game* looks at gender ambiguity, which accounts for the shock-value of the film.

The identity between women and masquerade (as dissimulation) in Western discourse dates back to Jewish legends of the creation of the first woman, and Christian teachings of the Church Fathers in the second and third centuries. It recurs periodically throughout the Renaissance in courtesy literature as a chastising trope linking the woman with artifice and deception. It even features in psychoanalytic and psychiatric literature in the idea that cultural reasons compel the woman to mask in order to be herself (Riviere, 1929; Lacan, 1982; Doane, 1988/9). Following on the gender transgression motif, Ahuva Belkin takes us on a historical journey into early modern Europe and beyond, examining a double discourse of ethnic (Jewish) and gender (women) marginality in the Jewish folk theatre. In the tradition of European carnival from the Roman Saturnalia to the Italian Renaissance even subversive festivities had their own 'Others'. Carnival often violently abused weaker, not stronger, groups – women, ethnic and religious minorities, those who do not belong – in a process of displaced abjection (Stallybrass and White, 1986, p. 19). In Renaissance Italy from the thirteenth century onwards, during carnival Jews were made the target of insult and abuse in the Christian passion plays, and the butt of jokes in the popular comic drama that was performed in the streets (Burke, 1978; Roth, 1959, chapter 11).

It is in this historical context that the cross-dressing form in the Jewish folk carnival theatre (the '*Purimspiel*') reported by Belkin is to be appreciated. The *Purimspiel* articulates two levels of identity construction simultaneously. Performed by those on the lowest social ladder in a community at the bottom of the European social order, it establishes its distance from yet a lower category: the woman.

Heyl and Ilan-Alter continue the historical foray by looking at actual face masks worn by women in France and England in public as a means of constructing an independent identity. Christoph Heyl focuses on the black masks worn by seventeenth- and eighteenth-century women in England in non-masquerade contexts. Ann Ilan-Alter looks at society women masking to go to the opera balls in eighteenth-century France during the July Monarchy. Both examine face masks as a liberating device in a society which had been guarding women's bodies and movements rather closely. Subverting the public gaze, the face mask provided a private space free from surveillance which enabled the woman to engage in pursuits otherwise denied to her.

Finally, Efrat Tseëlon's contribution looks at contemporary women's use of clothes and words as rhetorical strategies of speech and silence, out of a repertoire of identity-forming sartorial materials readily available for feminine use. It then draws an analogy between the strategic choices of the woman and her a kindred spirit, the proverbial carnival fool.

REFERENCES

Andersen, Benedict (1983) *Imagined communities: Reflections on the origin and spread of nationalism*, London, Verso.

Austin, J.L. (1962) *How to do things with words*, Oxford, Oxford University Press.

Bakhtin, Mikhail (1968) *Rabelais and his world* (trans. Iswolsky, H.), Cambridge, MA, The MIT Press (originally published 1965).

Barthes Roland (1979) *A lover's discourse*: fragments (trans. Miller, R.), New York, Yill & Wang.

Bauman, Zygmunt (1990) 'Modernity and ambivalence', *Theory, Culture & Society* 7, 143–69.

Bauman, Zygmunt (1991) *Postmodernity: Change or menace?* Lancaster, Centre for the Study of Cultural Values Papers Series, University of Lancaster.

Bauman, Zygmunt (1998) 'Allosemitism: premodern, modern, postmodern', in *Modernity, culture and 'the Jew'* (ed. Cheyette, Bryan and Marcus, Laura), Cambridge, Polity.

Billig, Michael (1997) 'Discursive, rhetorical, and ideological messages', in *The message of social psychology: Perspectives on mind in society* (ed. McGarthy, Craig and Haslam, Alexander S.), Oxford, Blackwell.

Burke, P. (1978) *Popular culture in early modern Europe*, London, Temple Smith.

Butler, Judith (1990a) 'Performative acts and gender constitution: an essay in phenomenology and feminist theory', in *Performing feminisms* (ed. Case, Sue-Ellen), Baltimore, MD, Johns Hopkins University Press.

Butler, Judith (1990b) *Gender trouble: Feminism and the subversion of identity*, London, Routledge.

de Lauretis, Teresa (1986) 'Issues, terms, and contexts', in *Feminist studies, critical studies* (ed. de Lauretis, Teresa), Bloomington, Indiana University Press.

Doane, Mary Ann (1988/9) 'Masquerade reconsidered: Further thoughts on the female spectator', *Discourse: Journal for theoretical studies in media and culture* 11, 42–54.

Edwards, Derek and Potter, Jonathan (1992) *Discursive psychology*, London, Sage.

Eliade, Mircea (1990) 'Masks: Mythical and ritual origins', in *Symbolism, the sacred and the arts* (ed. Apostolos-Cappadona, Diane), New York, Crossroads.

Elias, Norbert (1978) *The civilizing process*, Vol. 1, The history of manners, (trans. Jepchott, Edmund), Oxford, Blackwell (originally published 1939).

Elias, Norbert (1982) *The civilizing process*, Vol. 2, State formation and civilization, (trans. Jepchott, Edmund), Oxford, Blackwell (originally published 1939).

Ewing, Katherine, P. (1990) 'The illusion of wholeness: Culture, self and the experience of inconsistency,' *Ethnos* 18, 251–78.

Felman, Shoshana (1987) *Jacques Lacan and the adventure of insight – psychoanalysis in contemporary culture*, Cambridge, MA, Harvard University Press.

Fletcher, John (1988) 'Versions of masquerade', *Screen*, 29, 43–70.

Foucault, Michel (1980) *The history of sexuality*, Vol. 1, an introduction, New York, Vintage.

Garber, Marjorie (1992) *Vested interests: Cross-dressing and cultural anxiety*, London, Penguin.

Gilman, Sander (1986) *Difference and pathology: Stereotypes of sexuality, race, and madness*, Ithaca, NY, Cornell University Press.

Gilman, Sander (1991) *The Jew's body*, London, Routledge.

Gilroy, Paul (1997) 'Diaspora and the detours of identity', in *Identity and difference* (ed. Woodward, Kathryn), London: Sage.

Goffman, Erving (1959) *The presentation of self in everyday life*, New York, Anchor Books.

Harré, Rom and Stearns, Peter (1995) *Discursive psychology in practice*, London, Sage.

Heath, Stephen (1989) 'Joan Riviere and the masquerade', in *Formations of Fantasy* (ed. Burgin, Victor, Donald, James and Kaplan, Cora), London, Routledge. (originally published 1996).

Jenkins, Ian (1994) 'Face value: The mask in Greece and Rome', in *Masks and the art of expression* (ed. Mack, J.), New York, Harry Abrams.

Johnson, Paul (1987) *A history of the Jews*, London, Wiedenfeld Nicholson.

Hollis, Martin (1985) 'Of masks and men', in *The category of the person: Anthropology, philosophy, history* (ed. Carrithers, M., Collins, S. and Lukes, S.), London, Cambridge University Press.

Lacan, Jacques (1982) 'The signification of the phallus', in *Feminine sexuality: Jacques Lacan and the 'Ecole Freudienne'*, (ed. Mitchell, J. and Rose, J.; trans. Rose, J.), New York, W. W. Norton (originally published 1966).

Laqueur, Thomas (1990) *Making sex: Body and gender from the Greeks to Freud*, Cambridge, MA, Harvard University Press.

Mack, John (ed.) (1994a) *Masks and the art of expression*, New York, Harry Abrams.

Mack, John (1994b) 'Introduction: About face', in *Masks and the art of expression* (ed. Mack, J.), New York, Harry Abrams.

Malik, Kenan (1996) *The meaning of race*, London, Macmillan.

Matlock, Jann (1993) 'Masquerading women, pathologized men: Cross-dressing, fetishism, and the theory of perversion, 1882–1935', in *Fetishism as cultural discourse* (ed. Apter, Emily and Pietz, William), Ithaca, NY, Cornell University Press.

Mauss, Marcel (1979) 'A category of the human mind: the notion of person, the notion of self', in *Sociology and psychology* (ed. Mauss, M., trans. Brewster, B.), London, Routledge and Kegan Paul (originally published 1950).

Modleski, Tania (1989) 'Some functions of feminist criticism, or the scandal of the mute body', *October*, 49, 3–24.

Napier, David (1986) *Masks, transformation and paradox*, Berkeley, University of California Press.

Potter, Jonathan (1996) *Representing reality: Discourse, rhetoric and social construction*, London, Sage.

Riviere, Joan (1929) 'Womanliness as masquerade', *The international Journal of Psychoanalysis*, 10, 303–13.

Roth, Cecil (1959) *The Jews of the Renaissance*, Philadelphia, Jewish Publishing Society of America.

Silverman, Kaja (1986) 'Fragments of a fashionable discourse', in *Studies in entertainment: Critical approaches to mass culture* (ed. Modleski, Tania), Bloomington, Indiana University Press.

Stallybrass, Peter and White, Allon (1986) *The politics and poetics of transgression*, London, Methuen.

Stephan, Nancy (1982) *The idea of race in science: Great Britain 1800–1960*, London, Macmillan.

Tseëlon, Efrat (2000) 'Is the presented self sincere? Goffman, impression management, and the postmodern self', in *Erving Goffman: Sage masters of modern social thought*, (ed. Fine, G.A. and Smith, G.W.H.), London, Sage (originally published in *Theory, Culture & Society*, 9,115–28, 1992).

Tseëlon, Efrat (1995) *The masque of femininity: The presentation of woman in everyday life*, London, Sage.

Tseëlon, Efrat (1998) 'Fashion, fantasy and horror: A cultural studies approach', *Arena Journal*, 12, 107–28.

Tseëlon, Efrat (2001a) 'Women and the gaze', in *Formations: 21st century media studies*, (ed. Fleming, Dan), Manchester, Manchester University Press.

Tseëlon, Efrat (2001b) 'Revisiting the spectatorial gaze in film', *Studies in Symbolic Interaction*, vol. 24, 299–319

Turner, Victor (1982) *From ritual to theatre: The human seriousness of play*, New York, PAJ Publications.

Woodward, Kathryn (ed.) (1997) *Identity and difference*, London, Sage and The Open University.

Žižek, Slavoj (1997) *The plague of fantasies*, London, Verso.

1

REFLECTIONS ON MASK AND CARNIVAL

Efrat Tseëlon

A society which believes it has dispensed with masks can only be a society in which masks, more powerful than ever before, the better to deceive men, will themselves be masked.

(Claude Lévi-Strauss, 1961, p. 20)

Covering the human face is as old as humankind. Evidence of the practice has been found in the artefacts, literature and lore of every society. Be it playful as in Halloween children's parties or serious as in religious ceremonies, based on tradition or myth, democratically open or exclusively guarded – some form of masking has been known in every culture ranging from antiquity to the present, and from tribal cultures to the late capitalist West. Masks are made and used in various religious ceremonial cycles or events performed in association with numerous events: rites of initiation, rites of passage, mortuary rites, celebrations of the agricultural cycle, ritualised healing, warding off danger, parties and festivities. It is generally considered that masks are a type of artefact existing in cultures which practice magico-ritual activity (sometimes developing into a theatrical form). In Europe dressing up and the wearing of masks has been associated with the celebration of festivals since Roman Saturnalia, through medieval Carnival, up to eighteenth-century Masquerades.

Masks may seem emblematic: meaningful even when abstracted from their appropriate cultural setting. Gregor (1968) and Napier (1986), who have studied the anthropological literature, point to the mask's common association with transformation and categorical change (represented, for example, in initiation rites, mourning rites, annual and seasonal changes, impersonation of animals, ancestors and deities). It applies to all masks used in ritual, theatre or carnival, even in sexual perversions.

In spite of the evidence and the argument in favour of the universality of the mask, the meaning of masks is contextually bound and depends on use. Lévi-Strauss (1983) suggests that masks cannot be interpreted semantically outside their 'transformation set', whose lines and colours they echo. The reason is that masks are 'linked to myths whose objective is to explain its legendary or supernatural origin and to lay the foundation for its role in ritual, in the economy, and in the society'. Thus, masking is not just about certain kinds of artefact: it is a cultural institution embedded in knowledge, traditions, beliefs and practices (cf., Mack, 1994a for an exhaustive collection). What is the appeal of mask and masquerade?

Plate 1.1 Mask shop in Venice. The masked mask sustains the illusion that whatever is deeper is somehow more true.

Source: Photo by the author.

EFRAT TSEËLON

Mask and death

We respond to the mask with a mixture of fascination and avoidance. We regard mime artists as reaching perfection when their pale made-up faces appear like masks and their gestures mimic a clockwork doll. But we admire dolls for their capacity to look like a real baby.

We want to speak to the mask because it is like us, but it responds with strangeness because it is not like us (Raz, 1995). Like the uncanny, it is familiar and unfamiliar simultaneously. The mask stands in an intermediary position between different worlds. Its embodiment of the fragile dividing line between concealment and revelation, truth and artifice, natural and supernatural, life and death is a potent source of the mask's metaphysical power. The earliest masks have funerary associations. Mummy masks represented the deceased in the divine state they aspired to attain after death. The mummy masks first appeared in Egypt at the beginning of the second millennium BCE in Egypt, but their precursors can be recognised in burials dating back to the Old Kingdom (2686–2181 BCE) (Taylor, 1994). They had a major influence on the development of the anthropoids (human-like burial coffins decorated with clay funerary masks depicting an idealised face of the deceased). Those were widely used by Egyptian and Philistine civilisations from the Late Bronze Age (thirteen centuries BCE) (Dothan, 1982; Ornan, 1986; Ziffer, 1992). Golden death masks which are modelled on the faces of the deceased were found in the Cretan-Mycenaean age (second millennium BCE). Death masks were also involved in a Roman ritual tradition. When a member of the noble families died, a wax model was cast from his face to be worn by a person impersonating him at the funeral. The earliest evidence of masquerade in Mesoamerica (Mexico and Olmec civilisation) dates back to the middle pre-classic period (first millennium BCE). The Maya masks have mortuary or underworld associations. The Aztecs cremated their priests and rulers with burial masks representing deities with whom the ruler was affiliated (Shelton, 1994). In the Andes, masks were widely used to cover the faces of the dead. The ancient Peruvians (c. 500 BCE) placed a rude wooden image, usually fashioned when the person was still alive, upon the case in which the body was mummified, and in Melanesia the skull itself served as a mask during the sacred dances (Eliade, 1990). In Europe death masks became a widespread practice by the fifteenth and sixteenth centuries (Ariès, 1981). The mask, observes Sorell, 'truly reflected the mystery of being which is the other side of the mystery of death' (1973, p. 11). Indeed, from its origins in death it moved to the heart of life. In Western history the mask moved from the ritual to the

20

theatre and ultimately to the streets. It appeared first in Dionysian festivities of antiquity and then, in direct descent from these, in the carnivalesque manifestations of the Christian era.

The mask is simultaneously animated and inanimate, living and dead: an expressionless mass transformed into expressive being. On its own it is a lifeless piece of matter, like the marionette without the puppeteer. But as soon as the mask is worn, or the marionette is pulled on a string, they come to life. Human interaction infuses them with spirit. The effect of the mask on the wearer is a well-known phenomenon in theatre and ritual: the wearer wishes to be identified with the mask they wear (Gregor, 1968). This is evidenced from ancient ceremonial masks as well as contemporary ones. The complete identification with the mask is what relates it to its very origins – in animal cults. In totemic

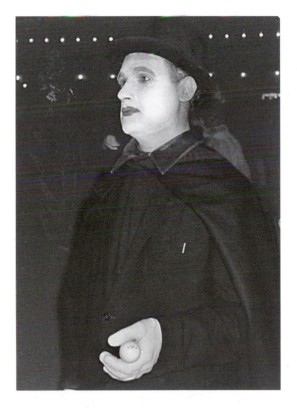

Plate 1.2 A mime artist in the Venice carnival. It takes only a coat of paint to transform a human face into a mask-like face.

Source: Photo by the author.

cultures the earlier masks depicted animals. They were believed to have demonic power. These powers are then transferred to the mask. The masked man who impersonates the spirit truly believes himself to possess its demonic powers (Sorell, 1973, p. 8). Masks were believed to be inhabited by spirits, but also to be the means of driving them away. Thus, animal masks were used in mediating communication with supernatural forces for the purpose of securing an abundance of crops, preventing illness, curing disease, succeeding in war or hunt, and expelling evil spirits.

Mask and face

Its proximity to the face creates a peculiar relationship between the mask and the face. When the face is covered, awareness shifts to the body and different registers are used. The lifelessness of any mask becomes strangely animated when the body moves. This is obvious enough when the mask is expressive, as are the Trestle theatre giant-size masks, but it is also the case when the mask is inexpressive, as are the Noh theatre masks (see Plate 1.3). The masks of the Japanese Noh theatre are generally neutral in expression. Within a 600 year unbroken Noh tradition – where every movement is highly controlled and limited, no editing or adaptation is permitted and an actor has no liberty of physical expression – it is the skill of the actor that brings the mask to life. The actor has to learn to express variations in feeling through subtle changes in his physical movements, and by symbolic representation. It is the actor's internal creative force which creates the intensity of his expression (Sekine and Murray, 1990).

This creative force is also shared by children, who are capable of being so absorbed in the mask as to bring out a character from even an inexpressive mask. Face masks have generated explanations about the psycho-philosophical properties of masks, and their power to transform and liberate the creative imagination of players donning them (Richards and Richards, 1990). Peter Brook observed that 'The actor, having put the mask on, is sufficiently in the character that if someone unexpectedly offered him a cup of tea, whatever response he makes is totally that of that type, not in a schematic sense but in the essential sense' (Brook, 1987, p. 221). This is characteristically typical of the actor of the Noh theatre who first dons the costume and sits in front of a mirror, studying the mask and 'becoming one with the character he is about to perform'. When he wears the mask he stands in front of a mirror 'letting the mask take over his own personality' (Irvine, 1994). The founders of the Ophboom theatre, a contemporary *Commedia dell'arte* group formed in

1991 (modelled on the spirit of the original sixteenth-century Italian improvisational dramatic performance) describe this as 'the madness of the mask'. 'Using masks as a performer alienates one from one's own body and this alienation frees the mind from normal, rational thought, until the performer becomes as it were, possessed by the mask' (Beale and Gayton, 1998, p. 176).

Each mask generates its own characteristic repertoire of gestures and poses. Kobi Versano recounted to me a North-African folk story he heard from his grandfather about the string instrument player whose range of tunes became more and more limited with every string that expired. Until in the end, when the last one expired he was finally liberated from the constraints of the medium and could play any tune in the world. Paradoxically it is the expressive which is pre-determined and limited. And it is the expressionless which is the most expressive as it brings out multiple potentials.

This, of course, is what links masks to imagination. The mask, says

a   b

Plate 1.3 The Trestle Theatre mask's expressive potential is limited by the emotion inscribed on it. The Japanese Noh mask is a neutral mask, hence capable of expressing any emotion. Both come to life *only* through the actor's body. a) Trestle Theatre masks in the production *Top Storey*. b) A Japanese Noh mask.

Source: a) Courtesy of Trestle Theatre, b) Courtesy of the Pitt Rivers Museum, University of Oxford.

Gregor, who has studied many masks all over the world, stands for the plenitude of creative power. A related motif runs through the fantastic tales of the Danish writer Isak Dinesen. Contrary to the bourgeois attitude which is preoccupied with questions of true identity and self-actualisation, Dinesen's aristocratic view places a high value on artistic creativity, adventure, dreams and imagination, not on truth. It is expressed, for example, in the words of the character in *The Deluge of Norderney* Miss nat-og-dag (night and day) who challenges the valet's idea that god wants the truth from us: 'why, he knows it already, and may even have found it a little bit dull. Truth is for tailors and shoemakers' (Dinesen, 1963, p. 141). Instead, she maintains, god prefers the masquerade. Kasparson observes that the mask is not all deception in that it reveals something of the spirit which life conventions conceal. Therefore, god might say that the person is known by the mask that they wear (Johannesson, 1961). One can detect here the influence of Nietzsche, who regards the mask as a device for releasing a power just as valuable as truth: 'it could be possible that a higher and more fundamental value for life might have to be ascribed to appearance, to the will to deception, to selfishness and to appetite' (1987, p. 16). Yet there is not only deceit behind the mask, but also necessary cunning. Since every deep spirit is bound to be misunderstood, a mask is continuously growing around it, due to the shallow interpretation people make of its word and deed. Hence 'everything profound loves the mask' (*ibid.*, p. 51).

Identity

Already its earliest sources in Western civilisation mark the mask as closely connected to the notion of the person. The Romans borrowed the concept of mask from the Greeks via the Etruscan civilisation where it represented face, or person. Mauss sees the human actor who is a carrier of roles, rights and responsibilities as a social creation, hence transient and changing (e.g. for the Hellenes the obverse of the person is the slave, for the Christian the unsouled, and for the Kantian the non-rational (Rorty, 1987)). Mauss argues that the idea of the individual is unique to Western thought, and attributes to the Greek roots of our civilisation a notion of the actor behind the mask. Originating in the masked drama of Athenian theatre, mask was used as identification of character, not as a deception or disguise. Mask and face were interchangeable (Jenkins, 1994).

The idea of the individual was later translated into the idea of the soul. From the Greeks the idea travelled to the pro-Hellenic Jewish sects of the

Pharisees and the Essenes in the first century BCE and later on to the sect which became Christianity (Dimont, 1994). The idea of the individual as a locus of personal accountability and moral obligation has always been at the heart of Judaism, reinforced by the sayings of Isaiah and Ezekiel (Johnson 1987). But it was Protestant Christianity which made the soul, a metaphysical category (Hollis, 1985) and a touchstone of its faith . The Roman 'person' was a judicial category more than a name or the right to a role and a ritual mask. The Stoics added moral obligations to the personal rights. From the second century BCE the word *persona* (Latin for mask) acquired the sense of an image which signifies a person. It contained a notion of artifice but also a notion of one's role, character, 'true' face (Mauss, 1979).

Contemporary approaches to personhood talk about identity. Identity is a construction by which a person is known, and disguise is almost a design feature of that construction. The philosophy of the mask represents two approaches to identity. One assumes the authenticity of the self (that the mask – sometimes – covers). The other approach maintains that through a multitude of authentic manifestations the mask reveals the multiplicity of our identities. Of course, the preoccupation with selves and identities is uniquely Western. It is an epistemology based on a belief in a single reality and unity of experience. The concept of identity, however, is not exhausted within the parameters of authentic and inauthentic or single and multiple. Other approaches introduce notions of reality and fantasy, as well as truth and fiction. The traditional mask, says Peter Brook, provides a hiding space. This fact 'makes it unnecessary for you to hide. Because there is a greater security, you can take greater risks; and because here it is not you, and therefore everything about you is hidden, you can let yourself appear ' (1987, p. 231). In contrast, Sorrell regards the mask as an imaginary shield that protects us against reality, a symbol of escape into a make-believe reality 'the persona is the mask which protects us not only against the other people behind their masks, but also against our own real self' (1973, p. 13); 'the mask contains the magic of illusion without which man is unable to live' (*ibid.*, p. 15). For Yeats the retreat from the reality self is not to a fantasy creation but to an heroic ideal one. The antithesis of conventionality, he sees the mask as a voluntary constraint or discipline imposed on the self in order to achieve victory over circumstances (1962, p. 108). For him the mask signifies 'active virtue, as distinguished from the passive acceptance of a code, [it] is therefore theatrical, consciously dramatic' (1972, p. 151).

Psychoanalytic reality, for example, created tolerance to various states of mind, and levels of existence. Dr Jekyll and Mr Hyde need not be an expression of a pathological personality. Psychoanalitically speaking, identity is an unconscious fantasy, an illusion of wholeness that covers splits. More precisely it has two meanings: the dynamics of the integrative efforts of the ego, and the relationship between unconscious actions and reality (for a review, see Graafsma, 1994a, 1994b). The search for identity reflects wishful thinking. An alternative model views identity as a story that reflects the person's search for the meaning of actions and experiences. Here the sense of identity is derived, not from the assumption of continuing correspondence between an inner wish and an external reality, but from the organisation and the narrative structure of the whole (Harré and Gillett, 1994; Ricoeur, 1991). Masking, from those perspectives, moves away from the epistemology of deception into that of fantasy and fiction.

Taylor (1980), for example, reports a case study where the mask is a magical device to facilitate the release of repressed instincts, thus blurring the boundary between man and animal. Moreover, the mask may also function to externalise split-off personality organisations. Taylor's analysis is of a transvestite who also wore masks fetishistically. His childhood was characterised by insensitive mothering (she dressed him in girls' clothes until the age of 5, against his wishes) and neglectful fathering. By making masks with animals shapes (based on comic books where animal characters increase their power by wearing human masks) and wearing female clothing he fantasised that he was empowered enough to overcome his sense of weakness and helplessness. Masking nourished his fantasy that he was 'blotting out his own identity' and being transformed into a powerful fearless 'other'.

Abstract or specific

The traditional mask, says Peter Brook, is actually not a 'mask'. It is an image of the essential nature. In other words, a traditional mask is a portrait 'of a man without a mask' – a soul portrait. Indeed, ancient theatre masks tended to present stereotypes, defining the general category of person to be portrayed, rather than individual personalities. (Individualising the mask was used to satirise well-known Athenian personalities (Mack, 1994b)). Here Brook touches on a quality of the mask which conveys the general, without reducing it to the universal. This is best captured in Barthes' reading of 'the face of Garbo'. As a language he sees Garbo's singularity as being of the order of an 'Idea', while the individualised face of Audrey Hepburn is presented as being of the order of an 'Event'. The snowy thickness of Garbo's mask-like make-up, like the white mask of the mime artist has the effect of transforming her face into an idea of the human creature, and aligns her with the absolute mask. . . . 'the absolute mask (the mask of antiquity, for instance) perhaps implies less the theme of the secret (as is the case with Italian half mask) than that of an archetype of the human face' (Barthes, 1989, p. 62).

Bakhtin also refers this ability of the mask to capture an abstract quality without being frozen into a stereotype. In *The Dialogic Imagination* he compares an epic hero and the hero of popular masks, like the *Commedia dell'arte*. According to him, while the dramatic hero is constrained by his destiny or the plot, the *commedia* hero is free. Paradoxically, despite the singularity of the dramatic hero as opposed to the stereotypic nature of the *commedia* character types, he views them as: 'heroes of free improvisation and not heroes of tradition, heroes of a life process that is imperishable and forever renewing itself, forever contemporary – these are not heroes of an absolute past' (Bakhtin, 1981, p. 36).

In a similar spirit, Urban and Hendricks (1983), who have studied masking in Amerindian Brazil, report one commonality despite a marked diversity in function: masks are a means of concretising a linguistic reality. Jedrej observed that even similarity in appearance does not guarantee similarity of meaning. For example, Jedrej compared masks from various tribes in different continents. He found that while those from Nigeria, Sierra Leone and North America structurally embody notions of transition and of crossing of boundaries between categories of space and time, the New Guinea mask does not mediate such categories, but rather represents them. Jedrej argues that a mask is not an entity but a signifier of a relationship between inside and outside. He identifies three such relationships: where the mask is of minimal significance and the masked is important (veil, screen); where the masked person is unimportant and the mask is significant (spirit masks); and where both mask and masked are important.

European carnival and masquerade

Carnival developed from the fertility and renewal rites that agrarian societies performed at the beginning of the year. The legacy of the carnival is a festive occasion characterised by indulgence in the pleasures of food and disguise, as well as an upside-down world: reversal of hierarchical relationships of masters and slaves, and replacement of refined and serious language of high culture with the obscene language of popular culture (Bakhtin, 1968). Geertz (1973) and Turner (1969) suggested that festivals of misrule institutionalised collective disorder while reifying ordering categories. By posing a reversal, the festivals comment on those categories. It is only by breaking rules that one discovers which rules exist.

Dressing up and wearing masks and face disguises have been features of European festivals for many centuries. But the carnival tradition gave rise to the development of the masquerade, the public masked ball where gentry and common folk intermingled. The masquerade was adopted enthusiastically across Europe. The classic features of the masquerade are traditional carnival motifs and these hint at the historical connection with the Saturnalia of Roman antiquity, the medieval Feast of Fools, and similar 'festivals of misrule' in Europe throughout the early modern period (documented by Frazer in *The Golden Bough*, 1963). It was no historical accident that the masquerade became so popular in the eighteenth century. The growth in international trade and the resulting changes in urban life created a society of strangers, where people could be placed only by virtue of identifying sartorial codes. Clothes, and particularly make-up and face masks (which became popular for everyday use), did not attempt to enhance the individual character. Rather, they were made to blot out individuality (Sennett, 1976).

In European history the masquerade was a space where people could enjoy fleeting liberty from social, sexual and psychological constraints. Here they could discard their private, sexual, social and hierarchical identities and choose whichever identity they desired. The carnivalesque as a liberating space does, as Bakhtin would have it, 'celebrate temporary liberation from the prevailing truth of the established order . . . [and] . . . marks the suspension of all hierarchical rank, privileges, norms and prohibition' (1968, p. 104). This is only part of the story. As a ritual strategy on the part of subordinate groups, carnival was rather a licensed affair, a permissible rupture of hegemony. Such a form of contained release may just be a form of social control, a domesticated parody which apparently opposes but actually affirms cultural hegemony (Eagleton, 1986, p. 148). In the tradition of European carnival, even subversive festivities excluded weaker, not stronger, groups – women, ethnic and religious minorities, those who don't belong. In Renaissance Italy from the thirteenth century onwards during carnival Jews were made the target of insults and abuse in the Christian passion plays and the target of mockery in the popular street comic drama. Like the pigs in the Venice carnival which were chased across the Piazza San Marco and stoned, in Rome Jews were forced to race at carnival time and were stoned by onlookers. During special races (*Corso degli ebrei*, 'the race of the Jews') Jews were forced to participate in the role of the 'hobby horse' to Roman soldiers or as carnival fools (Roth, 1962, chapter 11 Burke, 1978, p. 200). Ritual execution of the sacrificial victim was part of end-of-carnival festivities. Usually played by criminals, in Rome, Jewish convicts were actually put to death (Poppi, 1994). Thus the Jew, the archetypal "other" of medieval Christian society was at times made an enforced symbolic focus to the jeering violence of carnival (Stallybrass and White, 1986, p. 53–5).

The idea of the masquerade became a potent cultural symbol, a modern emblem, carrying multiple metaphoric possibilities: as a site of excess, ecstasy, intrigue and moral danger harbouring erotic, riotous and mysterious associations. In many novels, poems and operas the liberating, sensuous, rebellious and licentious charm of the mask has been celebrated, even giving rise to a genre of a Masquerading Romance (Castle, 1986; Schofield, 1990). Masquerades exploited a host of symbolic oppositions between human and animal, natural and supernatural, past and present, the living and the dead. The masked assemblies of the eighteenth century were a kind of collective meditation on self and other, and on the cultural classification of eighteenth-century life. One became the other in an act of impersonation or engaged in different forms of self-presentation: the experience of doubleness, the alienation of inner from outer.

In the course of 'the civilising process', Elias (1978, 1982) taught us, actual acts of aggression were transformed into ritual aggression in the form of intrigue or diplomacy. Eighteenth-century masquerade provided a model for the civilising process. It was sometimes an occasion for playing out diplomatic and court intrigue; later it became a natural stage for political satire. On close examination, the apparent anarchy and the upside-down world were not quite as egalitarian as they appeared. When role reversal is carried out by the powerful impersonating the powerless, travesty has a comic effect (like the burlesque appeal of male transvestism in patriarchal culture). But parodies of the powerful by the powerless are perceived as a threat to the social structure. This is the rationale behind a number of sumptuary laws and regulations on proletarian attire that were still enforced in eighteenth-century England. The fear of somebody 'dressing above their station' was that it would encourage people to join those ranks, and would delude them into adopting a revolutionary belief that rank is as easily changed as outward signs. For these reasons we find ideological prohibitions on women participating in masquerades, as well as real prohibitions put by eighteenth-century masquerade organisers in an attempt to maintain pretensions of exclusivity by limiting access of members of the lower orders to their entertainments (Castle, 1986, p. 92–3).

EFRAT TSEËLON

Masking and power

Masquerades were often used as a setting for political critique. If you add to this the possibility of deceit and the preoccupation with body adornment inherent in disguise, as well as the mask's pagan origins that link it to evil spirits, it is small wonder that masquerade was a target of moralising and condemnation of the Church. The religious conception of the mask shows continuity from antiquity to the Middle Ages. The Christian mystery could not do without its demon (the devil). For the Church, masquerade occupied the space of the conventional emblem of hypocrisy and moral duplicity.

Masking lends its object of disguise an enigmatic quality. Often this quality is associated with erotic and romantic fantasies. This is partly because the mask mystifies the object of desire. Masked individuals were often seen as fetishistically exciting (Steele, 1996, and see this volume, Chapter 4). By the eighteenth century the mask was a classic prop in pornographic representation, it had become part of the subterranean sexual iconography of the period – a sign of perversely intensified Eros (Castle, 1986, p. 40). Transvestite costume was also symbolically charged, evoking realms of perverse and ambiguous sexual possibility. Ecclesiastical travesties were similarly erotically appealing. The ironic contrast between the chaste costume and the desiring body underneath held a peculiarly tantalising promise. The hyper-sexuality of nuns and priests, has become another eighteenth century pornographic convention (see Plate 1.4).

To some extent the romantic reputation of masquerades was based on fact and not on fiction, as the masked balls were indeed the scene of amorous adventures. Moreover, protected by disguise it was the only opportunity for society women to go unescorted and experience erotic encounters. Nevertheless, women who went to the balls, especially fashionable women, risked losing their reputation of virtue (Ribeiro, 1984). Many critics equated going to a masquerade with the sexual act; the metonymic relation between masquerades and sex became metaphoric (Castle, 1986, p. 43).

The enigma of disguise suggests also a sinister dimension. A cloak of anonymity can provide the scene for staging petty crimes (as was indeed the case in eighteenth-century masquerades, especially in the darker alleys of the pleasure gardens where the balls were held). Further, mask of anonymity can relax the safeguards of controls and inhibitions and shield one from one's own morality. For many people their own anonymity or the facelessness of the other washes away all their humanity. Is it surprising that so many atrocities, as well as smaller scale crimes are carried out

30

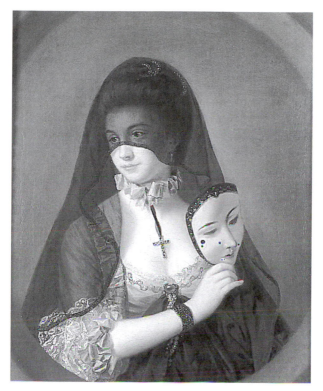

Plate 1.4 The Fair Nun Unmasked, Henry Moreland *c.*1730–1737, Leeds Museums and Galleries.

Source: Courtesy of the Courtauld Institute of Art, University of London.

by masked or uniformed individuals? (as is depicted in Kenny Hunter's "military figure", see Plate 1.5).

Such, indeed, was the suspicion of psychologists who carried out 'deindividuation' studies in the 1970s. Deindividuation was achieved by means of baggy coats and hoods (similar to those worn by the Ku-Klux-Klan). A series of studies confirmed a link between masking and aggressive behaviours. It was as if the disguise, by removing personal identification, also removed personal responsibility (cf. Zimbardo, 1969).

The ambivalence that the masquerade aroused in public life was replicated in its fictional representations. If seventeenth-century dramatic disguise (where the heroines of Shakespeare and Calderón de la Barca dress as men to gain achievements unavailable to them as women) is more equivocal, the masquerades of the eighteenth-century Masquerading Romance are depicted at once as the sign of depravity and freedom, corruption and delight. From the nineteenth century masquerades become a narrative trope for intrigue, deception and menace. Verdi's opera *The Masked Ball* tells of Richard, the governor of Boston in the early Colonial period, who desired the wife of his loyal secretary and friend Renato. Renato, who secured the escape of the careless governor from the conspirators, takes care of the veiled lady who was in his company only to find out inadvertently that it was his wife. Renato's love and devotion to his master turns into rage. Joining the conspirators, he murders Richard in a masked ball, in the course of which he learns, to his distress, that despite their passion neither his wife nor his friend have betrayed him, and Richard had prepared his promotion to a high position in London

Plate 1.5 Military Figure, Kenny Hunter, 1998.
Source: Courtesy of the artist.

(Davidson, 1929). Edgar Ellen Poe's *The Masque of the Red Death* staged at the time of the Plague tells the story of Prince Prospero who, in the midst of the misery and in defiance of death, plans a masquerade to celebrate life and pleasure. Into this assembly of the phantasmic and the bizarre, Red Death intrudes disguised with a corpse-like mask, his costume dabbled in blood. In the petrified silence that ensues, the Prince is murdered and all the revellers drop dead (Poe, 1982). The people inside the castle thought they could escape death, but Red Death defied closure and the boundaries of inside/outside. Heinrich Böll's (1975) Katharina Blum meets Gotten, a radical on the run from the police, at the city carnival, and this fatal brief encounter of the masked stranger opens the gates to a series of troubles that results in *The Lost Honour of Katharina Blum*. These are just a few illustrations of what Eliade calls 'the morphology of terror-producing masks', whose major inspirations sources are death myths, nightmares, demonology, and images of terror which express the 'Otherness' of the dead (corpses, skeletons, ghosts) (1990, p. 68). Contemporary genres of best-selling murder mysteries in books and films have made masking almost exclusively a metonomy of a crime or murder scene. (For example films such as *The Mask* exploit the sinister semiotic currency of disguise; Edward Sklepowich's detective novels *Farewell to the Flesh,* and *Death in a Serene City*, are both staged in Venice. One is described by *The New York Times* book review as 'intriguing . . . sinister . . . an enchanting spectacle', the other as 'a thoroughly civilised mystery . . . with a nice macabre touch'). Even popular culture draws on the collective stock of menacing images associated with the mask. In the 1996 British election campaign the conservative party, in an attempt to create a Labour scare coined the slogan 'new Labour, new danger' accompanied by photos of the Labour leader wearing a demonic mask.

Masquerade, then, is a measure of power in social relations. Both in rituals and in theatre, masking is often confined to men, the women remaining maskless. Information from a variety of anthropological sources reveals the mask as a special male privilege, offering access to power and secret knowledge. In African and Oceanian cultures, in ancient Greek and Japanese theatres, for example, men control, own and dance masks, even if the masks sometimes represent women. Yet, remarkably many masking societies identify women as the inventors of the entities portrayed in masking (Mack, 1994c). Masking seems to operate as a symbol of prestige or as an exclusionary practice from powerful sites. This might also explain the moral outrage provoked by female attendance of the masquerade in the eighteenth century. Much of the fear the masquerade generated throughout the century is related to the belief that it encouraged female sexual freedom and female emancipation generally. Respectable women were free to attend unescorted, their reputation protected by masks and disguise. But for all its lewd and mysterious shades masquerades never really survived the coming of electric light at the turn of the century. They needed candlelight to obtain their full effect!

Finally, I would like to end this brief sketch with an insight from Napier who studied the relationship between mask and transition. Discussing pre-classical masks he resists the temptation to fix their meaning through a typological approach. Grouping masks according to types is too general, he says, and derives more from 'our need for organizing artefacts rather than from categories of Greek thought' (1986, p. 45). Rooted in a 'metaphysics of ambivalence' he sees their meaning as in principle unfixed.

REFERENCES

Ariès, Philippe (1981) *The hour of our death* (trans. Weaver, H.), New York, Oxford University Press (originally published 1977).

Bakhtin, Mikhail (1968) *Rabelais and his world* (trans. Iswolsky, H.), Cambridge, MA, The M.I.T Press (originally published 1965).

Bakhtin, Mikhail (1981) *The dialogic imagination* (trans. Emerson, Caryl and Holquist, Michael), Austin, University of Texas Press.

Barthes, Roland (1989) 'The face of Garbo', in *Mythologies* (Barthes, R.; trans. Lavers, Annette), London, Paladin (originally published 1957).

Beale, Geoff and Gayton, Howard (1998) 'The drive to communicate – the use of language in *Commedia dell'arte*', *Theatre Research International* 23, 174–8.

Böll, Heinrich (1975). *The lost honor of Katharina Blum. Or: How violence develops and where it can lead* (trans. Vennewitz, L.) New York, McGraw-Hill.

Brook, Peter (1987) 'The mask: coming out of our shell', in *The shifting point: Theatre, film, opera 1946–1987*, New York, Harper & Row.

Burke, P. (1978) *Popular culture in early modern France*, London, Temple Smith.

Castle, Terry (1986) *Masquerade and civilization: The carnivalesque in eighteenth century English culture and fiction*, London, Methuen.

Davidson, Gladys (1929) *Stories from the operas*, London, Werner Laurie.

Diderot, Denis (1957) *The paradox of acting* (trans. Pollack, W. H.), New York, Hill & Wang (originally published 1830).

Dimont, Max I (1994) *Jews, god and history*, London, Penguin (originally published 1964).

Dinesen, Isak (1963) *Seven Gothic tales*, London, Penguin (originally published 1934).

Dothan, Trude (1982) *The Philistines and their material culture*, Jerusalem.

Eagleton, Terry (1986) *William Shakespeare*, Oxford, Blackwell.

Eliade, Mircea (1990) 'Masks: mythical and ritual origins', in *Symbolism, the sacred, and the arts* (ed. Apostolos-Cappadona, Diane), New York, Crossroads.

Elias, Norbert (1978) *The civilizing process*, Vol. 1, The history of manners (trans. Jepchott, Edmund) Oxford, Blackwell (originally published 1939).

Elias, Norbert (1982) *The civilizing process, Vol. 2, State formation and civilization*, (trans. Jepchott, Edmund), Oxford, Blackwell (originally published 1939).

Frazer, James George (1963) *The golden bough: A study in magic and religion*, London, Macmillan (originally published 1922).

Geertz, Clifford (1973) *Person, time, and conduct in Bali: An essay in cultural analysis*, New York, Basic Books (originally published 1966).

Goffman, Erving (1959) *The presentation of self in everyday life*, New York, Anchor Books.

Graafsma, Tobi L. (1994a) 'Identity and the human core: The view from psychoanalytic theory', in *Identity and development: An interdisciplinary approach* (ed. Bosma, Harka A.; Graafsma, Tobi L., Grotevant, Harold D. and de Levita, David J.), London, Sage.

Graafsma, Tobi L. (1994b) 'A psychoanalytic perspective on the concept of identity', in *Identity and development: An interdisciplinary approach* (ed. Bosma, Harka A., Graafsma, Tobi L., Grotevant, Harold D. and de Levita, David J.), London, Sage.

Gregor, Joseph (1968) *Masks of the world: An historical and pictorial survey of many types & times*, New York, Benjamin Blom (originally published, 1937).

Harré, Rom and Gillett, Grant (1994) *The discursive mind*, London, Sage.

Hollis, Martin (1985) 'Of masks and men', in *The category of the person: Anthropology, philosophy, history* (ed. Carrithers, M., Collins, S. and Lukes, S.), London, Cambridge University Press.

Irvine, Gregory (1994) 'Japanese masks: ritual and drama', in *Masks and the art of expression* (ed. Mack, John), New York, Harry Abrams.

Jedrej, M. C. (1980) 'A comparison of some masks from north America, Africa, and Melanesia', *Journal of Anthropological research* 36, 220–30.

Jenkins, Ian (1994) 'Face value: the mask in Greece and Rome', in *Masks and the art of expression* (ed. Mack, John), New York, Harry Abrams.

Johannesson, Eric O. (1961) *The world of Isak Dinesen*, Seattle, University of Washington Press.

Johnson, Paul (1987) *A history of the Jews*, London, Weidenfeld Nicolson.

Kaplan, Charles D. and Weiglus, Karl (1979) 'Beneath role theory: Reformulating a theory with Neitzsche's philosophy', *Philosophy and Social Criticism* 6, 291–305.

Lévi-Strauss, Claude (1961) 'The many faces of man', *World Theatre* 10, 3–61.

Lévi-Strauss, Claude (1983) *The way of the masks* (trans. Modelski, Sylvia), London, Cape.

Mack, John (ed.) (1994a) *Masks and the art of expression*, New York, Harry Abrams.

Mack, John (1994b) Introduction: About face, in *Masks and the art of expression* (ed. Mack, John), New York, Harry Abrams.

Mack, John (1994c) 'African masking', in *Masks and the art of expression* (ed. Mack, John), New York, Harry Abrams.

Mauss, Marcel (1979) 'A category of the human mind: the notion of person, the notion of "self" (trans. Brewster, B.), in *Sociology and psychology*, London, Routledge & Kegan Paul (originally published 1950).

Napier, David (1986) *Masks, transformation and paradox*, Berkeley, University of California Press.

Nietzsche, Friedrik (1987) *Beyond good and evil*, Harmondsworth, Penguin (originally published 1886).

Ornan, Tali (1986) *Man and his land: A selection from the Moshe Dayan collection*, Jerusalem, Israel Museum.

Poe, Edgar Allan (1982) *The masque of the red death*, in *The complete tales and poems of Edgar Allan Poe*, Harmondsworth, Penguin (originally published 1938).

Poppi, Cesare (1994) 'The other within: masks and masquerades in Europe', in *Masks and the art of expression* (ed. Mack, John), New York, Harry Abrams.

Raz, Yaacov (1995) 'The mask', in *Carnivals: Islands in the ocean of routine* (ed. Ronit Yoeli Tlalim), Tel-Aviv, Masa Acher (Hebrew).

Ribeiro, Aileen (1984) *The dress worn at masquerades in England, 1730 to 1790, and its relation to fancy dress portraiture*, London, Garland.

Richards, Kenneth and Richards, Laura (1990) *The Commedia dell'Arte: A documentary history*, Oxford, Blackwell.

Ricoeur, Paul (1991) 'Narrative identity', in *On Paul Ricoeur; narrative and interpretation* (ed. Wood, D.), London, Routledge (originally published 1988).

Rorty, Oksenberg Amelie (1987) 'Persons as rhetorical categories', *Social Research* 54, 55–72.

Roth, Cecil (1959) *The Jews of the Renaissance*, Philadelphia, Jewish Publishing Society of America.

Schofield, Mary Anne (1990) *Masking and unmasking the female mind: Disguising romances in feminine fiction, 1713–1799*, Newark, University of Delaware Press.

Sekine, Masaru and Murray, Christopher (1990) *Yeats and the Noh: A comparative study*, Gerrards Cross, Colin Smythe.

Sennett, Robert (1976) *The fall of public man: On the social psychology of capitalism*, New York, Vintage Books.

Shelton, Anthony (1994) 'Fictions and parodies: Masquerade in Mexico and Highland South America', in *Masks and the art of expression* (ed. Mack, John), New York, Harry Abrams.

Sorrell, Walter (1973) *The other face: The mask in the arts*, London, Thames & Hudson.

Stallybrass, Peter and White, Allon (1986) *The politics and poetics of transgression*, London, Methuen.

Steele, Valerie (1996) *Fetish: Fashion, sex and power*, New York, Oxford University Press.

Taylor, John, H. (1994) 'Masks in ancient Egypt: The image of divinity', in *Masks and the art of expression* (ed. Mack, John), New York, Harry Abrams.

Taylor, Graeme J. (1980) 'Splitting of the ego in transvestism and mask wearing', *International Review of Psychoanalysis* 7, 511–20.

Tseëlon, Efrat (2000) 'Is the presented self sincere? Goffman, impression management, and the postmodern self', in *Erving Goffman: Sage masters of modern social thought*, (ed. Fine, G.A. and Smith, G.W.H.), London, Sage (originally published in *Theory, Culture & Society*, 9,115–28, 1992).

Tseëlon, Efrat (1995) *The masque of femininity: The presentation of woman in everyday life*, London, Sage.

Turner, Victor (1969) *The ritual process: Structure and anti-structure*, Chicago, University of Chicago Press.

Urban, Greg and Hendricks, Janet Wall (1983) 'Signal functions of masking in Amerindian Brazil', *Semiotica* 47–1/4, 181–216.

Widdershoven, Guy A. M. (1994) 'Identity and development: A narrative perspective', in *Identity and development: An interdisciplinary approach* (ed. Bosma, Harka A., Graafsma, Tobi L., Grotevant, Harold D. and de Levita, David J.), London, Sage.

Yeats, William Butler (1962) *Explorations*, London, Macmillan.

Yeats, William Butler (1972) *Memoirs* (ed. Donoghue, Denis), London, Macmillan.

Ziffer, Irit (1992) *A touch of the past*, Tel Aviv, Eretz Israel Museum.

Zimbardo, Phillip G. (1969) 'The human choice: Individuation reason and other versus deindividuation, impulse, and chaos', in *Nebraska symposium on motivation*, (ed. W. J. Arnold & Levine, D.), Lincoln, University of Nebraska Press.

2

STIGMA, UNCERTAIN IDENTITY AND SKILL IN DISGUISE

Christie Davies

Most people have neither the skill nor the motivation to adopt a drastic disguise. They cannot adopt a new and very different identity in order to deceive others. They are bad actors in the sense that they have only a limited repertoire of roles, a repertoire bounded by a tight grid of age, sex, family position, social status, occupation, ethnic origin and social class. Even if they try radically to alter their costume and appearance, their speech patterns, gestures, manners and general bearing immediately give them away. Although the presentation of self is of central importance to every individual, it is typically done within a very narrow and often stereotypical range that comprises what the person thinks he or she 'is'. If forced to go beyond this range people become awkward, embarrassed, shuffling and incompetent. But then they very rarely need to do so, since even those occupations which require skills in persuasion, rhetoric and the creation of an image (as in the case of a lawyer, car salesman or air hostess) are either bounded and structured by rules and expectations, or operate within a narrow band of human behavior. Possibly the range of presentation of self is even narrower for men than for women in modern industrial societies, for even their appearance is held within the strict utilitarian confines of occupational or conventional clothing. Most of us could never succeed as actors or actresses, spies or undercover agents; our upbringing and social training have had much too limiting an effect. Those who habitually wear 'masks' to hide a stigma or to resolve an uncertain identity are more likely to have the makings of a good performer on the stage, even before they have been trained. The rest of us can only act out restricted versions of ourselves.[1]

By contrast there is a minority of individuals for whom disguise is central to their lives. This is because their identity is uncertain or because they possess a stigma which is defined by Goffman – as 'deeply discrediting' (Goffman, 1968, p. 18),

> an attribute that makes him different from others in the category of persons available for him to be, and of a less desirable kind . . . he is thus reduced in our minds from a whole and usual person to a tainted, discounted one.
>
> (Goffman, 1968, p. 12)

In some cases the stigma is obvious, visible or well known and the individual is 'discredited'; in others it is concealable and the individual is 'discreditable' (*ibid.*, p. 14). In the latter case people's attitudes and behaviour towards him or her will change markedly for the worse if he or she is found out. It is the latter case that is to be considered here and particularly in relation to illegitimacy and male homosexuality. During the 150-year period 1817–1967 in most of Western Europe and North America to be illegitimate or homosexual was to bear a discreditable social stigma that had to be concealed from most of a person's associates, with the exception only of those who shared the same stigma and the 'wise', i.e., 'persons who are normal but whose special situation has made them intimately privy to the secret life of the stigmatized individual and sympathetic with it' (*ibid.*, p. 41). It should be noted, though, that even Victorian representations and experiences of these problematic social constructs were varied and fluid. They depended on an individual's social position, the differing kinds of authority imposed on them in the various circumstances of their lives, and the choice of discourses and narratives available to them (Taylor, 1996, p. 119).

Goffman (1968) has described in detail the skills and strategems that those with a discreditable stigma need to employ in order to lead a reasonably smooth and unembarrassed existence. What I wish to suggest here is that these skills in disguise and in the management of identity (which 'normals' only rarely need to possess) are transferable to other activities. This, perhaps, is the crucial reason for the high concentration of illegitimates and of male homosexuals in the theatre and the entertainment industry, and in espionage. These professions differ from the general run of occupations in that they require their members to be able to play radically different parts on different occasions and to segregate incompatible parts of their lives. When Sir Ian McKellen successfully played Richard II and Edward II in Leeds, the Wood Demon in Bath and Harold the 'queer' antique dealer in *Black Comedy* in the West End, it required a very skilled transformation indeed on his part to move successfully between such disparate characters.[2] Likewise, Sir Anthony Blunt had to keep apart his totally incompatible roles as distinguished estab-lishment art-historian, confidante of the British royal family and trusted member of the British intelligence service on the one hand, and Soviet mole on the other. It seems very likely that the considerable professional skills of these two knights, one on the stage and the other as a secret agent of a foreign power, respectively, owed a great deal to their need for part of their lives at least, strictly to disguise and manage their homosexual incli-nations and identity.

Another factor that illegitimates and homosexuals have in common that motivates them to acquire techniques of disguise is the uncertainty and ambiguity of their identity (Davies, 1975, 1982, 1993). In a patrilin-eal society men and, to a lesser but substantial extent, women derive their identity and even their names (not just surnames but patronymics and pedigrees) from their fathers. But what if the mother of an illegiti-mate child doesn't know who the father is, or refuses to tell? What if the father is a distant figure who refuses to acknowledge and/or wishes to have no contact with his own children? What if the child is moved at a young age back and forth between the household of the father and that of the mother? Under these circumstances how does the child know who he or she is, particularly in the case of a fatherless male child who will lack a father to imitate or even a father's reputation to emulate? If such an unrecognised and disenfranchised person grows up in a society where identity is defined in terms of kinship rights and obligations, how can this *filius nullius* (the son of no one) know where and to whom he belongs? This is especially a problem if paternity is unknown or denied. What could a Welshman in Tudor times in this latter position say, when even a relatively humble neighbour would proclaim his own identity as Dafydd ap Rhys ap Myrddin ap Grufydd ap Wmfre ap Huw (David the son of Rhys the son of Merlin the son of Griffith the son of Humphrey the son of Hugh; today one of these patronymics will have long ago been turned into an Anglicised surname, such as Price, Bumphrey or Pugh).

The suggestion advanced here is that the person who has not inherited a part in such a patrilineal society is forced to act a part instead, possibly by moving away, taking on a new name and adopting a simulated identity, rather as, at a much later time, Henry Moreton Stanley (born Rowlands) the explorer did. But to act a part in a society where most people merely inherit a part at birth is to acquire transferable skills. In most cases in Wales, where naming and identity was (and in Iceland still is) defined by paternity and paternal ancestry, the illegitimate child would have taken the father's name and pedigree and been acknowledged, but others would be known as the son of someone or other, the son of a soldier or that son of a gun. Also in some cases paternity could not be properly acknowledged because the father was a celibate priest and the child a *fils du prêtre* or *Pfaffenkind*, as in the case of Erasmus (Bainton, 1972), whose entire life may be seen as a tale of uncertain identity. Likewise the Jewish category of *mamzerim* (where the parents are not merely not married to each other but could not marry because such a marriage would be incestuous or adulterous) is a category of exclusion and nullity. It would have been regarded not merely as a source of stigma but also of non-identity in all respects. Not only may *mamzerim* not marry non-*mamzerim*, they may not even marry one another (at any rate not in a Jewish religious ceremony). Such people are non-characters in search of a producer.

A similar problem has arisen historically in regard to male homosexuals and transvestites in those societies where they have been condemned and persecuted. In many countries practising male homosexuals have been denounced by religious leaders and punished by the exercise of the criminal law or of the disciplinary regulations of the armed forces (Davies 1982, 1983). Displays of public affection between males have led to severe social censure and even violence, and men dressing in women's clothing have been prosecuted and held up to public ridicule. In all these respects lesbians and women in male attire have been much less harshly treated (Davies, 1975). It was and is the case that an active female tomboy would be less persecuted in childhood than a male child behaving in a manner seen as effeminate. This difference clearly indicates that the more vigorous moral condemnation of male as against female homosexuality has its origins not in the defence of the family but in the protection of the male *de jure* or *de facto* celibate hierarchies that exercised such considerable power in the past, notably the army and the Church (Davies, 1982, 1983). Yet careers in these two hostile institutions are likely to have been attractive to male homosexuals, because they provided distinctively male roles that denied or at least did not require the active heterosexual behaviour demanded of a paterfamilias. A voluntarily celibate Anglo-Catholic priest is called Father, even though he has promised not to be one and can choose his attire from a wardrobe of colourful frocks that are forbidden to the dull-trousered modern male. It is likely that these distinctly male positions and preserves are and were attractive to those whose sexuality is 'a grey area'. For those whose masculinity (defined in sexual terms) is uncertain, membership of an exclusively all-male organization with a distinctive uniform (such as a combat unit or the priesthood) solves the problem of uncertain male identity with which they are faced. It is not surprising that homosexually inclined priests in the Church of England were so strongly, indeed bitterly, opposed to the ordination of women (Davies, 1987; Treasure, 1992), even though it represented a major boost to the values of toleration and equality from which they stood to gain most. Stigma and uncertainty of identity haunted the lives of homosexuals as much as it did the lives of those who were illegitimate.

The centrality of disguise for the stigmatized and for the uncertain of identity, and the consequent acting skills that they acquire, accounts for a phenomenon that is well expressed but badly explained by Ashworth and Walker (1972). They say that 'the ratio of homosexual males to heterosexual males appears to be higher in this occupation [the theatre] than in any other occupation known to the authors. An interesting fact is that female homosexuals are far less common.' (ibid, p. 150)

Ashworth and Walker go on to explain this phenomenon (as class-obsessed British sociologists tend to do) in terms of 'the positions occupied by male and female entertainers within the social stratification system of the U.K.' They argue that male actors and entertainers are unable to marry because most of them have low and uncertain incomes but come from middle-class backgrounds and, in common with any potential spouses they might seek, have middle-class tastes and expectations. By contrast, 'the fact that the female entertainer, having desired physical qualities, is sought after for erotic purposes, direct and indirect, and for companionship and marriage by males outside the theatre (or elite males within it) means that male entertainers have to compete on very unequal terms with males of higher economic status' (ibid., p. 152). In consequence, argue Ashworth and Walker, actors turn to homosexual relationships for both sexual gratification and emotional satisfaction, rather in the way that men or women may turn to homosexual or lesbian practices when in prison, where they have no access to members of the opposite sex. They fail to recognize that the nature of this adaptation is very different in women's prisons, where couples may form affectionate and stable relationships, at least for the duration of the prison sentence. In contrast sex in men's prisons tends to involve calculated exchanges often including illicit commodities such as alcohol, tobacco or other drugs and the use of coercion against young prisoners or prisoners known to be homosexual by nature and preference (Ward and Kassebaum, 1966). The 'Alcatraz Birdman' used the alcohol from a still hidden behind his smelly (and thus unlikely to be searched by prison officers) bird cages to pay for sexual favours from younger prisoners in this way.

Ashworth and Walker (1972) also claim, on the basis of quite inadequate evidence, that homosexuality is both rife and tolerated in the Muslim world because the polygamy of the rich means that there are not enough women to go round. Islam condemns homosexuality (Doi, 1984, pp. 241–3) and Muslim societies vary enormously in their attitudes to homosexuality: from toleration in Morocco and much of the rest of the

Maghreb, to great hostility in the Gulf States and Iran. Very few Muslims can afford more than one wife, and the only likely consequence of polygamy is that men would marry slightly later in life, and marry wives who are much younger than they are. The situation is no different from that experienced by the Victorian professional man who postponed marriage until he could afford to support a wife in middle-class comfort, or the son of an Irish peasant family who could marry only when he inherited the farm. There is no evidence that such men (who often did not marry until their late 30s or 40s) consoled themselves during their younger and most sexually vigorous years with homosexual practices. On the contrary, it is more likely that they were serviced by a sizeable population of relatively inexpensive female prostitutes. They may not have established a great deal of emotional rapport through these brief mercenary encounters but, then, how does this differ from the experience of homosexuals who go cottaging or cruise around promiscuously. Old and ugly homosexual actors have been reported as complaining that they are forced to pay for their sex (Williams, 1993), much as a male client pays a female prostitute. The number of stable Darby-and-Darby-type lifelong homosexual relationships between poverty-stricken, insecure, incessantly travelling, elderly actors is probably very small, far smaller than the number of marriages entered into by heterosexual actors who finally decide that love on the dole is better than none. Ashworth and Walker's model simply doesn't work.

Male heterosexual actors may find it difficult to marry, but it does not follow that they lack sexual partners in the short run. Actresses, female stage managers, usherettes or stage-struck female fans are all likely to be more appealing than a gay colleague to an actor whose orientation and preferences do not lie in that direction. Accordingly it is far more likely that most heterosexual men faced with the actors' dilemma would combine long-term male, female and kinship-based friendships with a succession of short- to medium-term sexual relationships with women, both partners knowing that these will lead neither to marriage nor to children. Such arrangements are common, particularly for men in occupations that require frequent geographical movement. Ashworth and Walker (1972) provide no evidence that homosexual relationships in general are any more stable or satisfying than the alternatives suggested above, and that those of a heterosexual disposition will choose the heterosexual version of the various unsatisfactory kinds of sex life open to them. Besides, there is some chance that the heterosexual version will culminate in marriage and children, even if this means penury, a change of occupation, supplementary jobs or living off the wife's earnings or on social security. There are after all many families who combine high social status with very low incomes, for example those of Protestant clergymen. Homosexual actors are far more likely to have been that way inclined long before they joined the theatre than to be converts from heterosexuality induced to be bisexual by poverty and permissiveness.

By contrast, the 'skill in disguise' model, postulated here as the reason for there being disproportionately large numbers of male homosexuals on the stage, has far superior explanatory power. It also explains why actresses are so successful in entering a higher social class through marriage, why the theatre is such a remarkably tolerant institution, and why people of illegitimate birth also use the entertainment industry as 'a queer ladder' of social mobility. Ashworth and Walker's (1972) explanation of the success through marriage of actresses is only partly true. Allure is only half the story. In the nineteenth century 13 female stage players married peers in Britain, and between 1900 and 1935 so did a further 21. Only seven of these marriages ended in divorce (Bullock, 1935). The key factor in sustaining and maintaining, as well as obtaining, such marriages is the actress's ability to play the part of a peer's wife as the peer expects it to be played. An attractive ex-barmaid married to a peer might well wantonly and shockingly swear at his lordship's associates, whereas a former actress in this position, even one of plebian origin, would only tell someone to 'fork orf' when it was strictly necessary and appropriate. An imaginary marriage broker would advise, 'she will be able to act her part to give every satisfaction, my lord.'

The theatre is attractive to the stigmatized and to those of uncertain identity because it offers a tolerant and amorphous refuge from an often hostile and rigidly structured and bounded world; it is tolerant and amorphous because it is the home of disguises. In the theatre no one has an essence, only a disparate series of 'masks', costumes, make-up and illusions that can be donned and doffed according to the tastes of an audience and the demands of a production. Those with a stigma can take refuge in the view that they have the freedom to represent themselves as, or indeed to be, whatever they choose. It can well be argued that when adopting a theatrical model of social life (like Goffman's, 1959) there would be no difference between acting and being (Tseëlon, 1992, 1995). Likewise, those tormented by an uncertain identity can take comfort in the view that all identities are uncertain in a theatre world where identities can be chosen and changed. Indeed, in a totally theatrical society like the one suggested by Goffman's theoretical model, there would be no difference between acting and being. However, while actual social life is never like that, some situations and some institutions approach the model more closely than others.

Disguise lies at the very heart of the work of the professional entertainer. Actors and actresses appear in many disparate and changing parts from one performance to the next or even quickly change their role or appearance in a single production. A player can in principle abandon his or her age-grade, sex, social class, ethnic, national and religious community and be whatever is called for on the night. Indeed, this has always been one of the bases of the puritans' dislike of the theatre, for the theatre affronted and threatened the puritan view that the self was or ought to be fixed, stable, uniform and distinct (Levine, 1994). Men in women's clothing were especially disturbing, not just because they were breaking down basic habitual boundaries (Davies, 1975), but also because the female attire was seen as effeminizing the man who wore it on the stage (Levine, 1994). However, that which shocked the puritans is salvation for the stigmatized and uncertain. For the uncertain it provides, at least for the time being, a part in a partless world and for the stigmatized an egoistic and anomic liberation from the prison of group and fate. The other side of the theatrical Weltanshauung is that male out-of-work actors are willing to work as domestic servants in private households, a job which even the long-term unemployed are unwilling to take on because they perceive such tasks as demeaning. However, actors do not become the second footman or the groom, the man who cleans the billiard room, they merely play the part of these flunkies.

The disguise model has the further advantage that it explains the disproportionate presence of illegitimates as well as male homosexuals in the theatre on the basis of the same sociological variables. People of uncertain or marred identity such as the illegitimates Sarah Bernhardt, Charles Brookfield, Daniel Chatto, Grevinde Danner, Peter Finch, Sophia Loren, Marilyn Monroe, Eva Peron, Sir Carol Reed and Kenneth Tynan (Bernhardt, L.S., 1949; Bernhardt, S., 1907; Berton, 1923; Bingham, 1979; Brandon, 1992; Craig, 1957; Faulkner, 1979; Flores, 1952; Jordan, 1989; Lanchester, 1983; Meisner, 1990; Summers, 1986; Verneuil, 1942; Whitaker, 1956) are to be found disproportionately among the ranks of successful entertainers and the designers and producers whose imaginations sustain them. The point is not that illegitimates are disproportionately represented relative to their numbers in the population, but rather that in the great age of stigma, the 150-year period 1817–1967, this was the main sector in both Europe and America where they visibly succeeded in large numbers. The fluid nature of the work and the rapid changes and deceptions employed by entertainers make it a tolerant world in which a person's peculiar social background or private life are unimportant and ignored. Furthermore the talent for disguise and deception developed by the illegitimate, which might be seen as suspicious in a solicitor, is an asset to an entertainer.

Illegitimates and homosexuals are experts of disguise in another significant sphere of life: that of the spy or undercover agent. The importance of homosexuality in the double lives of such agents as Burgess and Maclean, Blunt, Vassall, and Driburg is well known (Boyle, 1979; Costello, 1988; Pincher, 1978, 1989), though it is ironic that they all spied for the Soviet Union, a country notorious for its cruel persecution of homosexuals (Davies, 1975, 1982). The importance of illegitimates as spies is less well known and will be considered here in relation to the detailed biographies of specific individuals.

Case histories of illegitimates rather than homosexuals are used here because they are closer to being an 'ideal type' (in the Weberian sense) than are the homosexuals; there are fewer possible alternative explanations. A further advantage of focusing on the illegitimate in this way is that it focuses attention on the centrality of the skill in disguise displayed by the agents. Focusing on the illegitimate avoids the distractions that exist in accounts of homosexuals acting as spies, such as blackmail, as in the case of Vassall (a pressure to which many heterosexuals are vulnerable as well). Finally, concentrating on the illegitimate also avoids the widely held fantasy that there exists a great network of treasonable homosexuals, determined to undermine the bourgeois society that spurned them. Most British homosexuals were shrewd enough to have known that their Soviet equivalents were liable to spend several years in a Soviet labour camp for an entirely victimless offence. Presumably it is skill in disguise and not inclination to spy that is the key to success, though one is forced to wonder how the drunken Burgess and the reckless groping Driberg ever got away with anything.

The first illegitimate master of disguise to be considered is T. E. Lawrence (Lawrence, 1935, 1955), Lawrence of Arabia. Lawrence's father, Thomas Chapman, was a member of the Anglo-Irish gentry who eloped with his children's governess; divorce and remarriage were not possible. Lawrence's parents took the name Lawrence by deed poll, but Mrs Lawrence could never bring herself to say 'my husband' and referred to Mr Lawrence as 'the boys' father' or 'Tom' (Knightly and Simpson, 1969, p. 11). From the age of 10 Lawrence knew that he had a shameful secret to hide. As a youth he was already elusive and eccentric, an enigmatic outsider for whom acting was an integral part of his nature (*ibid.*, pp. 17, 215). In later life, when famous, he was terrified that the secret disgrace of his illegitimacy would become widely publicized, and this inspired him to play elaborate games of hide and reveal.

Even before the First World War, when Lawrence was an archaeologist in Syria, he was probably a British agent spying on the Turks. In 1911 he wrote to Hogarth: 'I may live in the district through the winter; it strikes me that the strongly-dialectical Arabic of the villagers would be *as good as a disguise* to me' (*ibid.*, p. 38) (emphasis added). During the First World War he became famous as the British agent who immersed himself in the Bedouin way of life and wore Arab clothing. In his manual for political officers dealing with the Arabs he wrote:

> If you can wear Arab kit when with the tribes you will acquire their trust and intimacy to a degree impossible in uniform . . . It is, however, dangerous and difficult. You will be like an actor in a foreign theatre playing a part day and night for months, without rest, and for an anxious stake. Complete success, which is when the Arabs forget your strangeness and speak naturally before you, counting you one of themselves, is perhaps only attainable in character; while half success (all that most of us will strive for – the other costs too much) is easier to win in British things, and you yourself will last longer, physically and mentally, in the comfort that they mean . . .
>
> (P.R.O. Foreign Office 882/7, see also
> Knightly and Simpson, 1969; Liddell Hart, 1934)

Lawrence had been able to succeed because his previous life had been spent in disguise as 'an actor in a foreign theatre', hiding his shameful background and creating myths. It was this that enabled him to mix and merge with the Arabs and to pose as a Circassian when spying behind the Turkish lines. For more conventional British officers from uncomplicated backgrounds only 'half success' was possible, for they were too satisfied with being what they already were, to want, dare to or even to be able to transform themselves as he had done.

Lawrence became an ambivalent hero, fascinated yet frightened by his own fame. On several occasions he sneaked unrecognized into Lowell Thomas' illustrated lectures on 'Lawrence of Arabia'. He had helped Thomas prepare the lectures and the book *With Lawrence in Arabia*. However, he insisted that Thomas should preface the book with a denial that Lawrence had assisted him in any way. Lawrence was also fearful that his fame would result in the exposure of his illegitimacy, if, for instance, the truth about his parentage was published in *Who's Who*.

Characteristically, he tried to escape by adopting a disguise. First the ex-Colonel Lawrence joined the RAF as Aircraftman John Hume Ross. When the press found out, he left and joined the Tank Corps as a private, before returning to the RAF as Aircraftman Shaw. His talent for *disguise* became an obsession, as he tried to hide in humble positions and distant places under a false name. His strategy of retreat and hide, disguise and flight, when faced with fame, is the response of a man who had been managing a shameful secret since he was 10 years old.

A similar pattern may be seen in the life of Willi Brandt. Born in 1913 as Herbert Frahm, the illegitimate son of a shop assistant, he eventually became German Chancellor. The scandal of his origins both aroused the prejudices of polite society in Germany and was exploited by his opponent Konrad Adenauer, who would pointedly refer to him as Herr Frahm (Harpprecht, 1972, p. 51), thus reminding audiences of Brandt's illegitimacy and odd career.

Soon after the National Socialists came to power in Germany in 1933, Brandt fled to Norway. He took the name Brandt, signifying a burning brand that would provide a light in the political darkness of the time (*ibid.*, p. 42). It is also the name of the hero of Ibsen's play *Brandt the Iconoclast*. Brandt soon returned in disguise to take charge of the underground organization of the banned Social Democrat party in Berlin. He travelled on false papers using the passport of a fellow student in Norway, having memorized his friend's personal data and copied his signature (*ibid.*, p. 83). Back in Germany he lived the life of an 'illegal' person, a life of perpetual disguise, pretence and mistrust, in which all acquaintances were feared as potential informers and meetings organized with great secrecy. When the Germans invaded Norway in 1940, Brandt, as a political refugee from Germany was particularly vulnerable, so he disguised himself in a Norwegian army uniform and 'hid' in a prisoner of war camp. After the war, he returned to Germany and officially changed his name to Willi Brandt, the name he had used in his political activities.

Brandt, like Lawrence, set aside his name, origins and nationality in order to be able to operate with a disguised identity for political reasons. He could do this because the personal identity he abandoned was an uncertain one and one regarded by others as disgraceful. A person with a more secure, valuable and unproblematic identity would have been less willing and able to make such a change and to let go part of his or her inner self and personal biography. It is also possible that Brandt's decision to masquerade as a Norwegian (rather than, say, as a Dutchman or an Englishman) was influenced by the rumours (*ibid.*, p. 72) he had heard that the man thought to be his father had a Scandinavian name. A man uncertain of his identity, he clutched at this small increment of identity and rootedness.

Although I have indicated in an almost causal way the connection between stigma, skill in disguise and going underground, it was only the chance outbreak of war between Britain and Turkey and the unfortunate rise to power of the National Socialists in Germany that led Lawrence and Brandt to use their talents in this way. The same tendencies towards disguise and self-erasure may be seen operating in the lives of other illegitimates, such as Sir Henry Morton Stanley and Leonardo da Vinci, for whom they were, if anything, dysfunctional forms of behaviour. The important point is that the pattern is there anyway and precedes any putting of skill in disguise to practical use.

H. M. Stanley, born John Rowlands in North Wales, was illegitimate, abandoned by both his parents, brought up for a time by relatives, then dumped in the workhouse at the age of six (Bierman, 1991; McLynn, 1991; Stanley, 1909). He himself refers to his birth as dishonourable and knew he had been rejected by all his kin. As a child he was mocked at school for being a bastard. Stanley fled from this situation and acquired a new name, a new country and a new family. Distance is a great help for those seeking a disguise. It pays to go where you are not known. Stanley became in turn an American, a soldier in the army of the Southern Confederacy (his adoptive father, Stanley, being a merchant of New Orleans) and finally an Englishman and Unionist MP, as well as an explorer of the most remote and inaccessible parts of Africa. Like Lawrence, he hid himself abroad in far and unknown places and both loved and feared fame and publicity. He became a renowned explorer and reporter, yet feared gossip, calumny and slander because of the shamefulness of being base-born in a world of Victorian disapproval. He laid great stress on the values of honesty, truthfulness and straighforwardness and yet like Lawrence he manufactured lies and fantasies about himself and his origins, including incredible tales of disguise and deception by others. Like Lawrence of Arabia (Knightly and Simpson, 1969; Liddell Hart, 1934) and Leonardo da Vinci (Freud, 1965; Taylor, 1927), Stanley (Wasserman, 1932) was suspected of being both a homosexual and a sado-masochist. It is significant that such accusations should be made, even though proof was lacking. They indicate the kind of suspicions that those who are able to live in an 'open' and 'ordinary' way, because their identity is unproblematic, held about men such as Lawrence, Stanley and Leonardo da Vinci, whose birth circumstances had given them an obsession with disguise and exposure, with concealing and revealing, with fame and shame.

In Leonardo da Vinci's case it was not shame but confusion about his identity that was crucial. In Renaissance Italy illegitimates were accepted (Burckhardt, 1940; Taylor, 1927) without moral disapproval. None the less the peculiar circumstances of his early years left him with a confused and uncertain sense of identity which expressed itself through an obsession with secrecy and concealment. He was the illegitimate son of a prosperous notary who had a child by a peasant woman. At first he lived with his mother but at an early age was taken from her to be brought up in the house of his father and childless stepmother. Freud (1965) has suggested that Leonardo's indifference as to what happened to his artistic works, his 'children', copied his own father's initial indifference to the fate of his illegitimate son. Much of Leonardo's work remained unfinished, as he gave priority to the recording of his secret ideas in notebooks filled with forms of disguised writing, such as mirror writing, that were very difficult to decipher (McCurdy, 1907; Taylor, 1927; Zubor, 1968). There is yet another kind of link here between illegitimacy and an obsession with disguise and secrecy; an implicit statement to the effect that: 'I don't know who I am, so you shan't know either.' It was born neither of shame nor of ignorance of his ancestry, but from his experience of abrupt change at an early age, which produced an uncertainty as to where he belonged and who he was.

A detailed examination of aspects of the worlds of the theatre and of espionage tends to support the hypothesis that people with a discreditable stigma and/or an uncertain identity acquire skills in disguise that can be put to use in other areas of life. In order to fully demonstrate the validity of the hypothesis, it would be necessary both to provide quantitative evidence demonstrating that there is or used to be a disproportionate number of illegitimates and of male homosexuals in the business of entertainment and of espionage. One would also need to show that the illegitimates and homosexuals gravitated there because there was a demand for the special skills in disguise they had acquired earlier in life, as a way of managing stigma or as a response to an uncertain identity. It is a hypothesis that would have to be tested upon the basis of data from the past, and particularly the period 1817–1967 that I have termed the great age of stigma. During the last 30 years the social stigmatization of the illegitimate and the homosexual has markedly declined in most of Europe. Consequently, there will have been a decline in the number of people who have acquired skills in acting and disguise from their need to pass in a critical world. On the other hand, this growth of toleration is the result of a general weakening of identities and boundaries in society as a whole (Davies, 1975). This may lead to many more people exploring a wider range of disguises and ways of presenting themselves to the world.

The aim of this essay has been to show that the central hypothesis running through it about stigma, uncertain identity and skill in disguise is sufficiently plausible to make it worth testing, and that the evidence in favour of the hypothesis is better than in the case of the alternative theses criticized above. However, it should also be clear that general discussions and disagreements in sociology concerning the nature of the self are largely futile. There can be no answer to the question 'Are we what we are or merely the sum of the ways in which we present ourselves to the world, and the way these presentations are perceived by others?' The interesting problem, rather, is why there are differences in the way people in different social locations (in terms of stigma, occupation and possibly gender) would answer such a question and others like it. At the centre of any further investigation of the problem lie questions of disguise and non-disguise, liking for and dislike of disguise and of what is seen as a fitting and appropriate degree of disguise.

NOTES

1 At the *Mask, Masquerade and Carnival* conference organised by Dr Efrat Tseëlon in Venice, 1994, it was demonstrated that the wearing of an actual physical mask, such as those used in *Commedia dell'Arte*, immediately gave people untrained in theatre skills the confidence to competently act out the otherwise alien part suggested by the mask.
2 The use of the word 'queer' to describe Harold is Joe Orton's (Lahr, 1978). The point Orton is making is that the part of Harold is written as a piece of conventional stereotypical comedy.

REFERENCES

Ashworth, A.E. and Walker, W.M. (1972) 'Social structure and homosexuality: a theoretical appraisal', *British Journal of Sociology* 23, 146–58.

Bainton, Ronald H. (1972) *Erasmus of Christendom*, London, Collins Fontana.

Bax, Clifford (1932) *Leonardo da Vinci*, London, Peter Davies.

Bergson, Henri (1971) *Laughter: An essay on the meaning of the comic*, London, Macmillan.

Bernhardt, Lysiane Sarah (1949) *Sarah Bernhardt, my grandmother*, London, Hurst & Blackwell.

Bernhardt, Sarah (1907) *My double life: Memoirs of Sarah Bernhardt*. London, Heinemann.

Berton, Thérèse (1923) *Sarah Bernhardt as I knew her*, London, Hurst & Blackwell.

Bierman, John (1991) *Dark safari: The life behind the legend of Henry Morton Stanley*, London, Hodder & Stoughton.

Bingham, Madelaine Mary (1979) *The great lover: The life and art of Herbert Beerbohm Tree*, London, Hamish Hamilton.

Boyle, Andrew (1979) *The climate of treason: Five who spied for Russia*, London, Hutchinson.

Brandon, Ruth (1992) *Being divine: A biography of Sarah Bernhardt*, London, Mandarin.

Bullock, J.M. (1935) 'Peers who have married players', *Notes and Queries* 169, 10, 92–4.

Burckhardt, Jacob (1940) *The civilization of the renaissance in Italy*, London, Allen & Unwin.

Costello, John (1988) *Mask of treachery*, London, Collins.

Craig, Edward Gordon (1957) *Index to the story of my days: Some memoirs of Edward Gordon Craig 1872–1907*, London, Hulton.

Davies, Christie (1975) *Permissive Britain*, London, Pitman.

Davies, Christie (1982) 'Sexual taboos and social boundaries', *American Journal of Sociology* 87, 5, 1032–63.

Davies, Christie (1983) 'Religious boundaries and sexual morality', *Annual Review of the Social Sciences of Religion* 6, 45–77.

Davies, Christie (1987) 'Witches at the church door', *The Times*, 21st February.

Davies, Christie, (1993) 'Aspects of illegitimacy', *Social Biology and Human Affairs* 58, 1, 34–44 and 58, 2, 26–37.

Doi, Abdur, Rahman I. (1984) *Shari'ah, the Islamic law*, London, Ta Ha.

Faulkner, Trader (1979) *Peter Finch: A biography*, London, Angus & Robertson.

Flores, Maria (1952) *The woman with the whip*, New York, Doubleday.

Freud, Sigmund (1965) *Leonardo da Vinci and a memory of his childhood*, Harmondsworth, Penguin.

Goffman, Erving (1959) *The presentation of self in everyday life*, New York, Anchor.

Goffman, Erving (1968) *Stigma: Notes on the management of spoiled identity*, Harmondsworth, Penguin.

Harpprecht, Klaus (1972) *Willi Brandt: Portrait and self-portrait*, London, Abelard-Schuman.

Jordan, Ted (1989) *Norma Jean: A Hollywood love story*, New York, Morrow.

Knightly, Phillip and Simpson, Colin (1969) *The secret lives of Lawrence of Arabia*, London, Nelson.

Lahr, John (1978) *Prick up your ears*, London, Allen Lane.

Lanchester, Elsa (1983) *Elsa Lanchester herself*, London, Michael Joseph.

Lawrence, T.E. (1935) *The seven pillars of wisdom*, London, Jonathan Cape.

Lawrence, T.E. (1955) *The mint*, London, Jonathan Cape.

Levine, Laura (1994) *Men in women's clothing*, Cambridge, Cambridge University Press.

Liddell, Hart, Sir B. (1934) *T .E. Lawrence in Arabia and after*, London, Jonathan Cape.

McCurdy, F. (1907) *Leonardo da Vinci's notebooks*, London, Duckworth.

McLynn, Frank (1991) *Stanley: Sorcerer's apprentice*, London, Constable.

Meisner, Morten (1990) *Grevinde Danner – en oprorsk kvinde*, Copenhagen, Politikens.

Pincher, Chapman (1978) *Inside story*, London, Sidgwick & Jackson.

Pincher, Chapman (1989) *Their trade is treachery*, London, Sidgwick & Jackson.

Smith, Leslie (1989) *Modern British farce*, Totowa, NJ, Barnes & Noble.

Stanley, Sir Henry Morton (ed. D. Stanley) (1909) *Autobiography of Sir H. M. Stanley*, London, Sampson, Low Marston.

Summers, Anthony (1986) *Goddess: The secret lives of Marilyn Monroe*, New York, NAL.

Taylor, Annard (1927), *Leonardo the Florentine: A study in personality*, London, Richards.

Taylor, Jenny Bourne (1996) 'Representing illegitimacy' in *Victorian England, Victorian identities: Social and cultural formations in nineteenth century literature* (ed. Ruth Robbins and Julian Wolfreys), Basingstoke, Macmillan.

Treasure, Catherine (1992) 'The enemies in the closet. Have homosexual priests queered the pitch for women?', *Guardian*, 10th November.

Tseëlon, Efrat (1992) 'Is the presented self sincere? Goffman, impression management and the postmodern self', *Theory Culture & Society* 9, 115–28.

Tseëlon, Efrat (1995) *The masque of femininity: The presentation of woman in everyday life*, London, Sage.

Verneuil, Louis, (pseud. Louis Collin du Bocage) (1942) *The fabulous life of Sarah Bernhardt*, London, Harper.

Ward, David A. and Kassebaum, Gene (1966) *Women's prison: Sex and social structure*, London, Weidenfeld & Nicholson.

Wasserman, Jakob (1932) *H. M. Stanley Explorer*, London, Cassell.

Whitaker, Arthur Preston (1956) *Argentine upheaval: Perón's fall and the new regime*, London, Atlantic Press.

Williams, Kenneth (1993) *The Kenneth Williams diaries*, London, Harper Collins.

Zubor, V.P. (1968) *Leonardo da Vinci*, Cambridge, MA, Harvard University Press.

3

LESBIAN MASKS

Beauty and other negotiations

Halla Beloff

This work is dedicated to Tessa Boffin, of happy memory.

In 1928 Marguerite Radclyffe-Hall published an explicitly lesbian love novel *The Well of Loneliness*, setting out her view that lesbianism is inborn and ought to be accepted because it cannot be helped. The 'scandalous' book was denounced as immoral and the author was prosecuted for obscenity (Ruehl, 1982). Its author, who called herself just 'Radclyffe Hall', wore well-cut masculine jackets, a stiff collar and tie, and a trilby hat. She had cropped her hair. We can see that the cultural aesthetic of such earlier lesbians was committed to a simple elegance that we at the distance of some eighty years can appreciate as 'classic'. Its timelessness depends on its distance from the vagaries of the feminine fashionable and on its sheer luxury.

In the mid 1990s 'lesbian chic' has been taken up by straight young women, while lesbians themselves may now want to use clothes simply to play.

As aspects of identity-work, such use of social codes and camouflage by straight as well as lesbian women is worthy of serious attention. These are transgressions of various kinds, some exciting more animosity than others, and codes of recognition are no longer reliable. And as Reina Lewis (1997) has suggested, 'when identity can no longer be decoded from appearances, fashion is both a newly available playground and a danger zone of irrecognisability' (*ibid.*, p. 109).

Such dynamic and provocative modes of creating ambiguous impressions through clothes can perhaps be best discussed through a similar elision of straight logic. A sideways glance at a set of visual arguments, forming a set of questions, may produce the self-reflexive attention that the subject deserves and this author is hoping for.

54

Plate 3.1 Radclyffe Hall by Howard Coster.
Source: Courtesy of the National Portrait Gallery, London.

We all know that certain identities, like that of a male Professor of Electronic Engineering, fit neatly into the centre of a community. Other constructions, for example being unemployed from any occupation, are put at the margin. Social value is high at the centre, and lower as we move from that favourable position to the edge. Goffman (1964) has given us the rich model of 'stigma' to start understanding the situation of a person disqualified from full social acceptance. Note that he does not want to label the person, only the context in which they find themselves.

Goffman helps us to understand what he called 'spoiled identities' and he started with the more straightforward 'discredited' groups, whose deviance is clearly there for all to see, say, those with a visible physical disability. Then it becomes clear as his thesis progresses that the most interesting analysis is applied to those who are 'discreditable'. By this he refers to those who are in a covert, only potentially discredited, state. First, we might think here about someone whose father is in prison or those who have, in the past, been psychiatric patients and also those with a lesbian orientation. But perhaps – and now the reader may have experienced a moment of enlightenment – we all have some shameful difference. We all have potential stigma and deserve to be insecure even in our seeming-central positions.

Such a model can lead us to a complex source of social dynamics and their understanding. Nothing need be what it seems. We have choices in the degree of transparency and the masquerade is all around us. Concepts like in-group and out-group take on a new power because we can naturally place ourselves into situations of the 'establishment' and also of deviants. It is not simply a question of inhabiting one total identity category. We may move smoothly from one to another.

Dress as a feature of self-presentation is seen as a way of expressing psychological distinctiveness which we choose and make for ourselves. By such creativeness we can give ourselves some positive attributes, whatever the stereotype others may apply to us. We may work to show a disparaged group to be more stylish than the mainstream and indeed in this way persuade the centre to admire our strange but also intriguing ways. A related movement of distinctiveness may be the passage of so-called lesbian 'butch' and also 'street style' from English subcultures to the high fashion of Manhattan. The critical matter of the rejection and acceptance of despised styles over time can be understood in new ways. With familiarity, the distinctive sabotage of dress rules by an out-group may be appreciated as psychological creativity and adopted as part of mainstream fashion. (The progress of the groups themselves from the edge to the centre may be a slightly different matter.)

It is Goffman's thesis that will be developed with respect to lesbian identities in modern Western history. The discredited/discreditable distinction refers to those who are open in their orientation and to those who are being discreet. And the argument will then be extended, fluently it is hoped, to the position of those in a less marginal position: all women. It will be argued that the understanding of 'normal deviance' is indeed widely applicable.[1] We are all in the business of information management. We are all 'passing' as something else, something better. Masquerade is a part of that.

This kind of dynamic analysis is, I believe, entirely consonant with Celia Kitzinger's (1987) pioneering explication of the social construction of lesbianism itself. Rather than the outcome of biological determination, Kitzinger views various lesbian identities as negotiations within and without straight gender stereotypes, enabling women to express their individual social and political ideologies. The degree to which such negotiations are to be explicitly 'on show' will itself depend on the justifying ideology. For example, one kind of political choice may make open espousal of the signs of lesbianism part of the point of the orientation. That is, if rejection of the whole traditional masculine tough-minded, aggressive, domineering social stance and distance from men is at issue, then one must be proud to show that. On the other hand, others may hold the identity to be a purely personal, private matter concerning preferences for intimate partnerships. Then it is no one's business but one's own in the public arena.

So coming out may be viewed and negotiated as a personal or a political matter. Either one is simply 'true to oneself' or one wishes to claim a right of difference as a social and political principle. As Tajfel (1982) pointed out from his perspective of intergroup-theory, the latter is related to social change, the former not. The social/political manoeuvre will question and indeed sabotage the clear relationship between sex and identity. Straight women who play their role in various assertive and not feminine ways similarly counter the essentialist script, but in less threatening ways.

Any social scientist who believes in the truth and value of their discipline finds this sort of discussion exciting. It holds a promise of extending the metaphor of making the invisible visible – which is the aim of all reasonable study. Such study is more than an exposé; it is of intellectual interest. The political and moral corollary from this perspective is emancipatory for individuals and liberating for the community. If we all possess some at least discreditable story in our lives, then the distinction between the 'satisfactory' and the deviant becomes fluid and we must acknowledge that we are all kin to those with a visible stigma.

Further, we can see that the question of what kind of selves are possible for us depends on the situation we find ourselves in. How do we accept that? How do we manage information? By hiding our stigma can we remain only potentially discredited and so only potentially marginalised? Are we willing to risk being discredited by showing who we really are? Can we sabotage the social sanctions by flaunting our difference? How can change in general terms be wrought?

When social psychologists study social identity in action they are thinking about communication as well as experience. Consider the language of clothes. It is one of the most obvious elements in the stories we tell about who and what we are – or rather who and what we hope people will 'take us for' (Barnard, 1996; Beloff, 1993; Hollander, 1988; Lurie, 1981). We are skilled at using dress to manage information; we flaunt, state quietly or hide our selves. We can choose to communicate only to our knowing in-group, even to overstate the stereotype, or try to confuse. All this is going on within the current fashion range. While the hierarchical language of clothing rules applies to middle-class businessmen, old university academics and football supporters, it has a specific meaning for people at the margin. Here clothes will demonstrate 'passing' as someone nearer the centre, acceptance of the stigma with pride, or simply the refusal to acknowledge the stereotypes. These positions are defined here as camouflage, using the code, and playing.

In our society sex determines clothing from infancy.[2] Dress is a part of gender, and can form a delicate comment on sex, reinforcing or contradicting it. And even within the rules of femininity/masculinity and sexual orientation there are choices open to us about the signs we use to signal our precise positioning in terms of gender and sexuality. And within such dimensions of variation women may hide our relative androgyny behind a soft blouse, claim power by means of big shoulder pads or not cut our hair short although we ally ourselves to Sappho. Men can wear a unisex polo shirt, a big leather jacket or go for the moustache and short hair of a gay solidarity.

What must be true is that we are constantly in the business of stating, maintaining, repairing or hiding our social identity. So it follows that we are also constantly in some state of danger. We have to keep up with work on the 'right' self all the time. Women have been particularly interested in these enterprises. This is not because they are biologically tuned to obedience to rules. Rather, it is that we play many of our roles more saliently. Daughter, wife, mother have been traditionally prescribed with more detailed responsibilities than son, husband, father. And then the authority of the patriarchs is more prescriptively stated for standards necessary for female physical appearance. Subordinates, like women, always have clearer obligations to obey such social by-laws, than do the masters. Any woman who cannot reach those standards, of youth, slimness and some level of current definition of beauty, must bear the stigma of spoiled identity and may be removed from deference of the worthy and indeed from 'the action'.

Considering the traditions of Western society, women as a whole are placed outside the centre of power. Then, bearing in mind the standards of worthy womanhood, we need the Goffman model of spoiled identity to understand how essentially all women must, for most of their lives, find themselves even further 'disqualified from full social acceptance' (cf. Tseëlon, 1992). Such insecurity can lead to fine creativity. It certainly motivates the identity games in which women artists have sometimes indulged.

The texts of Claude Cahun

The aim of the following discussion is to introduce an example of visual rhetoric which demonstrates the possible fluency of identity movement or passage, and the power of vigorous communication which moves us between different positions. What must be accepted is that the social hierarchy of gender identity is de-stabilised.

Consider the identity play of the French artist who gave herself the bisexual name of Claude Cahun (1894–1954). Born Lucy Schwob, into a literary family in Nantes (they were friends of Oscar Wilde), she was educated at the Sorbonne and briefly at Oxford. Under another pseudonym, Claude Corlis, she had joined surrealist circles in Paris, but has disappeared from that history. It is her portraits of a series of selves, made in the 1920s and early 1930s that have recently been unearthed (Cahun, 1994). As a lone pioneer in games of appearance, she produced in small black and white, seeming-snaps, a whole range of possible women, all played by herself.

The shock comes from the complexity of her imagination and the cool cheek of her changing persona. We see those different women and realise we could be all of them (see Plate 3.2). The construction that we have based on the accident of birth and social position seems indeed arbitrary. She toys with those roles and persuades us that we can range from the absolute doll-like feminine through the sophisticated harlequin to the androgynous aviator and the bow-tied man. The acclaimed American performance artist/photographer Cindy Sherman has done little more (Sherman, 1987, 1991; Beloff, 1997).

Most of the photographs were taken in Paris but the later ones were made in Jersey where Cahun and her companion, Suzanne Malherbe, lived. This is a repertory company of women presented for our interest. But more than that, they also disturb the customs of the gaze. Traditionally, the display is for the man. The gaze is a masculine, active stance which looks at a passive woman. What is happening here though? (David Bate in Cahun, 1994) Is not the domain of patriarchy deeply disturbed? We have some *mise en scène*, but a setting that is hard to place. Is it fact or fiction? What is truth in this world of hers?

In these photographs we seem to be seeing sites of desire. It may even be the place of our own fantasy work. If the self is a text (Edwards and Potter, 1992), whose self is involved? Not just Cahun's. I, as the spectator, seem to speak a series of texts. And how many selves? How many identities? Her fantasy, or perhaps we should say her logic, provides the unknown setting of some ambiguous desires, hers and mine.

So, women, as non-men, are notoriously the bearers of spoiled identities, at various levels of abstraction. But then we can hardly expect to fit in with all the rules involved. They are wider and certainly more strictly enforced, even for straight women than men. Consider just the category of the body. There are always, albeit varying, ideal measurements; there are the categories of Madonna and Venus (or is it Whore?). We bear the burden of the beauty mask and also the mask of death, analysed with so much learning by Tseëlon (1995). If we cannot or will not bear all those burdens, there is only one tactic.

Plate 3.2 Self-portraits by Claude Cahun.

Source: a) *c.* 1920, John Wakeham collection. b) *c.* 1929, Patrick Lazean collection. c) *c.* 1927 Musée des Beaux-Arts de Nantes collection. Courtesy of Jersey Heritage Trust.

a

b

c

We try to become inured to criticism and hope to be skilled at many forms of camouflage. We cleverly appear more stupid than we are; we may wear the liveries of the straight woman although we are lesbians; we feel we should spend money on 'anti-wrinkle' creams. Feminists certainly know that, being the spectre haunting the Western world, it might be wiser, in some circles, to reveal our ideas, if at all, with a hint of irony.

We begin to see that in any presentation or interaction, plain speaking is only one among many options. Always there is the option of using certain codes or even complete camouflage. Openness, plain honesty and impulsiveness are romantic ideals. Instead we are more likely, knowingly or unknowingly, to plan strategies that are suitable for specific settings. What tactical move is likely to be used in which kind of presentation? In so far as men believe themselves to be at the centre of positive identity structures, they tend to hold that plain speaking is good enough for them. They would like us to believe that there is no 'difference', no shame, in their identity constructions; no information to be 'managed', therefore. (If one observes the rituals of male self-presentations, either in the business meeting or in a public bar, one might doubt complete spontaneous simplicity.)

There are codes in all kinds of identity communications. For example, the shared insignia of academics is an open secret. Think of the traditional corduroy trousers of men, now replaced by 'black for everything'; the mention of post-modernist idols and the use of its short-hand; and the unkempt, impulsive hair. On the other hand, properly sensible women wear navy blue; while the code of metropolitan sophistication for women is, of course, also black. These signals are understood, even though not always expressed in words, by all the members of a community.

Information management

If an identity, were it known, would discredit me seriously, then I would seek to remain only discreditable. I would hide the shameful aspect of my autobiography by clever information management. I would not want my true position to be open to general scrutiny. Camouflage, then, is used by a marginal, despised, discreditable group that wishes to avoid being actually labelled. The social identity is hidden by the wearing/espousal of the 'ordinary', and therefore unnoticeable, uniform. This will maintain my better status and may reduce my own tension, but will hardly lead to political change. The attack on prejudice and social reform will be the result of group solidarity in the clear espousal and acceptance of the shamed stereotype. (The Gay Pride movement is one example.) Only then will the dominant majority see the foolishness of the discrimination which was based on the now-flaunted characteristics.

Lesbians during the twentieth century seem to have used the complete range of identity possibilities. They have camouflaged their group membership; they have spoken plainly following the general stereotypes; and they have sometimes used a set of private codes to communicate to their sisters 'in the know' while keeping others outside.

What is the point of appearing ordinary but at the same time telling the in-group who you really are? First of all, it keeps one within the accepted and acceptable community. It gets you past the social censors of respectability. Second, and perhaps more important, the insider signals are a refined way of giving and gaining support from the sisters. It is the equivalent of the wink of the eye. It gives the support of the knowing insiders, whom Goffman called 'the own'. Eventually the wider world will decode the message. Then there will likely be a change in the code or, if the time is right, the short hair and the manly jacket may be worn with pride.

The use of codes seems infinitely flexible and functional. And the effects of different uses will vary depending on whether it is individuals or groups that are engaged. A flamboyant expression of the lesbian appearance will likely lead to outrage, but when practised by many, that outrage may be transformed to provocation for thought. (We may make a comparison with the change in African Americans' espousal of the despised 'nappy' hair.) A long-term flaunting of group membership seems to make it difficult to maintain a traditional prejudice and discrimination. And it certainly makes it easier for other, covert members of the group to come out of hiding.

It is worth considering further the communication of the marginal lesbian identity through clothes and other means, which are more or less encoded. This will be described within the context of all womanly presentations, which are also fraught and generally discredited to a greater or lesser extent.

The rules of all womanly presentation are illustrated, described, but critically prescribed in images all around us (Goffman, 1976). The role of female models in newspapers and magazines, product advertising and the history of fine art is often discussed.[3] Traditionally many women have colluded with the social pressure to conform to the ideals, although some resisted. Think of the nineteenth century with its 'alternative dress' (Crane, 2000) subversively appropriating male accessories (e.g. ties, boaters) or rebellion into 'rational dress' of functional clothes – a counterstatement to corsetry and frills – and small groups of intellectuals and artists come to mind.[4] The acceptance of instructions for proper appearance – that is, one pleasing to men – is demonstrated by the numerous 'How to . . .' manuals produced profitably from the Renaissance onwards. These, of course, describe the social prescriptions and help to bring us all nearer the demanded shape, behaviour and attitudes: all three are necessary.

The visual argument of Rosy Martin

Rosy Martin (1991) has attempted to show how those 'How to . . .' manuals teach us how to lie. In the process she has demonstrated (see Plates 3.3 and 3.4) how all that can be subverted by their simple re-presentation. It is the re-telling that tells it. Martin is a London photo-theorist and with Jo Spence (1995) she devised a specifically active kind of re-creation of personal histories within a political mould which has become their form of British photo-therapy. This practice is not to alleviate clinical disorders, but to release any of us who want it, from the bondage of fashion in the wider sense.

She has written critically on the position of working-class girls who, because of their wits, were recruited to free places in private girls' schools and so removed from their class. This experience of becoming technically *déclassé* (classless) brought Martin to consider the whole question of the class of womanhood.

What is powerful here is that Rosy Martin has not really *done* anything. She has just shown us, with some irony, those 'How to . . .' instructions for worthy womanhood. What follows is explosive sabotage through juxtaposing the simple-minded commands to women, with photographs of herself desperately trying to follow them.

Erving Goffman himself was much given to using scientifically unrespectable real-life evidence as data to demonstrate his conceptual arguments. He would have much appreciated her work. This is the management of spoiled identities indeed.

Martin on lesbian codes

More specifically with respect to the lesbian situation, Martin's work must be considered within some historical context. While we will have here to ignore the rich earlier lesbian history in England, there was in the first third of the twentieth century a particular flowering of open lesbian presentations in costume among upper- and upper middle-class lesbian women. This has still a significant echo in present negotiations. These women with their own incomes (earned or unearned) were free to perform their chosen selves in public. They were able to show not only a fine

Plate 3.3 Rosy Martin, 'Even the plumpest girl can stand with poise and elegance' (inspired by Anne Webb, *Growing Up Gracefully*, 1956).

Source: Martin in collaboration with Spence, 1991, p. 98.

boyish/manly persona with its expensive costume and props, but to advocate an aesthetic which they saw as significantly superior to the general. Not for them the elaborately fussy dresses and the intricately worked hair and jewellery. They liked to wear plain silk shirts, tailored suits (breeches in the country), they cropped their hair and favoured an elegantly plain tie pin. Laura Doan (1996) has explicated the refinement of such social symbolism. They used their patrician position in the class hierarchy to break the rules of worthy womanhood. It seemed part of their natural claim to superiority.

The public performances and the erotic female boyishness is open for all to see, but there were also implications for female voyeurism (to see the usually hidden identity) and the stretching of boundaries of the cultural aesthetic into that bold but plain elegance. The fascination lingers for all women who want more than what lies within the limits of 'the feminine'. What is clear is that it involved something much more subtle than cross-dressing into collars and ties. The manners may have been gallantly

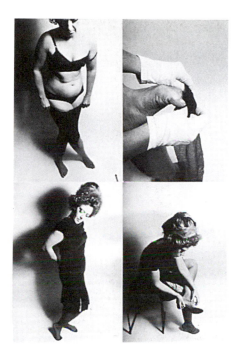

Plate 3.4 Rosy Martin, 'Women use their bodies far more than men to support their personality, even when they have a pretty face to attract attention' (inspired by Liselotte Strenlow, *Photographic Portrait Management,* 1966).

Source: Rosy Martin, in collaboration with Jo Spence, 1991, p. 99.

masculine (Rule, 1989) but it is not a crude masquerade of manhood. Rather it uses a kind of elegant austerity and an ideal of boyish slenderness to create an ambiguous cultural style. Here we are beyond the Goffman argument, that the management of spoiled identities must include a counterweight of some attractive attributes. Henri Tajfel's *Social Identity Theory* (1982) shows us how it makes sense for members of an oppressed group to choose their own criteria to turn their ascribed inferior identity to an achieved superior one. If others think us perverse, we might show them that our 'perverse' lifestyle includes the new aesthetic of advanced modernism which has progressed from their Edwardian traditional. We have made an alternative path to deserved worthiness.

Within the circle of 'the wise' (as Goffman (1964) called the intimates of a stigmatised group) this was successful. The codes, did provide validation for other lesbians' experience and practices. They recognised them. And, as we now see it, their presentations subtly

65

denaturalised and destabilised familiar gender signs (Garber, 1992). However, we also know that the medical and the sexology establishment entirely missed the fine nuances of lesbian presentations. As we see from the caption quotation in Martin's images (see particularly, Plate 3.5), they made crude interpretations about aping masculinity, to say nothing of penis envy, and used the subtle cultural style to fuel their anti-homosexual prejudice. It is this stance that Martin satirises, without bitterness.

Rosy Martin has addressed the issue raised by Walker (1993): 'The conflation of sexual style with sexual consciousness assumes a natural relationship between visible signifiers of sexual style and their signified sexual identities.' But, as Walker argues further, this can be deconstructed by a reconfiguration.

Plate 3.5 Rosy Martin, 'Transforming the Suit: what do Lesbians Look Like? Part 1, "Obsessed by their unobtainable goals to be men, they wore the most sombre uniforms: black tuxedos as though they were in mourning for their ideal masculinity"' (inspired by 'Brassai, "Sodom and Gomorrah"' in *The Secret Paris of the Thirties*, 1932).

Source: Rosy Martin, in collaboration with Jo Spence 1991, p. 100.

Like Jo Spence, Martin has also worked by means of presenting and re-presenting her own interactions, and needs and desires. She used an innovative way to communicate, performing or 'acting out' her identity work for the camera. This then involved thinking about the epithets she heard, or knew she would hear, when her relatives found out about her lesbian life. The cleverness or benefit of this technique is again that the audience can share her thoughts and feelings directly. We can empathise, or not, as the case may be. The access is so direct because the argument is simply visual.

Within the constraints of current fashion in dress, there remain certain echoes of those 1920s, pioneers. A certain element of masculinity was favoured. The social effects of such dress codes may provide several benefits. As in other kinds of uniform, they enhance solidarity. They are a signal of visibility to other members of the in-group. They show that members of a marginal group who wear such signals have the courage of their membership. The last point demonstrates that such benefits also incur costs. The openness puts you within the group which is discredited.

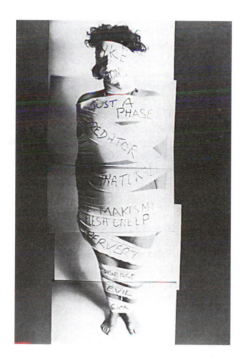

Plate 3.6 Rosy Martin, 'Unwind the Lies that Bind'.
Source: Rosy Martin, in collaboration with Jo Spence, 1991, p. 103.

Without it, you are safe in your ordinariness and remain only potentially discreditable.

If this is an understanding in terms of the lesbian tradition, there are now changes. It has been said that we now have 'the love that dares dress how it likes'. Is this an index of the acceptability? Is marginality no longer a badge to be worn with brave pride? Is it possible to just meld into the community?

Martin then has shown us the options that she understood to be offered her. She wants the right to distance herself from any kind of conforming uniformity, at least sometimes. She would seem to disagree with Elizabeth Wilson's view that all self-presentation is about power (in Steele, 1996 p. 184). She also seems uninterested in the general view that all fashion contributes to the subordination of women. She wants other possibilities, to use clothes to play with notions of identity (*ibid.*, p. 186).

What about the 'beauty' question?

This is not a triviality. I hold with Freud (1930), that we cannot live a reasonable life without beauty, and even Art. Art is a critical source of happiness and consolation. He wrote towards the end of his life, when he had strong reason to hold a deeply pessimistic view of the world, 'There is no very evident use in beauty; the necessity of it for cultural purposes is not apparent, and yet civilisation could not do without it.' (*ibid.*, p. 38) And further, 'The enjoyment of beauty produces a particular, mildly intoxicating kind of sensation' (*ibid.*, p. 39). But what is its relevance here?

Look again at those pictures from the 1920s. The tradition of severe, rigorous line in dress and decoration, its simplicity allied with quality provided beauty without prettiness and luxury without ostentation. It was above convention and ephemeral taste. This is art in the service of self-presentation.

Further, consider that tenacious war-horse of a novel, *The Well of Loneliness* (Hall, 1984), written in 1928. From it we know that Radclyffe Hall herself considered not only remarkable intelligence, great passion and intense religious feeling but beauty, elegant good taste and therefore some austerity to be an essential element of the Lesbian identity. It placed her group above the materialist bourgeoisie, *haute* or otherwise.

Stephen, the lesbian heroine did wear 'tailored suits' with matt silk neckties which were obviously sumptuously plain compared with the fripperies of her youth's dress-makers' dresses. And consider the important scene (*ibid.*, p. 163) where Stephen goes up and down Old Bond Street to find her beloved Angela the perfect present. It is the ring – 'just a thin band of platinum, holding a pearl without blemish', 'only the purest fit to touch her finger'. A fine standard of taste, although perhaps not untinged with some snobbery. While the language of love had to be camouflage, the aesthetic provided the easy code for the in-group, as well as a propaganda item for its periphery, the tentative perhaps-to-be lesbians.

No icons at the margins

Icons are works of art that presume the integrity and transcendental existence of their object (Lawson, 1989). From the history of Western art we know them as objects of worship and emulation. Let us be clear then that the life stories of the heroes of Western history are works of art in themselves. They 'presume' the truth. When Oliver Cromwell said, 'Paint me warts and all', his exceptional honesty entered folk lore. However, the point is that central members of the community, men, the in-group, have a whole repertory company from which to choose ideal persons, not only to follow but to bolster their own identities. Heroines are fewer but are, of course, increasingly recruited for straight women. It is lesbians who feel the lack of an extended company of icons. Tessa Boffin, the photographer, produced and published a body of work (Boffin, 1991) 'The knight's move' (see Plate 3.7), that at one stroke filled that lacuna and enlarged Lesbian history: if the company of the real lesbian role models was sparse, why stay there? Why remain frustrated by the disparagement of reality over fantasy? Create new icons, new transcendental existences.

Tessa Boffin's work moved history forward: by 'embracing idealised fantasy figures' and by 'placing ourselves into the great heterosexual narratives of courtly and romantic love: by making the Knight's move – a lateral or sideways leap' (ibid., p. 49). She threw the equation of photography with documentation of the real ('the camera never lies') into question.

These images are sites of fictions. And as Doan (1994, p. 154) has suggested, all fictions interrogate, trouble, subvert and tamper with gender. There is a negotiation of cultural history and identity that combines politics and beauty in a hermeneutic, liberating style. Here the pathology which was forced on lesbians in the past is abandoned. But Boffin says it is also more than an innocent rediscovery of a lesbian Golden Age. She has created a new past from present desires. She wanted a history that was both visible to us and was to be acknowledged by the general public. A creation that claims for the outsider at the edge a part of the centre empowers its own out-group. Those straight people in the mainstream will then be persuaded that such a beautiful formula of the past is something they can bear.

a   b

Plate 3.7 Tessa Boffin, 'My Knight, My Angel, from *Stolen Glances: Lesbians Take Photographs*, 1991.

Source: Courtesy of the Organisation for Visual Arts Ltd, London.

At this final point it is necessary for me to become personal – always a hard matter, especially for a British person. However, in the hermeneutic and feminist method of argument, it is accepted that we all start from a personal base and continue our arguments in some self-reflexive mode. Rigorous objectivity is not only a chimera, but is not even any longer hoped for.

I must admit that I am a straight woman, although marginal, discreditable and inferior from several other perspectives. I am aware of the fraught nature of seeking to represent others, or even worse, 'the Other'. I am aware of the danger that academics may do this unthinkingly, simply in their business of accumulating cultural and academic capital. This had been used to justify many things. However, taking my cue from Burman (1995), I am not so naive as to believe that I am in any general sense representing lesbian women. Rather, I attempt to disentangle our understanding of common kinds of Western social constructions around identity, which women have been doing with some panache. The more workers in the field, the more perspectives, surely the richer will be the outcomes. We are born into cultural traditions, but we do not need to remain within their bounds. And Western traditions need not be equated with some essential biological package.

I have wanted to emphasise my sameness not my difference, which does not come in a spirit of colonising nor romanticising, but comes of solidarity, because I recognise myself in 'others'.

NOTES

1 The fact that it is here applied to 'ordinary' women does not preclude its application to 'ordinary' men. It is simply the case that men have not yet been particularly interested in disassembling their own constructions.
2 Not only is blue 'appropriate' for a boy but there is the definite 'peril of pink'. While a baby girl may easily wear a blue garment, the development of a boy's gender identity is clearly so fragile, so fraught, that supposedly it cannot withstand the possible confusion that pink would bring.
3 Men who might be thought to have the obligation to fit the ideal of Classical Greek sculpture and the models of fitness of our own seem oblivious of it. Is that because women have not pointed out the discrepancies to them?
4 Examples may be seen among the artists called the 'Glasgow Girls' (Burkhauser, 1990). For men it was George Bernard Shaw who pioneered the sensible suits and woollen underwear of the firm of Jaeger.

REFERENCES

Barnard, M. (1996) *Fashion as communication*, London, Routledge.
Beloff, H. (1993). 'Les femmes de Cameron: rhetorique visuelle de "identité sexuelle"'. *Bulletin de Psychologie* 46, 580–8.
Beloff, H. (1997) 'Making and un-making identities: a psychologist looks at art work', in *Qualitative Analysis in Psychology* (ed. Hayes, N.), London, The Psychology Press.
Boffin, T. (1991) 'The knight's move', in *Stolen glances: Lesbians take photographs* (ed. Boffin, T. and Fraser, J.), London, Pandora.
Burkhauser, J. (1990) *The Glasgow girls: Women in art and design 1880–1920*, Edinburgh, Canongate.
Burman, E. (1995) 'The spec(tac)ular economy of difference', *Feminism & Psychology* 4, 543–6.
Cahun, C. (1994) *Mise en scène: Essays by David Bate and Francois Leperlier*, London, Institute of Contemporary Art.
Crane, D. (2000) *Fashion and its social agenda: Class, gender and identity in clothing*, Chicago, Chicago University Press.

Doan, L. (1994) 'Jeanette Winterson's sexing the postmodern', in *The lesbian post-modern* (ed. Doan, L.), New York, Columbia University Press.

Doan, L. (1996) 'The seductive lens: Sapphic performance and photography in the early twentieth century', paper presented at the conference *Masquerade and Gendered Identity*, Venice.

Edwards, D. and Potter J. (1992) *Discursive psychology*, London, Sage.

Freud, S. (1930) *Civilisation and its Discontents*, vol. 21, in *The standard edition of the complete psychological works of Sigmund Freud* (ed. and trans. Strachey, James), London, Hogarth Press, 1953–86.

Garber, M. (1992) *Vested interests: Cross-dressing and cultural anxiety*, London, Penguin.

Goffman, E. (1964) *Stigma*, London, Penguin.

Goffman, E. (1976) *Gender advertisements*, London, Macmillan.

Hall, R. (1984) *The well of loneliness*, London, Virago (originally published 1928).

Hollander, A. (1988) *Seeing through clothes*, London, Penguin.

Kitzinger, C. (1987) *The social construction of lesbianism*, London, Sage.

Lawson, J. (1989) 'The man who shot Garbo', *Scottish Photography Bulletin* 2, 30–1.

Lewis, R. (1997) 'Looking good: the lesbian gaze and fashion imagery', *Feminist Review* 55, 92–109.

Lurie, A. (1981) *The language of clothes*, New York, Random House.

Martin, R. in collaboration with Jo Spence (1991) 'Don't say cheese, say lesbian', in *Stolen glances: Lesbians take photographs* (ed. Boffin, T. and Fraser, J. London, Pandora.

Ruehl, S. (1982) 'Inverts and experts: Radclyffe Hall and the lesbian identity', in *Feminism, culture and politics* (ed. Brunt, R. and Rowan, C.), London, Lawrence & Wishart.

Rule, J. (1989) *Lesbian images*, London, Pluto Press.

Sherman, C. (1987) *Catalogue*, New York, Whitney Museum of Art.

Sherman, C. (1991) *History portraits*, New York, Rizzoli.

Spence, J. (1995) *Cultural sniping*, London, Routledge.

Steele, V. (1996) *Fetish: Fashion, sex and power*, London, Oxford University Press.

Tajfel, H. (1982) *Social identity and intergroup relations*, Cambridge, Cambridge University Press.

Tseëlon, E. (1995) *The masque of femininity: The presentation of woman in everyday life*, London, Sage.

Tseëlon, E. (1992) 'What is beautiful is bad: Physical attractiveness as stigma', *Journal for the Theory of Social Behaviour* 22, 295–309.

Walker, L.M. (1993) 'How to recognise a lesbian: the cultural politics of looking like what you are', *Signs* 18, 866–90.

4

FASHION, FETISH, FANTASY

Valerie Steele

Fashion has often been thought of as a kind of mask, disguising the wearer's 'true' identity. Indeed, in the eighteenth century, both fashion and masquerade were frequently used as metaphors for deceit. Henry Fielding, for example, described the world as nothing but 'a vast masquerade' where 'the greatest part appears disguised under false Vizors and Habits'. Yet, paradoxically, Fielding also observed with respect to actual masquerades that to 'masque the face' was 't'unmasque the mind'. And Addison agreed that masqueraders dressed as they 'had a mind to be' (quoted in Castle, 1995, pp. 82–3).

The connection between sexuality and masquerade apparently goes back to antiquity, when masked dances and theatrical performances accompanied ritual celebrations such as the Greek Bacchanalia and the Roman Saturnalia. Masked performances and carnivals continued to play a role in European popular culture for centuries, despite clerical ambivalence. In eighteenth-century Europe masquerades were entertainments at which the participants wore disguises. Many people chose to wear enveloping Venetian cloaks called dominoes accompanied by face masks to ensure anonymity. Contemporaries were well aware that the act of disguising oneself had erotic implications, because with anonymity came greater freedom. Cross-dressing was also popular, and revellers sometimes dressed as monks and nuns. Casanova believed that there was nothing quite so provocative as a fair nun unmasked (Fox and Ribeiro, 1983, p. 1; also *Columbia Encyclopedia*, 1950, p. 1237) (see Plate 1.5).

The construction of individualized sexual identities (as opposed to the performance of particular sexual acts) is a relatively modern phenomenon. Most historians believe that the eighteenth century marked a crucial phase in that process, which then crystallized over the course of the nineteenth century (Stanton, 1992, introduction; also Maccubbin, 1985). The influence of works like Richard von Krafft-Ebing's *Psychopathia Sexualis* (1886) popularized the use of medicalizing categories, and a nomenclature of words such as 'fetishist' and 'transvestite' was invented to describe people with 'deviant' sexual identities. Meanwhile, late nineteenth-century brothels increasingly catered to specialized sexual interests, often stocking fantasy costumes. Among the most popular were nuns' habits, bridal gowns, schoolgirls' uniforms and (in gay brothels) military uniforms. One of the necessary preconditions for this situation was, of course, the rise of fashion as a mass phenomenon (Steele, 1996, pp. 48–9. The present chapter draws upon and amplifies some material in the final chapter of that book, in a few instances using identical language.)

The categorization of minority or 'deviant' sexual interests and practices had the effect of stigmatizing their practitioners and driving them underground. The clothing and paraphernalia associated with such practices had to be obtained discreetly. In the late twentieth century, however, sexual fetishists have increasingly come 'out of the closet', developing a network of clubs, media and commercial emporia. Although many fetishists still utilize mail-order catalogues, fetish clothing stores are increasingly common. In recent years, the concept of fetishism has also assumed a growing importance in critical thinking about the cultural construction of sexuality. Works such as *Fetishism as Cultural Discourse* (Apter and Pietz, 1993) and *Female Fetishism* (Gamman and Makinen, 1994) complement or critique the clinical studies of fetishism as a sexual 'perversion'.

Although some fetishists are attracted only to individual objects (such as shoes), others adopt entire ensembles, which incorporate a variety of clothing fetishes: boots, corsets, rubber, uniforms, masks, etc. To initiates, these costumes convey rather precise messages about the kind of sex offered and/or solicited, and the theatrical play within which sexual contact will occur. The costume is thus part of an elaborate erotic drama, which often involves sado-masochism and transvestism. Participants in these ritualized sexual performances disguise themselves in costumes, among the most common being the dominatrix, the maid and the nurse. In what follows, I will attempt to analyze the psychological significance and cultural symbolism of these costumes.

Although the topic may seem bizarre, this type of sartorial role-playing bears obvious similarities to mainstream cultural phenomena. In the film *Batman Returns*, for example, Michelle Pfeiffer's Catwoman is costumed to resemble a dominatrix. The editors of the European sex magazine *O: Fashion, Fetish & Fantasies* responded enthusiastically: 'High Heels. Rubber Catsuit. Breast Harness. Face Mask . . . [Catwoman's] shiny black outfit . . . mak[es] fetish fashion internationally known. Thus speeding up its triumphal march and gaining general approval' (number 13, no date, p. 4). General approval may or may not be forthcoming immediately, but fetish style is visible throughout popular culture.

Fetishistic iconography is especially obvious in contemporary fashion. This is hardly surprising, since fashion often exhibits elements of fantasy, being inspired by ethnic dress, period costume and military uniforms. Since fashion implicitly refers to the body, sexual themes are often noticeable. Traditionally, sartorial eroticism entailed the exposure of selected body parts, the so-called 'erogenous zones'. Beginning in the 1960s, however, fashion also increasingly exploited the power of certain 'perverse' erotic fantasies. In the beginning of the 1990s, the fashion magazine *Harper's Bazaar* playfully captioned one photograph of an ensemble by Gianni Versace: 'Heavy metal, light bondage. The straps and stilettos of the dominatrix will not be denied' (September 1992, p. 319).

Let us begin then with the fetish costume of the dominatrix, which is one of the most important both in the world of sex and in the world of fashion. According to Madame Sadi, who was interviewed in the English fetish magazine *Skin Two*, a dominatrix should 'never bare her breasts and always wear elegant clothing (high heels, preferably boots, and gloves)' (issue 11, no date, p. 24). Although, in fact, a dominatrix may sometimes show a glimpse of naked thigh or bosom, it is more common for her to be almost completely covered by a second skin – from the mask that partially or entirely covers her face down to her stiletto heels.

If the dominatrix (or 'mistress') is clothed in power, the 'slave', by contrast, is stripped naked, or reduced to wearing clothing designed to expose underwear or soft vulnerable skin. There is a basic distinction, therefore, between clothing that signifies power and nudity that implies submission. But in any given case, the garment's symbolism is contingent on the overall context. If the dominatrix is masked like an executioner or torturer, the slave's mask or hood implies the victim. The boots of the mistress are cruel and empowering, while the slave is 'hobbled' by bondage shoes. Yet in terms of actual design characteristics, the shoes of mistress and slave are remarkably similar, usually with very high heels and often multiple straps and buckles.

Obviously, people who dress up as mistress and slave are acting out a fantasy of some sort, but how are we to interpret it? As commonly used, the word 'fantasy' denotes imagination, unreal or exaggerated images, illusion, and the like. Thus, the discourse in the fashion press stressed that Versace designed 'fantasy clothes' that should not be taken 'too seriously'. But fantasy also has a particular psychological meaning, involving the fulfillment of psychic needs. People might, for example, feel that sexuality is dangerous, and without really knowing why, their sexual behavior might be inhibited or otherwise altered. Behind their vague anxiety might lie a more-or-less unconscious fantasy that the vagina might strangle them, or that the penis will rip into the body like a knife. According to psychoanalysts, conscious sex fantasies overlie certain original fantasies on themes such as castration, seduction and the primal scene (i.e. the vision of parental intercourse) (Laplanche and Pontalis, 1986, pp. 18–20). Many psychiatrists believe that the 'Phallic Woman' is 'the ubiquitous fantasy in perversions'. By acting out the fantasy that this woman really does have a penis, the fetishist obtains an 'orgiastic affirmation of the truth of the primal fantasy'. In addition, '[b]y actually engaging dramatis personae, the fantasy becomes indisputable reality' (Bak, 1968, p. 35).

The costume of the dominatrix certainly incorporates a number of obvious phallic symbols, such as high-heeled shoes or boots, long gloves, a boned corset and such accessories as a whip or riding crop (Freud, 1927, pp. 152–4). Clothed in hard, shiny material, her entire body is transformed into an armoured phallus. Significantly, the visual history of fetishist pornography proves that the costume of the dominatrix has remained amazingly unchanged for decades. Since the vast majority of fetishists are men, this costume presumably appeals to certain male sexual fantasies and/or assuages male fears. According to Dr Louise Kaplan, the fetishist 'cannot introduce his penis into that temple of doom called a vagina without a fetish to ease the way' (1991, p. 54). But the fetish is much more than a phallic symbol.

'A fetish is a story masquerading as an object', writes Robert Stoller (1985, p. 155). Although the story's dialogue may be carefully scripted and endlessly rehearsed, the text itself (or rather, the subtext) may remain largely unconscious to the fetishist. Yet we do have some access, at least to the manifest content of these sex stories. Pornography, which has been notoriously difficult to define in legal terms, might be defined in psychological terms as a commercially produced sexual fantasy. The popularity of certain types of pornography provides at least a clue about the prevalence of perverse fantasy and behavior.

In fantasy, 'what is portrayed is not the object of desire, but a scenario in which certain wishes are presented', as Elizabeth Cowie writes in an essay on 'Pornography and Fantasy' (1993, p. 139). The pornographic image of a woman touching her genitals does not trigger an 'automatic stimulus-response' in a heterosexual male viewer. Rather, it is the staging of 'a scene of desire' and a 'sign' whereby the 'image of female genitals stands for something else, the man's pleasure' (*ibid.*, p. 138). Among the wishes expressed in this image, Cowie suggests, are the following: 'She waits for me, she is already excited, she is showing me her genitals because she wants to see mine' (*ibid.*, pp. 138–9).

The costume of a dominatrix also implies a scenario in which certain wishes are expressed. She wears a mask; therefore, she is anonymous: 'I don't want to know with whom I'm having sex, and if I don't know, then perhaps she doesn't know who I am either.' She looks menacing. In the pornographic literature, masks are associated with torturers, executioners and burglars. Therefore: 'I am the victim, so I'm innocent; or if guilty, then I'm already being punished for having sex, so I don't need to feel ashamed'. Black is overwhelmingly the most popular color for fetish clothing, evoking what fetishists call 'the dark side'. Black is also the color that has historically been associated with sexual ascetics, such as nuns and widows. It is also the color of power, as in the judge's robes, the biker's black leather jacket and the femme fatale's little black dress.

If the dominatrix wears boots, is the slave to be trod upon? Certainly this is what the pornographic stories tell us: He licks the boot and she kicks him. He sucks on the stiletto heel, and she inserts it in his anus. The tap-tap of her heels promises that someone is coming; the shiny patent leather already looks wet. The high heels make her buttocks sway; because high heels are a sign of femininity, he knows it is a woman coming (unless the story calls for the dominatrix to be a she-male). The boots are also hard and stiff and big; they will walk all over the slave, who loves this evidence of his submission.

But psychoanalytic studies of fantasy indicate that the subject may play different roles – may play all of the roles in any given story. The male viewer of a pornographic video does not necessarily identify only with the male character, but also simultaneously with the female character, with both characters, with the entire *mise en scène*, and with the role of the voyeur – he who watches (Williams, 1989). Even, perhaps, with the boot that is licked. Moving from male-oriented pornography to women's fashion magazines, we find that articles and photographs devoted to shoes also express fantasies: of male subjection to female sexual power.

A subcategory of the dominatrix is the amazon, or horsewoman, whose costume raises similar issues. Her jodhpur pants swell out at the sides or her Levis are crisp and hard. It was only in the twentieth century that Western women ceased to ride side-saddle while dressed in cumbrous, long riding skirts. Trousers, of course, are traditionally associated with masculinity, but the styles that the amazon wears are especially 'masculine'. Her clothing evokes not only masculinity but also sado-masochism. The amazon has something big and powerful between her legs, a beast that she controls with whip and spurs. A fashion photograph by Guy Bourdin showed a horsewoman whipping a man with her riding crop. The cowgirl, of course, has a gun.

Although this chapter focuses on fetish costumes for women, it is also true that some men wear phallic clothing. Within homosexual pornography, the cowboy and the motorcyclist are important icons. Key clothing items include motorcycle boots or cowboy boots, heavy belts (which can serve as whips), leather chaps, so-called 'master hats' and motorcycle jackets. All of these items have also been incorporated into the female fashion vocabulary and are frequently featured in fashion magazines, but this has not stripped them of their macho aura. Mark Thompson's book, *Leatherfolk: Radical Sex, People, Politics, and Practice* captions one photograph: 'Leathermen as urban knights . . . black leather as organic armor' (1991, p. 173).

By contrast, the maid plays a submissive role, which indicates the power differential implicit in traditional gender stereotypes. If the dominatrix is the quintessential Phallic Woman, armoured in power, the maid in her apron evokes an alternate model of the Veiled Woman. The fetish maid's costume is often reduced to a pair of high heels, a cap (symbol of servitude), and an apron, the last of which is both a symbol of femininity and a primitive *cache-sexe*. Unlike the dominatrix (and her colleagues, the amazon and the girl biker), the maid's costume has hardly influenced women's fashions at all, indicating perhaps that this submissive feminine image is not popular with fashionable women.

But the 'sissy maid' is a key role in pornography associated with transvestite S/M. Such pornography often features the male being humiliated by being put in women's clothing or underwear, and/or being forced to serve as a ladies' maid. Yet the cross-dressing boy-girl ultimately triumphs, since underneath his frilly apron, there is the unmistakable sign of manhood. One must ask: Do the fetishised images of the dominatrix and the maid support the gender stereotypes that disempower women? The short answer is probably not. In some cases they may actually subvert the 'normal' hierarchy of gender power.

In her brilliant essay, 'Maid to Order: Commercial S/M and Gender Power', Anne McClintock argues that 'contrary to popular stigma, S/M theatrically flouts the edict that manhood is synonymous with mastery, and submission a female fate . . . The bondage fetish performs identity and power as twined in interdependence' (1993, pp. 207–8). Within the subculture of consensual and commercial S/M, the vast majority of men seek to play the role of 'slaves', especially 'domestic slaves'.

In the land of Fem-Dom (Female Domination), these men pay large sums of money to cross-dress as women and perform menial domestic labour – washing the dishes, the floor and the laundry. 'By cross-dressing as women or as maids, by paying to do "women's work", or by ritually worshipping dominas as socially powerful, the male "slave" relishes the forbidden, feminine aspects of his personality,' suggests McClintock. Perhaps, also, this focus on the 'dirt fetish' may serve 'symbolically [to] absolve the "slave" of sexual and gender shame'. Moreover, she continues, 'in the ritual exchange of cash and the reversal of gender roles, domestic S/M stages women's work as having both exhibition and economic value' (1993, p. 213).

According to McClintock, 'Male TV (transvestite) "slavery" thus veers between nostalgia for female power, embodied in the awful spectacle of the whip-wielding domina, and the ritual negation of female power, embodied in the feminised male "slave" as the nadir of self-abasement' (*ibid.*, p. 214). Contrary to what many feminists fear, however, this type of drama is not simply a heightened version of traditional sex/gender roles, although it is true that the majority of fetishistic 'script-writers' are male while many female participants are professional sex workers.

The cult of the uniform has a wide appeal for men and women alike, hardcore fetishists and so-called 'normals'. Mainstream costume shops report a significant popular demand for uniforms, such as the 'French Maid' and the 'Policewoman'. Similarly, fetish clothing stores stock many uniforms, both those of submission (like the maid or 'naughty' schoolgirl) and the uniforms of authority (such as military, police and medical uniforms). Military uniforms have had a particularly significant impact on mainstream women's fashion, and fashion magazines frequently feature articles that portray women in styles reminiscent of military and naval uniforms. Until recently, however, fashion seemed uninspired by medical uniforms.

The nurse has long been a popular figure in pornography. In the commonest scenario, she plays what might be called the role of the 'naughty nurse', who helps the patient 'feel better' by engaging in therapeutic intercourse. As soon as she enters the room, dressed in a skimpy little white uniform, her resemblance to the virgin and the maid is obvious. Yet, as sadomasochistic pornography emphasises, the nurse is also a uniformed authority figure who inflicts pain on the patient. The 'nasty nurse' is erect and standing, hypodermic needle or enema in hand, while her victim lies passive in bed. The nurse costumes worn by fetishists are often made of rubber, a material associated with medical and childhood objects, such as rubber sheets, tubing and panties. Rubber, like leather, has certain sensory characteristics, including a hard, shiny feel and a distinctive smell. The 'ultimate fetish material', argues S/M activist Pat Califa, 'would combine the protective qualities of leather (its effect as armour) with rubber's ability to conform to the body's shape and heighten sensory awareness' (quoted in *Skin Two*, issue 11, no date, p. 29).

'Is fashion's fascination with nurses' uniforms . . . sick?' demanded the headline in the London *Sunday Times* (Steele, 1995). Certainly, the kinky nurse has begun to play an important role in the fashion world. At the

London fashion shows of Autumn 1995, models for Knightly, Versus, and Hussein Chalayan paraded down the runway in nurses' uniforms and medical corsets. Some licked bloody scissors or pretended to stab one another. One model from Versus wore an ensemble combining a nurse's cap and black fishnet stockings. A cropped white top and low-slung miniskirt bared her midriff, while around her neck was a stethoscope, hanging down to her navel. In place of a purse, she carried a plastic medical case marked, like her cap, with a large red cross.

Meanwhile, French *Vogue* featured erotic photographs of models dressed as nurses draped over surgical tables, and American *Vogue* had a fashion spread by Helmut Newton showing a doctor examining his female patient. And at the 1995 Goddess Ball in New York City (a part of Alternative Fashion Week), a tight-laced young woman appeared on the runway in a corset and a mint green rubber nurse's uniform, pretending

Plate 4.1 'Fetish Fashion'.
Source: Courtesy of the photographer, Aaron Cobbet.

FASHION, FETISH, FANTASY

to give herself a shot with a hypodermic needle. In real life, she is a nursing student. Thus, we find a telling metaphor for our time: masquerade and personal sexual identity can sometimes be impossible to disentangle.

REFERENCES

Apter, Emily and Pietz, William (ed.) (1993) *Fetishism as cultural discourse*, Ithaca, Cornell University Press.

Bak, Robert C., MD (1968) 'The phallic woman: The ubiquitous fantasy in perversions', *The Psychoanalytic study of the child* 23, 15–36.

Castle, Terry (1995) *The female thermometer: 18th-century culture and the invention of the uncanny*, New York, Oxford University Press.

Columbia Encyclopedia (1950), New York, Columbia University Press (second edition), 'Masquerade,' p. 1237.

Cowie, Elizabeth (1993) 'Pornography and fantasy: Psychoanalytic perspectives', in *Sex exposed: Sexuality and the pornography debate* (ed. Segal, Lynn and McIntosh, Mary), New Brunswick, NJ, Rutgers University Press.

Fashion, Fetish & Fantasies, number 13 (no date).

Fox, Celina and Ribeiro, Aileen (1983) *Masquerade*, London, The Museum of London.

Freud, Sigmund (1927) *Fetishism*, vol. 21, in *The standard edition of the complete psychological works of Sigmund Freud* (ed. and trans. Strachey, James), London, Hogarth Press, 1953–86.

Gamman, Lorraine and Makinen, Merja (1994) *Female fetishism: A new look*, London, Lawrence & Wishart.

Harper's Bazaar, September 1992.

Kaplan, Louise (1991) *Female perversions: The temptation of Emma Bovary*, New York, Doubleday.

Krafft-Ebing, Richard von (1886) *Psychopathia Sexualis with especial reference to the antipathic sexual instinct: A medico-forensic study* (F. J. Rebman, 1886), New York, Physicians and Surgeons Book Company, 1906, 1934.

Laplanche, Jean and Pontalis, Jean-Bertrand (1986) 'Fantasy and the Origins of Sexuality', in *Formations of fantasy* (ed. Burgin, Victor, Donald, James and Kaplan, Cora), London and New York, Routledge.

Maccubbin, Robert Purks (ed.) (1985) *'Tis nature's fault: Unauthorized sexuality during the Enlightenment*, Cambridge, Cambridge University Press.

McClintock, Anne (1993) 'Maid to order: Commercial S/M and gender power', in *Dirty looks: Women, pornography, power* (ed. Church Gibson, Pamela and Gibson, Roma), London, British Film Institute.

Skin Two, issue 11 (no date).

Stanton, Domna (ed.) (1992) *Discourses of sexuality: From Aristotle to AIDS*, Ann Arbor, University of Michigan Press.

Steele, Valerie (1995) 'Surgical Sex', *The Sunday Times* (12 November 1995), Style Section, p. 13.

Steele, Valerie (1996) *Fetish: Fashion, sex and power*, New York, Oxford University Press.

Stoller, Robert (1985) *Observing the erotic imagination*, New Haven, Yale University Press.

Thompson, Mark (ed.) (1991) *Leather-folk: Radical sex, people, politics, and practice*, Boston, Alyson Publications.

Williams, Linda (1989) *Hard core: Power, pleasure, and the 'frenzy of the visible'*, Berkeley, University of California Press.

5

IS WOMANLINESS NOTHING BUT A MASQUERADE?

An analysis of *The Crying Game*

Alkeline van Lenning, Saskia Maas and Wendy Leeks

Introduction

In the musical *My Fair Lady*, Professor Henry Higgins laments: 'Why can't a woman be more like a man?' Yet it is precisely when Eliza Doolittle refuses to conform to the confection of ideal womanhood Higgins has moulded for her that he voices his complaint. She refuses to be the perfect woman because she is a woman – irrational, emotional, unreasonable – unlike a man. In his complaint, as elsewhere in the film, Higgins exhibits the petulance, irrationality and stubbornness he ascribes both to Eliza and to femininity, so that, if Eliza both is and is not woman, then Higgins both is and is not man. Few would regard *My Fair Lady* as a radical or subversive examination of gender, even though an analysis of that film could reveal that the display of femininity as a masquerade is a key element within it. However, such a claim to radicality and subversion of conventional representations and understandings of both gender and sexuality would seem more sustainable for Neil Jordan's *The Crying Game* (1991).

Carol Clover (1992) has observed that 'filmmakers know that gender is more a porous membrane than an entrenchment'; still we are inclined to fall back on old wisdoms when we watch movies. Our assumptions about the gendered body and its direct connection with male or female are seldom disputed in mainstream films. *The Crying Game* thus stands out through its apparent challenge to these habitual and comfortable notions by disrupting them in quite novel ways. The movie unsettles conventions, and by doing so enables us to discover that they existed in the first place.

An analysis of *The Crying Game* can show how mask and performance function as a technology of gender, but it can further show how this deeply entrenched technology may function unimpeded behind a facade of unconventionality.

The secret

After a failed Hollywood adventure (*High Spirits* and *We're No Angels*) Neil Jordan returned to his native Ireland to shoot *The Crying Game*, in which the political situation served as a background. When *The Crying Game* started to circulate in the United States, the number of movie theatres initially showing the film was limited. After a couple of months, this number had to be expanded owing to the film's enormous success. This low-budget ($5-million-dollar) movie was not financed by Hollywood and was originally conceived as an arthouse movie. It is exceptional for such a movie to receive six Oscar nominations and an Oscar for best screenplay. The advertising poster said: 'The movie everyone is talking about, but no one is giving away its secret.' At the request of the makers of the film reviewers did not 'give it away'. This secret lured millions into the cinema, and will be central to our analysis.

The abduction

The movie starts at a fair in Ireland. Jude, a blonde woman, lures Jody, a slightly overweight, black British soldier to a desolate area for sex. There he is abducted as a hostage by the IRA. Fergus is given the task of guarding Jody and a friendship develops between them. Jody says of Jude: 'You know what the funny thing is, I didn't even fancy her. She's not my type.' Then he shows Fergus a picture of his girlfriend Dil. While looking at the picture Fergus says, 'She'd be anybody's type'. Fergus promises that he will visit Dil if Jody does not survive the abduction.

Jody initially confirms the stereotype of the overweight black man. He seems 'good natured' and not very smart and falls for the first skirt he sees. During the abduction we receive more information about Jody: he is a passionate player of the pre-eminently English colonial sport, cricket. On the one hand, as a black soldier, he is an outsider, yet on the other he has familiarised himself with things that are at odds with his underdog position. Jody therefore confuses Fergus. He also proves to be less bothered by physical intimacy than Fergus. When Jody needs to urinate, handcuffed, Fergus has to help him. Fergus finds handling Jody's penis embarrassing. Jody, however, reassures him that 'It's only a piece of meat'.

Every now and then Jody teaches Fergus life's lessons. Jody believes that it is not in Fergus' nature to be an active member of the IRA and explains this through a parable. A scorpion asks a frog if he can cross the river on the frog's back. 'No I won't do that', says the frog, 'because you will sting me and then I will die.' 'That won't do me any good', says the scorpion, 'because then I will drown too.' The frog thinks about it, finds the logic of the scorpion plausible and agrees. Half way across the river, the frog suddenly feels a stinging pain and realises that the scorpion has stung him anyway. 'Why did you do that? Now we will both drown', the frog shouts. 'Because it is in my nature', says the scorpion. 'What does that mean?', Fergus asks. 'It means what it says: a scorpion does what is in his nature.'

Jody does not survive. In an effort to escape, he is run down by British Army tanks that are trying to find the IRA's hiding place. During the course of the movie, this character remains present through pictures, dreams and memories, his image as the stereotypical representation of a tragic good-natured black man steadily fading.

The disclosure

Fergus breaks with the IRA and goes to England where he fulfils his promise to visit Dil. Dil is beautiful and slim: the ideal image of a woman. She[1] has a smooth brown skin, shoulder-length curly hair, long polished nails. She wears make-up and dresses in short tight skirts and shirts, and high heels. She has two typically female professions, in which the female appearance is aesthetically placed in the centre. During the day she is a hairdresser and at night she performs as a singer in a bar: the Metro. It is in this bar that Fergus and Dil meet. Dil pushes her boyfriend Dave aside and gradually a romance develops between Fergus and Dil.

One night Fergus and Dil are in Dil's apartment. When Fergus opens Dil's negligee he sees Dil's penis. In shock, he walks to the bathroom and throws up, then leaves.

The evening after the disclosure, Fergus goes to the bar again. The camera now presents the patrons of the bar differently, tracking their features to reveal a population of the transgendered, transsexuals or transvestites. Fergus crosses a border when he ventures into this domain, which undermines the comfortable expectations of heterosexual romance. Dil is angry and does not want to talk to him. Desperate, he puts a note in Dil's mailbox.

The next day Dil, dressed in short tight hotpants, a tight shirt and a short jacket, goes to see Fergus at the building site where he works. This appearance results in a lot of cheering and whistling. Even though he protests, Dil keeps calling Fergus 'honey', 'sweety' and 'dear'. They talk about the night of the disclosure. 'Never let the sun go down on an argument, as Jody used to say', Dil says. Because of his leave in London, where he lives under the name 'Jimmy', his visits to the Metro and his relationship with Dil, Fergus seems increasingly to internalise Jody's identity.

Plate 5.1 Dil and Fergus, *The Crying Game.*
Source: Courtesy of The Sales Company, London.

The IRA

When Fergus comes home, he finds Jude. After her appearances as the blonde, provocatively dressed woman who seduces Jody, and as an IRA member in jeans who provides the tea and sandwiches for the male members of the group, we now see Jude in her third guise. Her hair is dyed black, she is wearing a business suit, court shoes and leather gloves. This look seems either a mask of an evil being or the evil 'truth' unveiled from behind her previous mask. She calls it 'the tougher look'. Jude puts Fergus under pressure to carry out an assignment for the IRA. She threatens him saying that something will happen to his 'girlfriend' if he refuses. To keep Dil out of the hands of Jude and the IRA, Fergus wants to change Dil's looks into 'something new, that nobody recognises'. Dil wants to know if Fergus finds her attractive again, and says she will do anything for him.

Dil's hair is cut short and she puts on Jody's cricket outfit. We expect finally to see the man Dil is, but we get a confirmation of Dil's unclear gender. The outfit hardly fits her, and Dil looks like a woman in men's clothing. Payne remarks that this results in 'Neither turning Dil into a "man" nor affirming her "femininity". Dil's short hair and her adoption of male attire visually indicate the emergence of a "third": something new, something that nobody recognises – not yet' (Payne, 1994, p. 13).

That night they sleep in a hotel. Fergus stresses that Dil must under no circumstance leave the hotel, and himself goes to work in the morning. When he returns that night, Dil is gone. He finds her in her apartment, drunk and still dressed in Jody's clothes. Fergus confesses to Dil that he knew Jody. He tells Dil of the abduction. She feels too weak to respond. Only the next morning does it dawn on her what Fergus has told her. She takes Fergus' gun and ties him up, still asleep, to the bed. Fergus wakes up, realises he will be able to make it in time to carry out his IRA assignment, and begs Dil to let him go. Dil hears Jude come into her apartment. Dil wants to know if Jude was involved in Jody's abduction. She asks Jude if she seduced Jody and then shoots her. Now Dil wants to take her own life, but Fergus takes the gun from her and tells her to go away. He wipes Dil's fingerprints off the gun and resignedly waits for the police.

In the final scene, Dil visits Fergus in jail. Dil calls him 'honey' and 'darling', and Fergus still resists. Their relationship remains ambivalent. Dil thinks it is great that a man went to jail for her. Dil wants to know why Fergus let her escape. His answer is: 'it's in my nature', and then he tells the story of the scorpion and the frog. The parable, a recurrent motif in the film, is being used, here, in reference to moral behaviour. But it comments, ironically, on untenable assumptions about 'one's nature' through its connection with the gender disruptions of the film.

Gender and looking

Dil appears as a desirable (hetero)sexual object. Dil's image as a beautiful woman is constructed not only by her clothes, but mainly by her very 'feminine' motion and posture, and by the camera treating her as it conventionally treats an attractive woman. One of the first to theorise spectatorship, the cultural critic John Berger, argued that looking carries with it relations of power, access and control. He stated that 'women are depicted in quite a different way from men'. This is not because their femininity makes them so different but because 'the "ideal" spectator is always to be male and the image of woman is designed to flatter him' (Berger, 1972, p. 64). Although looking seems to be a rather neutral activity, many film theorists agree with Berger and many analyses (mostly feminist) are made of the instances of 'being looked at', and 'doing the looking' in films. One of the most famous is the analysis of gender, spectatorship and film by Mulvey. Drawing heavily on Freud, particularly his essay on fetishism, she argues that woman is created as a spectacle for male desire through the gaze of the camera, the gaze of the male in the narrative, and the gaze of the male spectator (Mulvey, 1975).

In *The Crying Game*, the male character, camera and spectator look at Dil in the same way. When we see her perform in the Metro we are invited to see Dil the way Fergus sees her and the camera forces us to gaze at Dil. At the moment of disclosure our gaze coincides with Fergus looking at Dil. The way in which Dil is visualised exemplifies how film is gendered: the woman is framed as an icon by the look of the camera (de Lauretis, 1984). Mulvey has noted that:

> The cinema has enhanced the image of feminine seductiveness as a surface that conceals. That is to say: the codes and conventions of Hollywood cinema refined the representation of femininity, heightened by the star system, to the point where the spectator's entrancement with the effects of the cinema itself became almost indistinguishable from the draw exerted by an eroticised image of woman.
>
> (Mulvey, 1996, p. 56)

This framing has far-reaching consequences for the way we look at Dil. We see Dil through the eye of the camera in love. The sexual meaning attached to the woman's body goes even further: 'The eventual availability of her breasts and other sexual areas as cinematic rewards have insured, by temporal contiguity, the essential content of her "mask"' (Straayer, 1990). We expect to receive this reward in the disclosure scene in the bedroom. The dual discovery – of Dil as a fantasy phallic woman, and of the penis which is cinematically historically absent – is doubly shocking.

The movie then has already lured the audience into sympathising with a relationship between Dil – the partner of the hostage – and Fergus – the former hostage taker. But that is not the only reason why the audience is misled. It is not just about a specific character, a woman who turns out to be a man, but about the conventional signifier of sexuality and of sexual differentiality which, by virtue of its sudden ambiguity, addresses precisely this convention. Ambiguities around other major and minor characters confirm this.

The impact of the disclosure

Half of the characters in the film are different from what is initially assumed. Jody's initial comments on Jude, 'she is not my type', take on a new meaning afterwards. Jody's character, however, remains not entirely filled in. He cannot simply be labelled a homosexual: he was charmed away by Jude and went along with her. He had a relationship with a man who dressed and behaved as a woman. What exactly is his sexual designation? Homosexual? Bisexual? Heterosexual? What does it mean that we cannot easily classify him? Does this undermine the viewer's belief in the validity of such categories or merely suggest that if we had seen more of Jody we would have found out, definitively, what he was?

And what about the character of Dave? After Jody's death, he becomes the possessive boyfriend of Dil. He keeps harassing her. Dave seems a stereotypical characterisation of a hetero blockhead who dominates his girlfriend with jealousy and violence. Yet his woman is biologically a man. Are the two just 'doing gender'?

The bar where Dil performs turns out to be filled with more ambiguities than we first thought. Through the crossing of borders between being a man or woman, not only is the difference between men and women debated, but also the classifying itself. Furthermore, the viewer could be watching a different kind of movie than was assumed; a movie which provides a commentary on the kind of movie the viewer thought s/he was watching.

The switching of a male into a female character and vice versa has been a theme of movies before. Still, *The Crying Game* can hardly be compared with classic transvestite movies in the mainstream, in which plot provides a motivation for the cross-dressing. In films such as *Tootsie*, in which Dustin Hoffman is disguised as a woman, and *Mrs Doubtfire*, with Robin Williams, the cross-dressing is presented as comic and grotesque. In *Victor/Victoria*, in which Julie Andrews impersonates a man, and *Yentl*, starring Barbra Streisand, this is less the case. However, in all these examples the sexuality of the lead characters is never in doubt, but rather is underscored by their clumsiness while playing the transvestite role. To see the male body appear in women's clothes in films such as these is humorous and does not destabilise gender coding and identity. Doane's argument in 1982 that: 'Male transvestism is an occasion for laughter; female transvestism only another occasion for desire' certainly held good at that time for the mainstream films produced for straight audiences, which were her concern. Perhaps more recent gay-aware, as well as queer-addressed productions (for instance *Priscilla, Queen of the Desert*), alongside the greater visibility of homosexual, transsexual and transgender peoples in the wider culture have made some inroads into the easy acceptance of such attitudes and stereotypes. In *The Crying Game*, the feminine appearance of Dil, even after the disclosure, is fully respected. Garber argues that an important aspect of cross-dressing, outside of film, is the way it challenges easy notions of binarity and questions categories of 'female' and 'male' 'whether they are considered essential or constructed, biological or cultural' (Garber, 1992, p. 23). In the film, Dil is not presented as a cross-dresser, and this does create space to move away from the binarity.

In the 'traditional' transvestite movie, the viewer knows the biological sex of the character: the disclosure of that biological sex to the other characters in the movie is the climax which is worked towards. In *The Crying Game*, the disclosure of Dil's biological sex, however shocking, does not herald the climactic resolution of the narrative. And unlike in mainstream transvestite movies, this male body in women's clothing, even after the disclosure, is not a figure of fun.

Femininity and masks

The narrative of *The Crying Game* involves a repetition of a triangular relationship, which can also be seen as an exchange of pairings.[2] Jody is seduced by Jude, who, we soon find, is Fergus' girlfriend. Jody's girlfriend is Dil. Later, a romance develops between Dil and Fergus. This switch can be shown to have deep significance for the impact of the film. It is the structure that sets up the sexual dilemma at the centre of the plot, revealed as a dilemma by the disclosure scene. But it also involves another pairing which is crucial in the film. It constitutes a relation between Jude and Dil, as first, Jody's 'women' and then Fergus's. The two unambiguously male characters, Jody and Fergus, serve as third terms linking the two 'women' in these triangular relationships. Furthermore, the repetition involves the motif of disguise.

Jody first appears in civilian clothing, masking his identity as a soldier. The stereotype of the black man also comes to seem a cloak that he wears over a different identity. Jody the cricketer is, at first sight, the colonised adopting the form of the coloniser, yet he tells Fergus that the real game was the one played at home, when he was a child, and not the game they played when he came to England.

Jody is the first to see through Fergus, recognising that being a terrorist is 'against his nature'. It is in the guise of Jimmy, the Scot, that he meets Dil. Dil, in her female occupations as hairdresser and club singer, makes herself up and changes the appearance of others for her living. Her feminine façade is shown to conceal male genitalia. To make her unrecognisable, she is 'made over' by Fergus/Jimmy turned hairdresser. Jody in his cricket kit might be read as the black man in white man's clothing. Dil, dressed in Jody's cricket 'whites' is a palimpsest of masks, veils or contradictory signifiers – a man who has passed himself off as a woman; a woman who must now pass for a man; a black wo/man who could pass for white, but now cannot measure up to being disguised as Jody.

Jude also comes under this trope of disguise. As the blonde in the short skirt she tricks Jody and delivers him to the kidnappers, the men who at first appear to just use her for this task. Next she is a figure of indeterminate sex in black leathers and helmet. In jeans and jumper she is tea-maker, guard and lover to Fergus; a little ill-kempt. On her appearance in London, Jude has been transformed into a brunette 'businesswoman', more sophisticated and well groomed.

On the face of it, this metamorphosis of Jude is marked and only slightly justified by the plot. We must presume that the change is necessitated by her escape from the army and her mission in London. In the section of the film set in Ireland, Jude exhibits some tender qualities and most of her actions are explicable in plot terms. The character, at this point, is believably human. In London, these qualities have been replaced by a virtual caricature of an ambitious, driven and dangerous woman. In retrospect, we can remember clues to this 'real' character of Jude from the Ireland sequence, particularly her manipulation and cruelty towards Jody. Lyrics early on in the soundtrack echo the activities of Jude towards Jody: 'When a man loves a woman, deep down in his soul, she can bring him so much misery', and 'If she's bad, he can't see it, she can do no wrong'.

Jude's disguise is, in one sense, the most visually marked transformation in the film, to the extent that we do not immediately recognise her as the same character. It is also the least complex and least ambiguous. She starts as seductress, a role at first presented as just that and then shown to be her 'nature'. While Jude in London is momentarily physically unrecognisable, her 'nature' is very familiar to the viewer. She is the stock film character of the femme fatale, the seductive woman who brings death. Manning describes this figure: 'By definition, she is beautiful, desirable, mysterious, ambivalent and dangerous, but also . . . active and ambitious and – in her most pure form – as the term indicates, fatal' (Manning, 1984, p. 96).

Duplicity is an essential element in the character of the femme fatale, and thus in itself a necessary and sufficient motivation for Jude's actions. This is what marks out Jude from the other central characters and, perhaps paradoxically, gives her the most derealised and the most secure identity in the film.

Through all the twists and turns, layers of disguise and revelation, the other three characters in the double triangulation retain an undecidability. They remain an enigma for the viewer: What is their identity? What are they? What do they (each) want? No such question remains with Jude, since viewers are sure to have seen her before; they know her like, and they know what she wants. The unreliability of Jude is a requirement of her function as femme fatale. This function fills the character, making it wholly recognisable, whereas the other three, neither filled nor emptied by a mythic function of this kind, retain a distinctness that is felt by the viewer to be their lived individuality.

What is it that the femme fatale wants and that viewers know (but not consciously) that she wants?

The repetition of the femme fatale function in film is an indicator of its appeal to the desires of male (heterosexual) spectators. She represents a threat to the male hero, through her seductiveness and her activity, which is overcome by her death. The counterpoint to the femme fatale in film is the good girl/wife, and together these form the conventional components of filmic representations of woman. While the good girl exhibits the passivity required by the active male subject in order to qualify as his object of desire, the femme fatale appears to be a passive object with no desire of her own, but is subsequently revealed as desiring, a subject who instigates action in pursuit of this desire. As Mulvey, among others who draw upon Lacan, has demonstrated, the male spectator's unconscious fantasies construct the desire of the femme fatale as, at one level, the castrated woman's desire to regain her lost phallus/penis by performing an act of castration on the male hero. At a further level, the active subjecthood, rather than passive objecthood of the femme fatale is perceived as the possession of masculinity. The femme fatale appears to be woman, but underneath she already has the phallus, the sign of masculinity, which gives her the power and authority to castrate. Žižek draws attention to this threat of the femme fatale by arguing that it is not Woman as an object of fascination that may cause men to lose their senses. Rather, it is 'that which remains hidden beneath this fascinating mask and appears once the masks fall off: the dimension of the pure subject fully assuming the death drive' (Žižek, 1989). Jude's status as potential castrator is repeatedly signalled in the film, not least by Jody's plea, 'Don't leave me with her, she's dangerous'.

At this deeper level, then, Jude and Dil can be seen to be paired, since both, in this regard, mask the possession of masculinity and the phallus/penis with a cloak of femininity. But more than this, it is in their similarities and their differences that the pairing of Jude and Dil, and particularly the presence of Jude as femme fatale, are fundamental to the effects of the film.

The mythic dimension of the femme fatale function and its relation to unconscious processes is evidence that this perception and conception is not confined to film alone. As feminist analysis has revealed, the image of the castrating female is an important component of what woman is understood to be in patriarchal cultures. The femme fatale is seen to really be woman. Jude is less ambiguous because she is recognised as 'real' woman in the film. The pairing of Jude and Dil, in their similarities, therefore adds to the network of significations which guarantee Dil's acceptance, by the viewer, as a woman. The 'problem' around Dil's womanliness may result in the very notion of 'real woman' being problematised, yet, as we shall show, the distinctions made between Jude and Dil have other, highly significant, consequences.

Femininity as masquerade

Recent feminist and queer theory has argued that woman is a social construct, internalised and reinforced by psychic processes. Lived understanding of the woman and by the woman is a product of representations. Grosz argues that there is no existence of woman outside discursive practices (Grosz, 1995). Irigaray claims that the female coincides with its representation; when female figures appear, that is considered to be femininity itself. And when these visions of femininity are viewed as the female, the female itself is completely wiped out by this representation (Irigaray, 1974). Butler radicalises the discursive thesis by stating that categories do not refer to essentials, but in their repetition give their shape to the things they name. She introduces the notion of 'gender as performance' and also of 'sexuality and sex as a cultural enforced performance' (Butler, 1990). Other theorists also hold that the visual image of the woman in different forms of appearances is a collective mythology. It forms a visual vocabulary and an iconography of gender (Tseëlon, 1995). The myth views femininity as something natural, and woman as highly dictated by her body. This contributes to the eternal mystery of the woman, and the urge to look at her appearance and to know her body: the supposed essence behind the masquerade. This enticing enigma is generally enormously exploited in films.[3] The space metaphor of a visual seductive surface and secretive dangerous core 'further locks women in all sorts of other auras of masquerade and appearances, with a strong emphasis on what can be seen. And that which can be seen takes the form of a veil' (Mulvey, 1992, pp. 50–1). The woman, therefore, often stands for the enigma, which is an important part of her attractiveness. When, as in *The Crying Game*, the image of the woman is embodied by a man, the mythological character of this representation is exposed, and the audience is taken by surprise for having misjudged Dil's gender so badly.

The idea of the discursive and performative character of femininity derives in part from a 1929 paper by the psychoanalyst Joan Riviere (1986). She observed femininity to be a strategy which masked a desire for (phallic) power with a charade of powerlessness. It is about femininity as style, as an artificial appearance, a masquerade, and, furthermore, 'genuine womanliness' and the masquerade are one and the same.

In *The Crying Game* Dil not only dresses, moves and behaves as a woman. She also takes on a classical female, heterosexual position in relation to men and women, in love and work. Partially because of this, it is almost impossible for the spectator to view Dil as a man even after the revelation. According to Deaux and Lewis (1984), gender stereotypes have four components: personality traits, appearance, role behavior and profession, which turn out to play a bigger role in our information processing than our knowledge of someone's biological sex. All four elements are filled in as feminine by Dil in a serious manner, without the cynical touch that is often attached to homosexuals or transvestites represented in a female role. The song at the beginning can be seen to refer to Dil and to Jude as the veiled woman. The man in love cannot see 'what' she is.

That the revelation was difficult for Fergus does not stop Dil from remaining faithful to him. Dil is in a dependent position in relation to the men, and takes every opportunity to emphasise her femininity by using cliche 'feminine' statements such as: 'Be nice to a girl and she's yours forever', or 'A girl has to have a bit of glamour', or 'I know you're lying [after soliciting an 'I love you' declaration from Fergus] but it's nice to hear'. Such statements underscore Dil's representation in or of a 'normative' female role and Fergus' uneasiness with it.

But what is Dil behind the masquerade? A homosexual, a transsexual, a transvestite, a heterosexual? A man, or a woman? And what is a woman? Dil's character raises many questions. Can a woman have a man's body? What is the definition of gender, and what is the relationship between the concepts biological sex and gender? Her/his character is a criticism of the unreasoned assumption of the man/woman duality. Dil seems to be beyond this duality, and seems to embody Butler's statement of sex as performance. Besides her gender, her ethnicity is also unclear. While adding to the mysteriousness of this character, Dil's exceptional ambivalence not only raises the issue of her own gender and ethnical identity, but also that of categorising itself.

Masculinity as masquerade

The theme of ambiguity that runs through the film is also expressed in language. Jody and Dil seem to distance themselves from themselves and continually to reconstruct their identity by referring to themselves in the third person. For instance, Jody says: 'Jody is always right' and

Dil says things like: 'Dil can't stand it'. Dil usually refers to herself as a woman: 'A girl has her feelings' and 'A girl has to draw the line somewhere'. When Fergus tells Dil he cannot view her as woman anymore, she says: 'You can always pretend'. Fergus, in this, is not quite capable of pretending. His identity is constrained by his body to a large extent. When we consider the acquisition of an identity as a process of inclusion and exclusion, this is about the continual defining of similarities and differences.

None the less, identity is not ruled only by the included but also by the rejected. The reject does not stand outside the identity but gives form to its completion (Butler, 1993). The masculine masquerade consists of the concealing of a disturbing presence of femininity and homosexuality. Homophobia, like a psychological defence mechanism, is connected with heterosexual masculinity.[4]

The character Fergus is the representation of this heterosexual masculinity and, as such, is familiar to the spectator. He is a classical figure frequently found in movies: the good, brave, lonely, unattached protagonist. He has no family ties which keep him from taking on a different identity and starting a new life in England. Many times in *The Crying Game*, Fergus is a traditional male hero. He protects Dil when she is harassed by her boyfriend Dave or slighted by his boss at the building site. Fergus is an ordinary, balanced man who shows little emotion. In the course of the story he loses his balance as a result of the disruption of his evident heterosexuality. This actually starts with the unlikely friendship between the guard and the hostage, and can be felt through the obsessive character of Fergus' thoughts of Jody after his death.

When Fergus throws up after the revelation, he is not so much disgusted by Dil, but more by his own desire. He realises he desired a man. Homosexuality is a threat to his fragile heterosexuality. Psychoanalytically speaking, desire and disgust are two sides of a coin. Even though Fergus keeps resisting a love affair with Dil, he is attracted at the same time and he keeps seeing her. When Fergus and Dil discuss the sex switch, the result is dialogues in which Fergus appears as an accomplice in Dil's game. For instance, Fergus says: 'You should have stayed a girl' and 'I liked you better as a girl', which affirms the credibility of Dil's sex as female before the revelation. Dil, therefore, is not the pseudo-woman who misled Fergus and has been discovered. Rather, Fergus seems to agree that Dil's sexual identity coincided with her appearance. He confirms, in fact, that femininity is identical with the masquerade. Similarly, the audience which has been lured into identification with Fergus' desire for Dil, has to acknowledge that this could not have been provoked by Dil's biological body but by Dil's 'performance'.

Conclusion

The masquerade, by creating a distance between self and image, problematises comfortable assumptions of gender, sexuality and categorisation as a system (Doane, 1982). In the character of Dil particularly, and elsewhere in the film, *The Crying Game* exhibits such resistance. This still leaves the question of its popularity. This contradictory story, which continuously undermines heterosexual assumptions about gender and sexuality, is told in a movie made without Hollywood financing and distribution. Is it possible that this movie was so well received by an enormous audience, given good reviews and accorded six Oscar nominations? Is this film as critical and subversive as it seems?

Even though the movie was advertised as a 'mystery thriller' it cannot be classified simply in one genre. It could equally well be seen as a romance and, if we take it that a woman, or even two women, are at the centre of the story, we could even regard it as a melodrama. And *The Crying Game*, like the classic melodrama, according to Mulvey (1981), while featuring female characters revolves around the desires of the man.

A large number of the vast audience of the film must have been male. It is not identified as a cult film or singled out as having appealed particularly to gay or queer audiences. In that case, a significant proportion of the audience must have been heterosexual men, the very category likely to be least comfortable and least pleased by its disruptions of gender and sexuality. How did they manage, not only to tolerate the film, but also gain pleasure from it?

It is evident that at key moments the male heterosexual viewer will identify with Fergus as hero. This puts the viewer in the position of having desired a man, a threatened homosexual relation that has to be disavowed. This Fergus duly does in his reaction to the revelation, a reaction that can be adopted by the viewer. The act of fellatio apparently performed on Fergus by Dil is the only sexual act between them in the film. This tends to confirm Dil's position as the woman who serves the man, but might also function to summon up the spectre of homosexuality. However, this spectre is effectively laid to rest by the remainder of the film where, significantly, no further genital activity takes place between them. Fergus is presented as ill at ease with his desire for Dil, enabling the male spectator to share this reaction too, while at the same time fully enjoying other aspects of their relation.

These mechanisms fall into line with Lacan's formulation of the (heterosexual) relation as hom(m)osexual (Lacan, 1982). The double 'm' here indicates that heterosexuality is not, at root, a relation between two different sexes. It is an affair entirely to do with the man, and with the socially-dominant fantasy of woman as a castrated being. The heterosexual relation is hom(m)osexual in two senses. At one level it arises from the earliest experience of alienation (conceptualised by Lacan as the famous Mirror Stage). This structures the male's desire, and more properly speaking desire itself, as the wish to be whole, unalienated and complete. The male desires to be complete in himself, a state which he imagines he once enjoyed but then lost. The woman thus functions, for the man, merely as the means by which he will complete himself. She, as the other element in the relation, serves only to make him a perfect whole: the sum of the two makes him the One.

The second sense of this hom(m)osexual relation lies in its overvaluation and misrecognition of the male organ, the penis. Its presence or absence is seen, in the social order, as the biological, natural ground of the cultural structures of sexual difference. Lacan draws attention to this misrecognition through use of the term 'the phallus'. The phallus takes the form of the penis, but is not possessed by the male. It is what he wants to have in order to complete himself. The phallus, therefore does not signify wholeness, power, and so on, but is rather a marker for, or signifier of, the male's state of incompleteness. Within a social order which is, precisely, phallocentric, the penis seems to be what the man has and the woman does not, yet for Lacan the penis is only the physical form (we could say the 'piece of meat') that marks the body as desiring, as experiencing lack. The overvaluation of the penis gains its social force from the social understanding of the woman as castrated. Woman is defined and determined by her lack of the penis, and is therefore taken, by the man, to desire to have it. The male desire to be complete and to be the only One or the One and only, involves fetishising the woman, making her *be* the phallus which he desires as his completion. He, and the culture, mistakes his having the penis as having the phallus. Thus, the heterosexual relation is a fantasmic relation of masks and misrecognitions.

The problem of the woman, or woman as a problem, arises from this. She is seen as castrated. Yet she does not want the man, only that part of him previously taken from her, that she threatens to reclaim. There is no place in this for any desire on the part of the woman that is not a fantasy construct built around the man's desire and around the mark of sexual difference. Her desire, constructed in this way, is dangerous and must be repeatedly denied.

Viewed from this perspective, the double triangulation and the pairing between Jude and Dil take on their full significance. Jude as femme fatale stands for 'real' woman, in the sense that she is the castrated who wants to reclaim her prize – the fantasy representation of woman that *is* woman in the culture and in the unconscious of male heterosexual viewers. Dil is contrasted with Jude, and at this deep level is man's ideal woman. Coded as object, she is both object of desire and undesiring. She is represented absolutely as woman and also as woman ought ideally to be, that is, without the threat posed to man by woman's castrated status. Jude does not want Fergus, she only wants to use him to get what she wants, her seductive masquerade being the ruse to achieve his castration. Dil really loves Fergus for himself. She does not need to take anything from him because she already has her own 'piece of meat'. She wants to do any-thing and everything for him, to be his absolute object, because she is herself without desire. She cannot threaten castration because she is not castrated, so that, after the revelation Dil's attraction is not diminished, but increased.

The relation between Dil and Fergus is perfectly hom(m)osexual, a ful-filment of the male's desire. It is not homosexuality at all, but heterosexuality perfected. Dil's love for Fergus guarantees Fergus as whole, as One and all-in-all, because as well as being the phallus for the man (being the woman) she also appears to have the phallus and thereby negates castration anxiety. To merely have the penis (be the man) in this heterosexual fantasy formation, would reactivate heterosexual anxieties over homosexuality. The character must convincingly and consistently be the phallus (the woman) as well.

Identification with Fergus on the part of the male heterosexual viewer thereby places the spectator as whole, as the One, and generates a pro-found narcissistic pleasure. In his possession of Dil, the spectator, like Fergus, is desireless. This makes any further representation of a sex act after the oral sex episode not only inadvisable, since it would bring back the issue of homosexual desire, but also unnecessary.

It is clear from this that the figure of Jude is pivotal in setting these mechanisms in motion. Her presence and the vital pairing with Dil set up another pairing that can now be seen as significant in another way. Fergus and Jody are also paired, and it is Jody who bequeathes Dil to Fergus. Furthermore, the fellatio sequence echoes the segment where Fergus han-dles Jody's penis. In this earlier episode, Fergus reluctantly serves Jody in circumstances where the sexual aspect of this service is debated and, largely, neutralised. Subsequently Dil takes the place previously occupied by Fergus and serves him by an act that is overtly sexual, presented in a heterosexual context. So, in this second sequence Fergus has taken Jody's place. This gives further weight to the idea that the hom(m)osexual relation is at stake in the film, and that it is this dominant structuration of desire and gender that is finally reasserted in the movie. As with patriarchal kinship structures, it is the exchange of the (ideal) woman here that cements the relations between the men. It was Jody who saw Fergus' 'nature', told through the fable of the frog. That 'nature' Fergus asserts again with the same story at the end – the self-sameness of Fergus and Jody, confirmed by the exchange of Dil. To an extent, it may be in the 'nature' of all three to be outsiders, the dominated not the dominating, rather like the film itself which, again to an extent, is subversive of dominant conceptions of sex, gender and sexuality. Yet behind this mask of subversion, dominant forms are reasserted. This is a key to explaining the popularity of the film.

NOTES

1 Because Dil is a woman, as we argue here, we refer to this character with the female pronoun.
2 For an examination of a similar structure of triangulations, pairings and exchanges in a very different context, and a discussion of these for hetero-sexual and queer spectatorship, see Leeks (1996a).
3 A useful examination of female figures in film using the Lacanian model also deployed here can be found in Silverman (1988).
4 On the fantasmic nature of the heterosexual relation and the subversive play on this fantasy in the gender performance of the drag king see Leeks (unpub-lished,1996b).

REFERENCES

Berger, J. (1972) *Ways of seeing*, London, British Broadcasting Corporation.
Butler, J. (1990) *Gender trouble: Feminism and the subversion of identity*, London, Routledge.
Butler, J. (1993) *Bodies that matter: On the discursive limits of 'sex'*, London, Routledge.
Clover, C.J. (1987) 'Her body himself: Gender in the slasher film', *Representations* 20, 187–228.
Clover, C.J. (1992) *Men, women and chain saws: Gender in the modern horror film*, London, British Film Institute.
Deaux, K. and Lewis L. L. (1984) Structure of gender stereotypes: Inter-relationships among components and gender label. *Journal of Personality and Social Psychology* 46, 991–1004.
de Lauretis, T. (1984) *Alice doesn't: Feminism, semiotics, cinema*, Bloomington: Indiana University Press.
Doane, M.A. (1982) 'Film and the masquerade: Theorizing the female spectator', *Screen* 23, 3/4, 74–87.
Doane, M.A. (1992) 'Masquerade reconsidered', in *Femmes fatales: Feminism, film theory and psychoanalysis*, London, Routledge.
Freud, S. (1923) *The Ego and the Id*, vol. 19, in *The standard edition of the complete psy-chological works of Sigmund Freud* (ed. and trans. Strachey, James), London, Hogarth Press, 1953–86.

Garber, M. (1992) *Vested interests: Cross-dressing and cultural anxiety*, New York, Routledge, Chapman and Hall.

Grosz, E. (1995) *Space, Time and Perversion*, London, Routledge.

Irigaray, L. (1974) *Speculum de l'autre femme*, Paris, Minuit.

Kotsopoulos, A. and Mills, J. (1994) '*The Crying Game*: Gender, genre and post-feminism', *Jump Cut* 39, 15–40.

Kuhn, A. (1982) *Women's pictures: Feminism and cinema*, London, Routledge & Kegan Paul.

Lacan, J. (1953) 'Some reflections on the ego', *International Journal of Psychoanalysis* 34, 11–17.

Lacan, J. (1982) *Feminine sexuality: Jacques Lacan and the Ecole Freudienne* (ed. Mitchell, J. and Rose, J.), New York, W.W. Norton.

Leeks, W. (1996a) 'Out of the maid's room: Dora, Stratonice and the lesbian analyst', in *Outlooks: Lesbian and gay sexualities and visual cultures* (ed. Horn, P. and Lewis, R.), London, Routledge.

Leeks, W. (1996b) 'Ame-ame-us: A sex performance', unpublished paper, Leeds Metropolitan University.

Manning, K. (1984) 'Out of the past – into the future? Film noir en de femme fatale', *Versus* 3/4, 96–105.

Mulvey, L. (1975) 'Visual pleasure and narrative cinema', *Screen* 16, 6–18.

Mulvey, L. (1981) 'Afterthoughts on "visual pleasure and narrative cinema" inspired by King Vidor's Duel in the Sun (1946)', *Framework* 15/16/17, 12–15.

Mulvey, L. (1992) 'Pandora: de topografie van het masker en de nieuwsgierigheid' in *Eenbeeld van een vrouw* (ed. Braidotti, R.) Kampen, Kok Agora.

Mulvey, L. (1996) *Fetishism and curiosity*, Bloomington, BFI and Indiana University Press.

Orbio de Castro, I. (1994) *Made to order*, Amsterdam, Spinhuis.

Payne, R.M. (1994) 'Crossed lines', *Jump Cut* 39, 7–14.

Riviere, J. (1986) 'Womanliness as masquerade', in *Formations of fantasy* (ed. Burgin, V. Donald, and Kaplan, C.), London, Routledge (originally published 1929).

Silverman, K. (1988) *The acoustic mirror: The female voice in psychoanalysis and cinema*, Bloomington, Indiana University Press.

Straayer, C. (1990) 'The she man: postmodern bi-sexed performance in film and video', *Screen* 31, 3, 262–80.

Tseëlon, E. (1995) *The masque of femininity: The presentation of woman in everyday life*, London, Sage.

Walters, S.D. (1995) *Material girls*, Berkeley, University of California Press.

Žižek, S. (1989) *The sublime object of ideology*, London, Verso.

6

THE SCARF AND THE TOOTHACHE

Cross-dressing in the Jewish folk theatre

Ahuva Belkin

The aim of this chapter is to examine the significance of cross-dressing and representations of femininity in the Jewish folk play the *Purimspiel.*[1] It will be argued that this traditional festival performance was a vehicle for social comment and protest, expressing resistance by the weak against the strong on two levels: by asserting the identity of an oppressed Jewish minority culture within a dominant Gentile culture, and by registering the perspectives of the poorest and least-powerful male members of the Jewish community within that community itself. However, I shall contend that while the inverted world of masks and disguise found in the topsy-turvey world of the *Purimspiel* afforded a means of expression and release of social tension for the men, it offered no such expression or release for women. On the plane of gender relations and positionalities, these ostensibly oppositional and even radical performances uncritically reproduced and reinforced the subordinated status of women within the Judaic culture of early modern Europe and beyond.

Like the festive plays of other communities, the improvised performances staged by Jews at *Purim* played with liminal symbols and role-reversal, and exhibited the typical characteristics of European carnival. As with similar phenomena in pre-industrial societies, the Jewish festive folk theatre was characterised by rituals involving dance, feasting, masquerades, mock weddings, mock fights, impersonation and cross-dressing. The popular customs manifested in the folk play included recourse to a spirit of anarchy and rebellion, evoking a world of chaos and the breaking of taboos, which also involved abandoning the banality of mundane clothing. The common practice of wearing masks and costumes in which men took on the roles and garb of women is particularly marked in the *Purimspiel.*

In early modern Europe, under the influence of the carnival pageant, the Jewish neighbourhoods resounded at *Purim* with dramatic games and theatrical presentations featuring the rituals of social reversal and clownish merriment, in which the ruled usurped the position of rulers and the rulers became objects of ridicule. The *Purim* celebrants, all male, would form groups composed of Yeshiva students, entertainers, jesters, bands of folk musicians, artisans and their apprentices, and even beggars and pickpockets. Masked, and with many of them in women's clothes, they would parade through the streets stopping at the richer Jewish households to demand food and money in exchange for entertainment.

In a previous study (Belkin, 1999) I suggested that disguise enabled the players to safely express their grievances against the 'establishment', because they used the masks of ethnic 'otherness' to express a mutiny of social 'otherness'. In effect, this masking emphasised, at one and the same time, the identity of the beggar and the merchant, of the poor and the mighty, the learned and the uneducated as members of a powerless Jewish community as well as their differences in status within that community.

Several theorists, notably Bakhtin (1984), have suggested that the inversion of carnival offered ordinary people access to a utopian sense of community, abundance, freedom and equality. However, Bakhtin indicates that the liberation sought in carnival and its associated genres is caught in perpetual tension between rebellion against the existing order and reinforcement of it. Victor Turner (1982), in his study of pre-literate societies, argues that the 'masking of the weak in aggressive strength', like the concomitant 'masking of the strong in humility and passivity' are devices used to cleanse society of its structurally engendered 'sins'. At the end of the festival or special occasion there is a sober return to a now purged and reanimated structure. The enactment of social subversion that is a major constituent of both carnival and the *Purimspiel* can thus be seen to be, precisely, an enactment, allowing the expression of social and political dissent and discontent within a confined and ritualised space.

In the *Purimspiel*, the temporary overthrow of the social order sent out two messages: one was utopian, allowing the individual to identify with the community; the other was potentially subversive. Jewish society was as anti-structured as it was structured, containing conflicts, contradictions and social divides as much as stability. The society itself exhibited features of liminality. This underpins the dual nature of the players and their messages. The players were the underprivileged, marginal, liminal or 'other', and they represented a social dissonance, taking advantage of the festive occasion to vent their resentments. Yet, although their activities crossed over the boundaries of the sacred values of Jewish society, both the transgression and reinstatement of these values highlighted their centrality to the identity of the community and its life.

Theatrical performance was transgressive in itself, and out of tune with the puritanical nature of Judaism. The biblical prohibition 'Thou shalt not make unto thee any graven images or any likeness' and the books of oral law that interpret it, contain vehement exhortations against the theatre, and such performances were banned. Once a year, however, the Jew did become *Homo Teatralis*, at *Purim*, when all prohibitions were lifted. It was the only holiday in the Jewish calendar that contained such Saturnalian elements as drinking, clowning, games, playacting and men wearing women's clothes.

Cross-dressing was ordinarily rigorously prohibited. The many regulations on dress in the Jewish code of sexual morality were backed by biblical injunctions, perhaps the foremost being: 'A woman shall not wear that which pertaineth to man, neither shall a man put on a woman's garment; for all that do so are an abomination unto the Lord thy God' (*Deut.*, 22:5). Commentators interpreted this as intending to safeguard the demarcations between the sexes, for otherwise the door would be open to immorality. It can be argued that adherence to codes of dress, as well as to dietary regulations and other observances and admonitions, not only regulated behaviour among Jews, but also signaled and guaranteed membership of the Jewish community and its exclusions. The prohibition on cross-dressing indicates that upholding a clear distinction between gendered behaviours or roles as well as appearances, and also, by inference adherence to heterosexuality, were important elements of this 'membership'. That this taboo was breached in the *Purimspiel* is therefore significant in itself. The manner in which it was breached demands investigation, since a performance which draws attention to transitivity of gender might be seen to open up the possibility of changing demarcated gender roles.

As Natalie Zemon-Davis has noted in her widely cited article 'Women on Top' (1985) the experience of social inequality was often expressed through sexual symbolism, in which the female position was used to symbolise hierarchical subordination as well as violence and chaos. Furthermore, feminist criticism has discussed the probability that some limited potential for women lies in the alternative worlds created by carnival. Theatrical cross-dressing has provided one way of playing with liminality and its multiple possibilities, and of extending the sense of that potential to the spectator. Postmodern theory has suggested that the masks of transgender stress the performativity of gender, and some have applied this to the study of carnival. Howard (1993) considers that carnival's inversion of order gave women momentary power, and carried it with the possibility of exposing that liminal moment, that threshold of questioning, that slippery sense of a mutable self. Zemon-Davis (1985) examines the inversion of roles in the carnivalistic mode in which males disguised themselves as grotesque, cavorting females. She speculates that these images of women out of their 'natural' place might have enriched the options of female behaviour beyond the privileged boundaries of the performance of the festival. However, another strand in feminist criticism concludes that this supposed model for potential change only served to reaffirm the normal, oppressed status of women. Mary Russo, for instance, in 'Female Grotesques: Carnival and Theory' (1986), considers Davis's example of transgression of boundaries in the 1641 riots in Wiltshire, led by male cross-dressers who called themselves 'Lady Skimmington'. She argues that this comic female masquerade, ostensibly an image of power which protected the men and stimulated them to action, was nevertheless an image that perpetuated dominant misogynous representations of women. Because of the particular characteristics of the *Purimspiel* and cross-dressing within it, it is this latter interpretation that will be argued here.

Chone Shmeruk (1979) traces the development of the *Purim* procession into a full play, in which biblical themes become central. The most common offering became an enactment of the *Book of Esther*, unsurprisingly, since this Book tells of the origin of the Purim feast itself. Broadly, the Book recounts how the wicked Haman, viceroy to the Persian King Ahasuerus, plots to massacre all the Jews. They are reprieved at the last moment through the ingenuity of the beautiful Jewish Queen Esther and her uncle, the wise Mordechai. It is interesting to see how and to what extent the *Purimspiel* remains faithful to and departs from the biblical text. Certainly, major elements of the story are reproduced in it. Principally, the story is about the oppression of the Jewish minority and their eventual triumph over that oppression. It can also be seen to be concerned with faithfulness, loyalty and law, particularly in terms of righteous transgression in the service of a higher loyalty or morality. These and other themes are reflected not only in the narrative or content of the *Purim* play but also in the social import or messages.

In the biblical tale, Ahasuerus gives a feast to celebrate his power, and during it commands his queen, Vashti, to come before the princes and show off her beauty. Vashti, who has been holding a feast for the women of the palace, refuses. The king is counselled that this act of disobedience is serious: 'For this deed of the queen shall come abroad unto all women, so that they shall despise their husbands in their eyes' (*Esther*, 1: 17). Ahasuerus is advised to put the queen aside and choose another from the most beautiful virgins in the kingdom, so that, when his decree is published;'all the wives shall give their husbands honour, both great and small' (1: 20). Esther is chosen. Unknown to the king, she is the cousin of Mordechai and has been adopted by him and brought up as his daughter. Mordechai then foils a plot by two of the chamberlains to kill the king, but is not rewarded for this.

Meanwhile, Haman rises in favour and everyone bows down and pays homage to him. As a Jew, Mordechai will not do this, which infuriates Haman. Hence, he hatches a plot to kill Mordechai and all the Jews by telling Ahasuerus that they obey their own laws and not his. So the king passes a law decreeing that on an appointed day his subjects may rise up against the Jews, kill them and seize their property. Mordechai, in mourning, tears his clothes and dons sackcloth and ashes, attire not allowed within the court. Esther sends him clothing, perhaps in an attempt to protect him, but he will not wear it and instead urges her to do something for her people.

A motif concerning clothing thus appears in the biblical story itself, and moreover it is connected to an idea of disguise. If Esther attempts to disguise her relative as 'not Jewish', then his reply to her underscores her status as a woman in disguise. When chosen as a candidate to be the king's consort, Esther did not reveal that she was Jewish. Mordechai had told her then to keep silence, now, when she tries to get him to hide himself, he reminds Esther of her higher duty and urges her to speak out:

> Think not with thyself that thou shalt escape in the king's house, more than all the Jews. For if thou altogether holdest thy peace at this time, then shall there enlargement and deliverance arise to the Jews from another place; but thou and thy father's house shall be destroyed: and who knoweth whether thou art come to the kingdom for such a time as this?
>
> (*Esther*, 4: 13–14)

The element of unmasking in the sense of revealing what is hidden is strong in the *Book of Esther*. The king discovers Mordechai's act of loyalty, which had been masked by Haman's lie regarding the disloyalty of the Jews. Esther reveals her Jewishness and Haman's perfidy to the king. Mordechai is raised up to become the king's chief adviser, and Haman is hanged on the gallows he had prepared for Mordechai. This last is just one of the many instances of reversal or inversion in the story. Queen Vashti disobeyed by refusing to go before the king when summoned; Queen Esther, in order to appeal for her people, disobeys by going in to the king without being summoned – a crime punishable by death. As Ahasuerus had decreed, at Haman's request, a day on which the Jews could be killed, he subsequently decrees, at Esther and Mordechai's request, a day (extended to two) when the Jews could stand up against and kill anyone who wanted to do them harm. The feast at the beginning of the story, from which the Jews were excluded, is mirrored at the end by the establishment, by Esther and Mordechai, of *Purim* as a feast for the Jews.

The *Book of Esther*, therefore, contains many of the themes and motifs found in the *Purimspiel*. To some extent the features of disguise, transgression and reversal seen in the performance could be said to have some justification in the biblical text itself. However, some key elements that characterise the *Purimspiel* are not in the Book. The *Purimspiel* was spontaneous and improvised freely on its source. The story of Esther was treated from very early on with a levity totally unthinkable on other occasions. The revellers resorted to parody as a strategy for inversion, and although the plot remained, the characterisations and atmosphere were greatly altered. The major difference lies in the characterisation of the women. All are played by men in bizarre versions of female dress. Not only do women literally lose their voice in the translation from the book to the play, but the women characters are given very little to say themselves; rather than speaking, they are essentially spoken about. Above all Esther loses her centrality, and her good character, in the folk play.

The fact that all parts were played by men in the *Purimspiel* might be expected to have an effect upon the female characterisations and the audience's perceptions of them, but this need not be a detrimental effect. The absence of women from the Jewish folk theatre is part of a long theatrical tradition going back to classical times. In ancient Greek and Roman, and in Renaissance theatre, men took all the parts in plays that were also written by men. However, critics differ as to how to interpret both the men-only enactment and the level of mysogyny in the contents of such plays. Leading Shakespearian scholars, for example, reject the historicist critical assumption of a correlation between women's status in Elizabethan society and the representation of women characters in the plots and their stage enactments. Phyllis Rackin, for instance, in her recent lecture 'Mysogyny is everywhere: Reflection on the current state of feminist Shakespeare criticism' (2000) repudiates what she considers to be an exaggerated feminist/historicist critical trend to find mysogyny as all-pervasive in Shakespeare. She demonstrates, rather, that women were part of public life in Elizabethan times and an active audience in the theatre, where they brought their own perspective to the action. Thus, to point merely to the fact that men played women's roles elucidates neither the form and meaning of the plays, nor their effects on their contemporary audience.

To understand the roots of gender bias in presenting images of women in a theatre where men played women's parts, we have to revert to the absence of women in the ancient Greek theatre, in a society where women were excluded from public life and confined to an interior, private or domestic world. The Jewish masculocentric society exhibits affinities, in this narrow sense, with ancient Greek society in which women had inferior status and were confined to an inner domain. The verse of the *Psalms*: 'The king's daughter is all glorious within the house . . .', for example, has been interpreted to bolster this discrimination. Women were traditionally denied access to theatrical performances in Jewish culture, as these were regarded as immodest, and their voices were not allowed to be heard. In 'Classic drag: The Greek creation of female parts' (1985), Sue-Ellen Case argues that feminist critics assume that images of women in the plays of Classical Greece represent a fiction of women constructed by a patriarchy – a fiction which does not correspond to the lives of actual women. She maintains that the purpose of men in female clothing playing women was to put on stage a vocabulary of male-originated signs and gestures engendering an image of archetypal 'Woman', institutionalised through a patriarchal culture. However, the purpose of men playing female parts in the *Purimspiel* was neither to create an illusion, as in the Renaissance theatre, nor because men were thought to be 'better' at playing women than women themselves would be. Nor was it in order to endow the female characters with specific and distinctive attributes which could be identified as feminine and were enacted by these characters, in the manner which Case's argument suggests. The male Greek playwrights put great heroines on centre stage, albeit in roles that might indeed have reflected only the experience of men attempting to dramatise the battle of the genders, as Case indicates. But in the festive play of the Jewish community, where women were also excluded from public life, the active female protagonists of the *Book of Esther* were reduced to non-entities; rather than the female characters being filled with characteristics constructed as feminine, so that they projected some sort of feminine subjectivity, they were emptied of attributes and effectively objectified. This 'emptying' and degradation of the female image served to validate male authority . Even when portrayed as clowns, the male characters of Mordechai, Ahasuerus, Haman and the courtiers still had control over the unfolding of the plot, whereas Esther, Vashti and Haman's wife, Zeresh, had no such control and were enacted by the cross-dressed players as grotesque caricatures, becoming objects of derision.

Roger Baker (1968) distinguishes between 'real' and 'false' disguises of cross-dressing male actors, that is, between a man playing a female role in all seriousness and expecting the audience to accept him as such, and a man playing a female part where the audience is expected to realise he is a man. He suggests that the 'false' disguise puts the female impersonator into a different category, as a type of comic curiosity. Certainly, the cross-dressing elements of the *Purimspiel* fall into this 'false' category, and were a staple component of the buffoonery. The male characters engaged in monologues, songs and jokes at the women's expense, in which lack of chastity, humility and modesty were ascribed to the women characters. The men in the *Purimspiel* gave the women a 'voice' by imitating supposed feminine small talk on intimate sexual experience, offered in coarse language and parodic mode. At the same time, the men themselves, especially the 'pious' Mordechai, freely made mention of female genitals and their own pleasure in sex.

Queen Esther's role as the saviour of her people is taken from her in the *Purimspiel*, and she is presented as a grotesque, passive, humiliated and inferior object. In the Bible she is beautiful, in the play she is a pale, skinny girl, dressed in rags and the butt of comic barbs. The practice of matchmaking, a serious business in Jewish society, often performed by women, is given farcical treatment in the *Purimspiel*. In many versions of the play, Mordechai acts as matchmaker, Esther as object for exchange. Gorin (1929) cites his description of Esther, given to Ahasuerus:

> [She is] a good housewife who cleans the pots and pans with her sleeves, sweeps the floor with her apron and, instead of lighting the stove and making the beds, will make the stove and light the beds. Her father is a thief from here to Siberia, and her mother – a whore.
>
> (*ibid.*, p. 59)

In another version we find a parody of the imagery of beauty from the *Song of Songs*: 'Her nose is as large as a house. Her mouth gigantic. Her brow is like a bear's behind, her ears like those of a donkey. Her breasts are pointed, the nipples like pinheads.' An exaggerated nose is a common carnival feature and frequently symbolises the penis. In the *Purimspiel*, where man is playing Esther, the big phallus is in fact his own.

Chastity disappears altogether and, as so often happens in comedy that is obsessed with the female body, that body is repeatedly alluded to, described and thus verbally exposed. In the *Purim* play published by the ethnographer Samuel Weissenberg (1904) *Dus Purimspiel – Du Spielt die Rolle Humen in Mordche*, known as the Purimspiel of Elisabethgard, Queen Vashti is not only summoned before the princes in her finery, she is commanded to appear naked. After her refusal, and when the death sentence is passed she kneels to plead with the king and says: 'My king, why have you forgotten the times you used to fondle my snow-white breasts . . . ?' Such a description might have shifted the show into the classical mode, in which the human body is perceived as complete and beautiful. But when the woman is played by a man with a beard, a kerchief around his shoulders, or a short and shabby dress, with a pair of large, coarse boots showing beneath – as Shalom Aleichem (1942a) describes one such performance – these breasts belong to the grotesque.

The Purimspiel often featured long mysogynous songs. Vashti's episode of disobedience was used as a pretext to insert the theme of women's infidelity to their male masters – their fathers, husbands and brothers. In Weisenberg's *Dus Purimspiel* biblical heroines are invoked by Vashti's executioner, and for each one a flaw is found: Eve was the first woman to eat the apple; Sara, the wife of pious Abraham, betrayed him and fell in love with Abimelech; Rebecca cheated Isaac, taking advantage of his blindness to extort the blessing for her beloved younger son Jacob; Rachel stole her father's idols; and Miriam gossiped about her brothers Moses and Aaron. Women are so dangerous that even Samson, the superman, was seduced by Delilah. After each stanza the refrain comes: 'Her end was dreadful death, women are damn nuisance and trouble!'

Throughout, it is the male characters who establish the 'nature' of the female characters – and women in general – by their comments about them. Even though Esther is played by a man, she still has no voice of her own. The great female protagonist of the Book hardly appears in the play. Indeed, even though she is given only a few lines to recite, she is represented by the men in the reverse mode of the play as talkative and unfaithful. When the Jews are facing impending disaster after the King has ordered their genocide, Mordechai asks Esther, according to the biblical text, to pray for her people. In Jewish culture all public rituals constituted a male domain. A woman could never be a cantor, leading the prayers of the community, and to think of doing so would indicate a shocking immodesty. That Esther is a man in female disguise underlines this immodesty, but his ludicrous appearance transforms the shocking into the ridiculous and increases the parody.

Lacking a theatre, a stage, scenery, or even an organised audience, the *Purimspiel* was a 'poor theatre' in every sense, stripped down to its barest elements. Everyday attire was transformed into a festive, theatrical garb. The mode of parody dictated the design of the costumes. Bell-Metereau (1985) interprets transvestism as always presenting a negative image of women since, in order to accomplish the imitation, the actor must focus on precisely those elements of female anatomy, dress, facial appearance and mannerism that are the most superficial. The masquerade in the

Purimspiel brought negative images of women even lower, and this degraded representation was reinforced by means of costume. In the spirit of the carnival the actors' appearance was exaggerated, surprising and ridiculous. Clothing was worn backwards or upside-down. While some effort was made to lend the male characters' costumes a measure of dramatic authenticity, even dignity, the drag players were costumed in rags. The players tried to imbue old clothes and rags with an additional quality of chaos, buffoonery and distorted fashion, thus creating a disproportion and sloppiness that produced the desired hilarity. The players' own clothes could frequently be glimpsed beneath the ragged costume. The slovenly female attire, combined with the misogynous text and stage business, caused the female characters to appear doubly distorted. They were not only voiceless, but in this parody of women's clothing they hardly looked like women at all. The actors would achieve the desired effect by padding themselves in the appropriate places with pillows, wearing wigs or scarves on their heads and adding other female accoutrements.

Descriptions can be found in all the sources on Purimspiel productions. The Yiddish writer Mendele Moykher Sforim inserted a *Purimspiel* scene in his play *Der Priziv* (Abramovitsh, 1913, pp. 76–80). In the third act a group of *Purim* players bursts into an assembly: Ahasuerus is clad in an old velvet *Parochet* (curtain of the Ark of the Law) with a paper hat on his head; Mordechai, riding a hobbyhorse adorned with bells, wears the traditional Jewish dress of *kapota* (black cloak) and *streimel* (fur hat), his beard is made of strings; Haman wears a military tunic, with a tricorn made of paper on his head. This style of hat is seen very often, probably as a reflection of the 'Ear of Haman', the traditional ear-shaped *Purim* biscuit. Vashti shows signs of a beard – her short dress is dirty and she wears a kerchief around an old straw hat. None of the actors bothered to hide their male identity. Shaul Sapir (1959), in his memoirs of a *Purimspsiel* from the beginning of the twentieth century, recalls how he played the role of Haman's wife, Zeresh. He was told by the Rabbi that it would suffice to wrap a shawl around his shoulders to appear like a woman. A stylised artificial beard of string was made for the role of Mordechai, whose Jewish identity was stressed. Such camouflage was preferable to the player's own beard, for it increased the theatricality. Concealing their natural beards when playing a female role was a problem encountered by the Jewish players, and attempts to hide them made them look even more ridiculous. Shalom Aleichem recalls (1942b) that in his youth he saw a *Purimspiel* in which Mottil the carpenter, who played the role of Vashti, wore a dress over his *kapota*, the edges of which could be seen underneath. To complete the look, he tied up his beard in a white kerchief to 'convince' the audience they were in the presence of a woman. According to another testimony from Soslowitch (Levin, 1959), a certain beardless old man used to play Vashti. When he died, the only replacement to be found was a bearded man who had played the other female roles and who would wind up his beard around his cheeks and tie a scarf over it, as though suffering from an aching tooth. Hiding a beard behind a scarf soon became a convention of the *Purimspiel*, as did Vashti's toothache – a sure-fire comic ploy. What began as a matter of necessity became a tradition: men in women's roles had their faces wrapped in scarves. In nineteenth-century Russia, a group of actors got together every *Purim* to perform the play for charity. Vashti was played every year by a young lad who, beardless and in a gown with a paper crown, made a nice queen. One year, just before *Purim*, the young man suddenly showed signs of a rather advanced beard. With improvised toothache and a scarf wrapped around his face, the text was amended on the spot to suit the situation. When the servant came to fetch Vashti to appear before King Ahasverus, the boy playing her part sang out: 'Go tell your master/ He's an idiot and a jerk/ I won't come/ because my tooth hurts' (Egoz, 1924).

Cross-dressing, the erasure and degradation of female characters in the *Purimspiel* serves to preserve the patriarchal culture, by underscoring the necessary exclusion of women from a position of centrality within that culture. Even in the fantasy world of the *Purimspiel*, borrowed from the world of myth, woman is not empowered. The players, who belong to the lowest stratum of society, may triumph temporarily over authority, but the laughter belongs to the men alone. The comedic pattern of movement from established order through an inverted upside-down-world and back to a re-established order gave the participants an opportunity to invert and subvert the norms. In Jewish homosocial culture, however, this did not provide women with a chance to achieve even a transitory higher status. They were always mocked and voiceless. The stereotyped, passive female image offered in such a gender masquerade in fact reiterates male anxieties, desires and interests, rather than subverting the status quo of Jewish patriarchal culture. In fact, transgressing the taboo on cross-dressing, and the manner in which this was transgressed – through a 'false' disguise – reinforced, rather than breached, the socially constructed demarcations between the genders. This indicates that the subordinated position of women was an essential feature of notions of Jewish community and identity, a law that should not and could not be broken, even in the *Purimspiel*. After all, in the *Book of Esther*, it is Vashti's wilful disobedience to male authority that marks the start of the trouble, and it is Esther's obedience to her 'father' Mordechai which saves the Jews.

NOTE

1 This Chapter is based on my research into the Purimspiel within the context of the Saturnalian-type festivities, to appear in my forthcoming book *The Purimspiel: The Jewish Folk Theatre*, Jerusalem, Bialik Institute.

The author wishes to acknowledge Wendy Leeks for her extensive invaluable editorial input.

REFERENCES

Abramovitsh, S.Y. (1913) *Der Priziv in Ale verke fun Mendele Moykher Sforim*, Warsaw, Farlag Mendele.

Baker, Roger (1968) *Drag: A history of female impersonation on stage*, London, Trinton.

Bakhtin, Mikhail (1984) *Rabelais and his world* (trans. Iswolsky, Helene), Bloomington, Indiana University Press.

Belkin, Ahuva (1996) 'Citing Scripture for a purpose: The Jewish Purimspiel as a parody', *Assaph Studies in the Theatre* 12, 45–61.

Belkin, Ahuva (1999) 'Masks and disguises as an expression of anarchy in the Jewish festival theatre', in *Theatre and the Holy Script* (ed. Levy, Shimon), Brighton, Academic Press.

Belkin, Ahuva (2001) *The Jewish folk theatre: The Purimspiel*, Jerusalem, Bialik Institute (forthcoming).

Bell-Metereau, Rebecca, (1985) *Hollywood androgyny*, New York, Columbia University Press.

Case, Sue-Ellen (1985) 'Classic drag: The Greek creation of female parts', *Theatre Journal* 37, 317–27.

Egoz, A. D. (1924) *Abisel Purimdiges Mazes*, New York (Yiddish)

Gorin, B. (1929) *Die geschichte fun Yiddishen teater*, New York (Yiddish).

Howard, Jean E. (1993) 'Cross-dressing, the theatre, and gender struggle in early modern England', in *Crossing the stage: Controversies on cross-dressing* (ed. Ferris, Lesley), London, Routledge.

Levin, Shmaryahu (1959) *Lexikon fun Yiddishen teater* vol. III (ed. Zilberzweig, Z.) New York, Farlag 'Elisheva'.

Rackin, Phyllis (2000) 'Misogyny is everywhere: reflection on the current state of feminist Shakespeare criticism', in *A feminist companion to Shakespeare* (ed. Callaghan, D.), Oxford, Blackwell.

Russo, Mary (1986) 'Female grotesques: Carnival and theory', in *Feminist studies/Critical Studies* (ed. de Lauretis, Teresa), Bloomington, Indiana University Press.

Sapir, Shaul (1959) *Lexikon fun Yiddishen teater*, vol. III (ed. Zilberzweig, Z.), New York, Farlag 'Elisheva'.

Shalom Aleichem (1942a) *Fun Pesach biz Pesach* (From Passover to Passover), New York (Yiddish).

Shalom Aleichem (1942b) 'In the house of the King Ahasuerus', in *Ale Werk*, New York (Yiddish).

Shmeruk, Chone (1979) 'Appendix I: The beginnings of the Purim play and its sixteenth century remnants', in *Yiddish Biblical plays 1697–1750*, Jerusalem, The Israel Academy of Science and Humanities.

Turner, Victor (1982) *From ritual to theatre: The human seriousness of play*, New York, PAJ Publications.

Weissenberg, Samuel (ed.) (1994) *Dus Purimspiel: Du spielt die rolle humen in Mordche*, Hamburg, Mitteilungen der Gesellschaft fur Judiche Volkskunde, Heft XIII.

Zemon-Davis, Natalie (1985) 'Women on top: Symbolic sexual inversion and political disorder in early modern Europe', in *Society and culture in early modern France*, Stanford, Stanford University Press.

7

THE METAMORPHOSIS OF THE MASK IN SEVENTEENTH- AND EIGHTEENTH-CENTURY LONDON

Christoph Heyl

This chapter deals mainly with the development and the functional role of masks worn by women in seventeenth- and eighteenth-century London. I shall focus on the practice of wearing masks in a non-masquerade context. Masked women in, for instance, London parks would once have been a fairly common sight. However, this cultural practice is not something to be taken for granted. How did it evolve? What was the status and purpose of these masks? Were they meant to provide a real, efficient form of disguise, or are we dealing with a more complex phenomenon? How did they affect patterns of behaviour, i.e. what were the effects these masks had both on their wearers and on others? These issues will then be related to both the masquerade and other uses of anonymity and disguise in the eighteenth century.

I shall argue that the split between private and public sphere (cf., passim: Habermas, 1992; Sennett, 1977; Stone, 1977) which took place among the English urban middle classes long before similar developments started in most other European countries, gave an altogether new meaning to a range of phenomena associated with masks and disguises. As a new demand for privacy progressively isolated people from each other, the use of, among other things, a mask, could offer a way out of this self-imposed isolation and inhibition. By means of deliberately obscuring one's own identity, relatively unrestrained and even new forms of social interaction could become possible.

A characteristic trait of premodern societies is the utter irrelevance of the concept of the individual's right to an inviolable private sphere. Although pockets of privacy always existed, this was very much a phenomenon which mainly affected privileged minorities. Premodern societies can be described as face-to-face societies (see Stone, 1977, pp. 6, 95f.) in which groups such as the extended family, the neighbourhood and the guild played a decisive role in guiding and controlling the actions of each of their members. As the concept of privacy was for all practical purposes almost non-existent, every action was conducted in what we today would regard as an atmosphere of publicity. How far this observation went in practice can be concluded from the thousands of detailed denunciations for domestic and moral transgressions received by the ecclesiastical courts between the middle of the fifteenth century and the seventeenth century (see Emmison, 1972).

In this type of premodern society, it could always be assumed that each member of a given community knew, and had a right to know, a good deal about other members of that community. Under these circumstances, an unknown person was either to be treated as a guest or be regarded as an outsider and a potential menace.

One of the basic functions of a mask is to conceal or at least to obscure a person's identity, to turn its wearer, at least notionally, into a stranger – and more often than not, it was not a good thing to be a stranger in a premodern context. This is why it was possible to use certain forms of masks as a feared shame punishment for women regarded as 'scolds'. In late medieval and Renaissance England as well as on the continent, a contraption known as a 'scold's bridle' or 'brank' was widely in use.

There were two types of scold's bridle. In its simplest form, it consisted of a plain metal cage fitting tightly round a person's head with a metal gag protruding inside. The second type was of a similar construction, but took the shape of a grotesque mask, often fitted with bells and such like to attract even greater attention. Women were exhibited in the pillory or led through the streets wearing these contraptions in a ritual of public humiliation.

Some examples of a particularly unpleasant variety of the 'mask' type are known. These were fitted with a screwing apparatus which, according to a nineteenth-century description, 'seems calculated to force the iron mask with torturing effect upon the brow of the victim; there are no eye-holes, but concavities in their places, as though to allow for the starting of the eye-balls under violent pressure' (Andrews, 1890, p. 60).

These 'masks' in a sense run counter to modern expectations about what a mask is there for: their purpose was not to protect and conceal, but to torture and expose. Scold's bridles of the 'mask' type were made for being stared at, and this is why it seems to stand to reason that the most

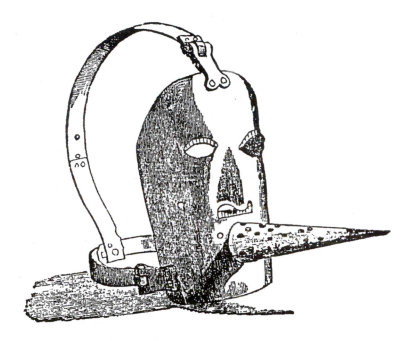

Plate 7.1 Scold's bridle, 'mask' type.
Source: Andrews (1890, p. 58), the author's collection.

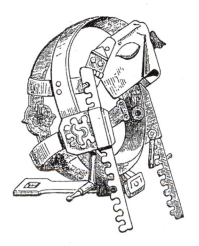

Plate 7.2 Scold's bridle, mask with screwing apparatus.
Source: Andrews (1890, p. 60), the author's collection.

cruel of these artefacts are masks without eye holes. They are in effect blind masks, not designed in any way to efface the wearer's presence, but to provide a focus for the hostile attention of a crowd of gaping spectators.

While a certain form of mask could assume these functions within the context of a premodern society, an altogether different use of masks evolved in the singular social setting of early modern London.

A far-reaching process of change was well under way here: as its population increased rapidly, London became the first European metropolis of the day. Urban mortality was so high that this growth was only sustainable by means of a steady influx of people from the rest of the country. Given its sheer size, London was populated by people who were and remained strangers to one another. Here, the days of local communities exercising an exceptionally high degree of social control were numbered, and the kind of urban anonymity we have come to associate with life in big cities came into being. It became 'normal' to live as a stranger among strangers, to accept and to respect the anonymity of others (see Sennett, 1977, pp. 48, 54f.) Under these new conditions, new ideas about acceptable patterns of behaviour spread especially among the urban middle classes. In this unique local and social setting, a demand for privacy first became a mass phenomenon.

It is under these conditions that new forms of masks began to appear which were soon to undergo a remarkable development. While the phenomenon of the masquerade in eighteenth-century England has been the subject of scholarly studies (Castle, 1986; Craft-Fairchild, 1993; Ribeiro, 1984), the equally interesting use of masks and disguises in a non-masquerade context during the same period and earlier has not yet been studied in depth. There is a body of evidence concerning these phenomena dating from the seventeenth and early eighteenth century, and I shall tentatively chart out what seem to be some relevant aspects of this material.

During the first half of the seventeenth century, a black half-mask (also called 'vizard mask'), covering the upper half of the face, was a common winter accessory worn by well-to-do women in London.

There are a fair number of prints by Wenceslaus Hollar depicting women wearing this type of mask.[1] Hollar obviously associated the wearing of such masks with England: there are no masked figures in his collection of prints depicting the costume of women from various European countries (Hollar, 1643). What is more, Hollar associates the wearing of masks (as a standard accessory rather than an element of fancy dress) with London. Women wearing masks appear, for instance, against a panoramic London background as in Plate 7.3.

Plate 7.3 Wenceslaus Hollar, *Winter* (from the full-length Seasons series, 1643).
Source: author's collection; cf. Pennington (1982, no. 609, p. 98).

Perhaps surprisingly, the winter costumes and groups of winter accessories shown in Hollar's prints include fans. One does not see these fans
in action, but contemporary texts imply that they were used to cover the
remaining part of the naked face. Mask and fan go together because
they both serve to protect the face, as a couplet from a poem by Samuel
Butler (1613–1680) suggests (Butler, 1928, p. 294):

> There are no Vizard-masks, nor Fans,
> To keep Age from a Countenance

Later pictorial evidence confirms that fans were indeed used to cover the
face and thus to interrupt eye-to-eye contact. (For a striking example see
William Hogarth's *The Rake's Progress*, no. VII, i.e. the Bedlam scene. Oil
on canvas, 1733, Sir John Soane's Museum, London.)

The main practical reason for wearing these winter masks as suggested
by their seasonal use and by sub-titles of prints seems to have been the

desire to protect the delicate skin of the face from the cold. (Three unti-tled small prints by Hollar show masks among winter accessories. See Pennington, 1982, nos. 1948, 1949, 1951; all p. 310.) A poem by Charles Cotton (1630–1687) entitled 'Winter' stresses such protective and even cosmetic purposes (Cotton, 1689, p. 62):

> [. . .] out of rev'rend care
> To save her beauty from the Air,
> And guard her pale Complexion,
> Her Hood and Vizard Mask puts on

However, apart from this primary purpose these masks were also a form of disguise. Of course the disguise must necessarily have been rather inefficient: it was still relatively easy to recognize the wearer of such a mask which, after all, just covered the upper half of the face. But then even this must have been more than sufficient to introduce the idea of anonymity and therefore to modify the behaviour of the wearer. After all, a mask deprives its wearer of certain modes of facial expression and thus affects one's ability to communicate.

These masks offered new possibilities of playing with anonymity, and they probably gave a sense of protection, a sense of almost being invisi-ble. Slowly and steadily, the more utilitarian aspects of wearing a mask became a mere pretext. What had been the mask's side-effect (the price a woman had to pay for 'guarding her complexion' was that it temporarily rendered at least part of her face invisible) now became its main attrac-tion. The mask obscures the wearer's identity, thus temporarily turning her into a stranger of sorts. Although this would have been a most unde-sirable predicament in a premodern community, in the new world of the metropolis it could be regarded as an attractive option. In an urban con-text where people were more at ease with anonymity than they had ever been before, these masks gradually took on some kind of life of their own which was worlds apart from the scold's bridle.

One should keep in mind that masks both obscure their wearers and attract attention at the same time. The half-masks depicted by Hollar and others could be more of a token disguise than a real one. This point is being made in a poem by John Cleveland (1613–1658) as he mentions the

> [. . .] Cob-web vizard, such as Ladies weare,
> When they are veyl'd on purpose to be seene
>
> (Cleveland, 1647, p. 33)

Several new developments in the late seventeenth century confirm that the anonymity (be it real or notional) conferred by the mask now became its main attraction and that even the pretence of cosmetic reasons for wearing it was eventually dropped. Under the influence of the new intellectual and moral atmosphere brought about by the Restoration, new informal rules concerning the wearing of masks began to apply. The overall role of the mask underwent a transformation: both its physical appearance and the time and places regarded as appropriate for wearing it changed.

The mask ceased to be a winter accessory and it began to be an option available at any time of the year. As its main function came to be its power to confer varying degrees of anonymity, its size increased from the half-mask to a mask covering the entire face. The use of such masks was governed by informal rules: they were only worn in special places, mainly London parks and theatres.

This new appreciation of anonymity reflected in the development of the mask can be traced in similar, parallel phenomena as it affected patterns of everyday behaviour in numerous ways.

A new phenomenon which could well be described as a virtual form of disguise is the incognito ritual. If you make it understood that you are incognito, people may well recognize you, but they are nevertheless expected to behave towards you as if you were completely disguised. This apparently bizarre but once common pattern of behaviour demonstrates that the privacy of strangers or of people who wanted to be treated as strangers had become something to be respected. Such a thing would have been unthinkable in a face-to-face society in which every stranger was inevitably incorporated into the existing group as a guest or expelled as an alien and a menace. (The word 'incognito' became current in the English language from the mid-seventeenth century. See *OED* on CD-ROM, 1992, q.v.)

Eye-to-eye contact among strangers rapidly became a taboo. The anonymous author of a list of 'Rules of behaviour' (*London Magazine*, February 1734, p. 66f.) advises his readers

> (6) To be cautious of Staring in the Faces of those that pass by us, like an Inquisitor general; for an over-bearing Look has the Air of a Bully, and a prying one that of a Bayley. If we do it by Mistake for a Friend, ask Pardon.
> [. . .]
> (8) Not to fasten your Eyes upon any Person entring [sic] into a publick Room, for Fear (by such a broad side) of Shocking his Modesty, and Dismounting his Assurance [. . .].

It was a common notion that looking closely at someone's face enabled one to 'read' this face and thus to find out about a person's abilities, inclinations and motivations. The new taboo concerning eye-to-eye contact really meant that it was now regarded as a violation of peoples' private spheres to snatch their secrets from them by 'reading' their faces.

The basic idea that faces can be 'read' was in fact an old one which, however, had developed into something like a science in its own right by the eighteenth century. In 1586, Della Porta drew attention to parallel characteristics of human and animal physiognomy in his illustrated work *De Humana Physiognomia*. The idea was taken up in Le Brun's hugely influential *Traité sur la physionomie* (1698) and works of a similar nature which were soon translated and became hugely influential in England. Numerous illustrations form an integral part of Le Brun's works. These demonstrate how specific passions affect the human face. Le Brun in fact provided a key, a kind of an alphabet which could eventually facilitate the 'reading' of faces in everyday life.

19

L'AMOUR SIMPLE.

LEs mouvemens de cette paſſion, lors qu'elle eſt ſimple, ſont fort doux & ſimples, car le front ſera uni ; les ſourcils un peu élevés du côté que ſe trouve la prunelle, là tête inclinée vers l'objet qui cauſe de l'amour, les yeux peuvent être mediocrement ouverts, le blanc de l'œil fort vif & éclatant, la prunelle doucement tournée du côté où eſt l'objet, elle paroîtra un peu étincelante & élevée, le nez ne reçoit aucun changement, de même que toutes les parties du viſage, qui étant ſeulement

B ij

Plate 7.4 Le Brun, 'L'amour Simple'.
   Source: Le Brun (1713, p. 19), author's collection.

161

TERROR.

as represented by Le Brun. The violence of this passion alters all the parts of the face ; the eyebrows rise in the middle ; its muscles are marked, swelled, pressed one against the other, and sunk towards the nose, which draws up as well as the nostrils ; the eyes are very open ; the upper eyelid is hid under the eyebrow ; the white of the eye is encompassed with red ; the eyeball fixes towards the lower part of the eye ; the lower part of the eyelid swells, and becomes livid ; the muscles of the nose and cheeks swell, and these last terminate in a point towards the sides of the nostrils ; the mouth is very open, and its corners very apparent ; the muscles and

P 3

Plate 7.5 G. Brewer, 'Terror'.
Source: Brewer (1812, p. 161), author's collection.

Later on, this notion was further developed by Johann Kaspar Lavater and others. Thus, belief in the practical value of the science of physiognomy developed from a body of specialist knowledge to a set of commonplace assumptions. Numerous English conduct books propagated these ideas, enabling people to 'read' the faces of others as well as making them aware of the constant danger of 'being read' themselves. A concise version of the popular view of physiognomy is given, for instance, in *The polite lady, or, a course of education in a series of letters from a mother to her daughter* (Anon., 1760, pp. 218–19):

But, my Dear, not only does the countenance receive a transient tincture from the passion which happens, for the present, to be most prevalent in the mind: what is still more, if we indulge that passion frequently and habitually, it will come at last to give the countenance such a particular cast and air, as it will not be in our power to alter or throw off at pleasure, but will continue fix'd and invariable through our whole lives, and will go a great way to determine our character, at least with the generality of the world, who have no other opportunity to judge of our tempers, but from our looks and appearance; so that we shall pass for proud or humble, peevish or good-natured, impudent or modest, just as our countenance is expressive of any of these dispositions.

Thus, you see, my Dear, there is at least some truth in physiognomy, and that it concerns every young lady to be very careful of her looks, since her character depends as much upon these as upon any other part of her behaviour. The only advice I can give you in this case is, never to entertain any lewd or immodest thought in your breast, and then you will never be in danger of expressing any thing of that nature in your countenance: if you would wish to have a modest look, you must endeavour to have a modest mind; for without the latter, the former can hardly exist.

It was thus a widely received idea that a face could be 'read'. Nothing demonstrates this so clearly as the curious device which was in use in the London criminal courts of the Old Bailey in the eighteenth century and which is shown in a print from *The Newgate Calendar*. While the defendant was being questioned, his face could be watched in a huge and specially lighted mirror installed for this purpose. The defendant's facial expression was apparently almost of as much interest to all other parties concerned as his or her words.

It became a part of a middle-class child's education as set out in conduct books to disguise one's feelings by turning one's face into a kind of expressionless mask. The following rules are given in *The School of Manners*, a book written for children and published in London in 1701:

> (18) If any immodest or obscene thing be spoken of in thy hearing, smile not at it, but settle thy countenance as though thou didst not hear it.
> (19) Let thy countenance be moderately chearful [sic], neither laughing nor frowning.
> (20) Laugh not aloud, but smile upon occasion.
> [. . .]
> (22) Look not boldly or wishfully in the Face of thy Superior.
> (Anon., 1983, p. 40f.)

Conduct books for adults continued to make the same point: one may frustrate peoples' attempts to 'read' one's face by deliberately trying to give no clues at all:

> [. . .] it is now-a-days considered as a sign of rusticity and igno-rance to allow the countenance to be an index of the mind, or to express those particular passions with which it is affected. A certain unmeaning uniformity of face is now studied and practised, or rather to have such an absolute command over our features, as to be able, on occasion, to assume any appearance [. . .].
>
> (Anon., 1760, pp. 219–20)

Given all these alarming assumptions about the countenance being read-able, it could indeed make good sense to wear a mask of the new type which covered the entire face. In the early eighteenth century, Baron von Pöllnitz, a German visitor, was astonished to see well-to-do women wear-ing such masks in London parks as a matter of course:

> The Ladies here have little to employ them; their Amusement being [. . .] to have the Pleasure of being seen, which really is of all Pleasures that which they seem to take most delight in. This is the Motive that carries them to the public Walks, Concerts, and Theatres; in all which Places, they are mightily reserved [. . .]. [. . .] As for the rest, the Women here enjoy great Liberty. They turn out in a Morning with a black velvet Mask on their Faces, a Coif on in Form of a Hat, with the Brims down, a round Gown, and a white Apron, and in this Trim they go to the Park, or where else they please.
>
> (Pöllnitz, 1737, II, p. 461)

Note that on the one hand the author thinks that English women are 'mightily reserved', while on the other hand they delight in the game of seeing and being seen. The mask made it easier for them to do both things at the same time: protected by a mask, an element of privacy could be maintained while frequenting public places.

The very thing described by von Pöllnitz can be seen in a painting attributed to Mario Ricci which shows *A View of the Mall from St. James's Park* (c.1710). Among the numerous figures promenading in the park, there are some women whose faces are entirely covered by black masks.

There are similar examples dating from the late seventeenth century such as two anonymous paintings showing the Horse Guards Parade, one of them including the King and his entourage.[2] In both of these paintings, among the numerous figures depicted, there is a woman wearing a black mask covering her entire face. The remarkable thing about these paintings is that, as in Ricci's painting, the masked figure (or figures) is given a most prominent position. In the painting showing Charles II on Horse Guards Parade, for instance, it is not the King with his group of attendants, dogs and a detachment of Foot Guards who provides the unquestionable focus of attention: the figure 'closest' to the viewer is a masked woman, i.e. the anonymous artist chose to diminish the figure of the King and to enlarge that of a nameless masked female figure.

Such images strongly emphasize the fact that masked women were present in these places. From the late seventeenth century, women wearing masks seem to have been a feature readily associated with, for instance, St. James's Park. Masked women were apparently stock characters connected with certain urban localities, much as foreign merchants in exotic dress were likely to be included in views of the Royal Exchange.

What these paintings strongly suggest is confirmed by a large number of contemporary texts. While early seventeenth-century evidence points to a seasonal use of masks for mainly cosmetic purposes, now the mask's function as a disguise is emphasized time and time again. Numerous references to the practice of wearing masks for the sake of enjoying a certain degree of (at least notional) anonymity can be found in poems, plays and prose texts such as essays, letters and diaries.

There are references to masked women walking in parks, references to masked women in theatres and there are, of course, plays featuring park scenes including masked women. Such scenes must have been of considerable immediate appeal as masked actors faced an at least partly masked audience. Given this type of situation, the audience could relate in a very direct sense to what was happening on the stage and issues related to the use of masks could be addressed easily. This may help to explain the fact that allusions to masks abound in some Restoration comedies: it must have been hard to resist the temptation to point out that what happened on the stage was essentially very similar to what went on among the audience. In a situation where part of the audience was masked, the distinction between players and audience almost broke down, turning the theatre into a gathering of professional and amateur performers.

One went to the theatre not only to see a play, but also to enjoy an extraordinary atmosphere characterized by the relative absence of restraints (which, by the way, never failed to shock foreign visitors). While the players were acting on the stage, members of the audience could don a mask too and assume an alternative persona, thus, escaping from the role they played in everyday life. The semiotic function of these masks was to denote that 'normal' rules of social interaction need not necessarily be observed, that people might approach each other more freely than elsewhere. Up to a point, the rules of everyday life (as regards morals and patterns of communication) were relaxed here, albeit only in certain environments such as parks or theatres.

The mask assumed a dialectic function of repellent and invitation, its message was both 'I can't be seen, I am – at least notionally – not here at all', and 'look at me, I am wearing a mask, maybe I am about to abandon the role I normally play'. One of the mask's paradoxical attractions was that it could both endanger and protect one's respectability. On the one hand, wearing a mask, one might allow oneself to do things which would otherwise be unthinkable. On the other hand, however, one assumed a different persona (the Latin word *persona* literally means mask), i.e., the mask at least notionally protected the identity and thus the integrity of its wearer.

The mask disguises – or more to the point: it pretends to be a disguise; instead of making one inconspicuous, it makes onlookers more inquisitive. This is made abundantly clear in Wycherley's *The Country Wife* (written in 1672) (act III, scene 1). Mrs Pinchwife has just arrived from the country and wants to explore London with all its delightful entertainments:

> *Mrs. Pin.* Well, but pray Bud, let's go to a Play to night.
>
> [. . .]
>
> *Mr. Pin.* So! the obstinacy already of a Town-wife, and I must, while she's here, humour her like one.   [Aside]
> Sister, how shall we do, that she may not be seen, or known?
> *Alith.* Let her put on her Mask.
> *Mr. Pin.* Pshaw, a Mask makes People but the more inquisitive, and is as ridiculous a disguise, as a stage-beard; her shape, stature, habit will be known: and if we wou'd meet with Horner, he wou'd be sure to take acquaintance with us, must wish her joy, kiss her, leer upon her, and the Devil and all; no I'll not use her to a Mask, 'tis dangerous; for masks have made more Cuckolds, than the best faces that were ever known.
>
> [. . .]
>
> *Mr. Pin.* [. . .] a Mask! no – a Woman mask'd, like a cover'd Dish,

gives a Man curiosity, and appetite, when, it may be, uncover'd, 'twou'd turn his stomack; no, no.

Alith. Indeed your comparison is something a greasie one: but I had a gentle Gallant, us'd to say, a Beauty mask'd, lik'd [*sic*] the Sun in Eclipse, gathers together more gazers, than if it shin'd out.

(Wycherley, 1675, pp. 34–5)

People were apparently very much conscious of the fact that one mainly played with anonymity as opposed to really achieving it. The cultural practice of wearing a mask (i.e. displaying a sign denoting 'I am incognito') while in fact being still very much recognizable can be compared the convention of the *aside* in the theatre. Once people get used to such rules, they begin to guide their perception and the entire situation very soon ceases to appear contrived and artificial.

However, true anonymity was certainly a possibility when perfect strangers first met and the woman wore a mask. In the correspondence of the second Earl of Chesterfield there is a letter addressed 'To one who walked 4 whole nights with me in St. James's Park, and yet I never knew who she was' in which the Earl requests to see this particular lady's face (Larwood, 1877, p. 107f.).

Parks, like the theatres, were obviously perceived as areas which were set apart in that otherwise unacceptable forms of behaviour were regarded as legitimate there – and only there. These are the places, as Wycherley puts it in *The Country Wife*, 'where the men are to be found' (Wycherley, 1675, act II, scene 1, p. 17). In Vanbrugh's *The Relapse* (1696) there is a reference to women wearing masks in 'that Babylon of Wickedness, Whitehall' (Vanbrugh, 1698, act V, scene 2, p. 59f.). St. James's Park being one of the prime venues for wearing masks in the open air, it is small wonder that Wycherley's *Love in a Wood, or St. James's Park* (1671, first published 1672) abounds with allusions to masked women and to the relatively free forms of behaviour associated with this practice. Men go to the park to chat up women wearing masks, and Lady Flippant, 'an affected widow', dons a mask to go out in search of a husband (Wycherley, 1694, act II, scene 1, p. 16). Of course one should take care not to take these comedies too easily at face value, but they would seem to confirm the evidence of other sources mentioned.

The fact that these forms of behaviour occurred 'in the open' probably served to control and limit them to a certain degree. All in all, what went on in the parks and theatres appears to be a case of society sanctioning comparatively uninhibited, transgressive types of behaviour in a clearly defined environment.[3]

CHRISTOPH HEYL

When discussing phenomena associated with masks and disguises, one has to keep in mind that, at least according to continental standards, a significant part of the English population habitually disguised themselves in everyday life. In, for instance, the principalities of eighteenth-century Germany, sumptuary laws were still widely being enforced, i.e., there was a clear correlation between the outward appearance of a person and his or her social status (see Wieacker, 1952, p. 108). Not so in England: there, the existing sumptuary laws had been allowed to lapse, and and hardly anyone even thought of forcibly preventing people of a low social status from imitating the costume and appearance of their betters if they could afford to do so. In many cases they could, as it was the custom to give even expensive clothes to servants because these clothes were after a short period of time regarded as being out of fashion.

Travellers from the continent were invariably confused by this state of affairs which was, from their point of view, completely irrational and even reprehensible. They positively resented what they regarded as mere underlings masquerading as fashionable people, especially in places of entertainment. (For one of many such examples see Alberti, 1752, vol. I, p. 297.) It is well worth pointing out that, in sharp contrast to most European states of the day, dress and outward appearance were no longer expected to be an almost infallible guide to peoples' status in society.

Something which would have been regarded as a masquerade, i.e., a highly exceptional phenomenon in most other countries was here being taken for granted as a part of everyday life. This points to a comparatively high level of tolerance towards an element of disguise and the potential confusion that went with it in English urban society which was indeed remarkable if seen in an international context.

This tolerance extended to what one might call virtual forms of disguise, and a good deal of imaginative use was made of these from the late seventeenth century onwards. A vast number of texts published during this period were anonymous or pseudonymous: their authors chose not to disclose their true identity; instead, they disappeared behind a virtual mask. A continual sort of masquerade was permanently going on in almost all the new periodicals such as John Dunton's *Athenian Mercury* (collected in Anon., 1703) and the vastly successful *Gentleman's Magazine* or the *London Magazine*. Readers frequently engaged in lengthy discussions conducted by means of sending anonymous or pseudonymous letters which were then published. The protection offered by a pseudonym (which is a functional equivalent of a mask) made them feel free to join in an uninhibited public discussion while they themselves remained safely hidden in their own private spheres.

Such a discussion would have been impossible without this deliberately

128

created artificial anonymity. It was commonly regarded as a grave breach of decorum to assert and defend one's own ideas against those of someone who occupied a superior position in society. An early eighteenth-century conduct book makes this point quite bluntly:

(11) Strive not with Superiors in Argument or Discourse, but easily submit thine opinion to their assertions.
(12) If thy Superior speak any thing wherein thou knowest he is mistaken, correct not, nor contradict him, nor grin at the hearing of it, but pass over the error without notice or interruption.

(Anon., 1983, p. 44)

Rules of this type which governed peoples' everyday behaviour and which gravely inhibited any type of rational discourse could be suspended if face-to-face contact was avoided, and if the discussion was transferred to a public and anonymous exchange of letters to the editor of a magazine.

A new use of actual masks became current from the 1720s in the shape of masquerades (cf. Castle, 1986, passim). Masquerades were events which took place in enclosed spaces such as the pleasure gardens. One gained access by purchasing a ticket at a fixed price. Both women and men attending masquerades were completely disguised; the types of masks and elaborate dress they wore usually ensured that they could not be recognized as long as they chose not to reveal their identities. Although these masquerades were first introduced by a foreigner in 1717 (the Swiss Count Heidegger – see Ribeiro, 1984, p. 3), their immediate success can only be understood if one sees it in the context of previous developments and preconditions which could already be found in London.

Bizarre as these masquerades might seem at first glance, people could rapidly get used to them because they represented an attractive amalgam of similar cultural practices which had been familiar to the London public for a considerable time. People were used to the notion of masks being worn in certain localities only: the introduction of enclosed spaces with access controlled by the purchase of tickets merely reinforced this element. The old combination of the mask and the park resurfaced in a slightly modified but easily recognizable form in the shape of masquerades held in London's pleasure gardens. The equally established combination of mask and theatre was not lost either as the element of performance by everybody in front of everybody became much more prominent. Just as in the theatre, the public (and now the entire public) got a chance of appearing masked. The 'performance' element was now provided not by professional actors but by the public itself for their own benefit.

The main attractions of the older cultural practices associated with wearing masks were presented in an intensified form. Now, one went a step beyond merely playing with anonymity. The masquerades definitely and openly offered a chance to adopt a new persona, an alternative identity expressed in an elaborate costume – and they offered this chance to women and men alike.

The underlying progression informing this development can be traced just by looking at the development of the mask: the early type depicted by Hollar in the first half of the seventeenth century was just a half-mask; in the late seventeenth century the mask covered the entire face; and the early eighteenth-century masquerade introduced elaborate disguises covering the entire body. Thus, the element of anonymity grew steadily.

The masquerade retained elements of what had happened in parks and theatres before. It was less of a new phenomenon than a continuation and culmination of earlier cultural practices associated with previous settings. These earlier practices are replaced by their new incarnation as part of the masquerade scenario. Sources documenting the wearing of masks in London parks (and similarly in theatres) peter out in the 1730s, and it is no coincidence that this was exactly the time when the masquerade had fully established itself in London.

Both the masquerade and its links with the earlier uses of masks discussed above can only be fully understood if one regards this phenomenon as closely linked to the new and extremely powerful concept of privacy which was rapidly gaining ground in late seventeenth- and eighteenth-century London. Age-old networks of intimate social contact and communication had been eroded by the mass retreat into innumerable isolated private spheres. The masquerade gave a new chance of satisfying the still existing desire for social contact and communication while at the same time it satisfied the new desire for privacy. By means of a strategy of complete disguise, one could break the new taboos imposed on modern urban society. One could approach strangers and communicate with them without any fear whatsoever of exposing oneself.

As the element of anonymity was increased to a maximum, unprecedented liberties, especially between the sexes, could be taken – a circumstance much commented upon in the eighteenth century. Without a doubt, part of the masquerade's appeal lay in the fact that rules of propriety which had otherwise to be obeyed were relaxed or dropped altogether. Hence there are numerous contemporary warnings against the dangers associated with masquerades:

A Masquerade is almost the only Place where a Man has an Opportunity of entertaining a Woman alone. 'Tis the only Place in which a man, who is an absolute Stranger, can speak to you. The Custom of the World allows a Liberty in the Discourse there, that cou'd not be permitted any where else in the World: There is an Air of great Pleasantry, and great security, in saying the most tender and the boldest Things between Jest and Earnest; and he will stop at nothing whose Insolence you encourage, while you suffer it, and whose Presumption is nothing, while in a moment he can turn it all to Raillery; and as soon as he finds he cannot succeed, pretend that he never design'd it. The Woman who is mask'd, under the Pretence of being between known and unknown, will bear a thousand Things, which if she was under a Necessity of confessing who she was, she cou'd not: And the Assistance of this to the Liberty which he takes, who pretends to be between Jest and Earnest, gives Opportunities to Things the most intolerable [*sic*].

(Seymour, 1753, p. 217f.)

On the one hand, the masquerade setting offered a higher potential of transgression than the park/theatre setting where wearing a mask had just been an option. On the other hand, however, this new practice was much more circumscribed and limited both spatially and temporarily than what had been going on in parks and theatres. Masquerades were commercially organized events which were planned for a certain day and which took place in architecturally enclosed spaces. One had to hire a masquerade dress and purchase a ticket in order to participate.

The boundaries between the masquerade and 'normal' everyday life were thus made very obvious. Blatant transgression 'inside' a sphere designated for masquerades in a sense affirms the status quo reigning 'outside'. Parks and theatres where one could but did not have to wear masks, in which one could just pretend to be an invisible observer or choose to become more active had been spaces characterized by a certain ambiguity. It was there that the world of the mask with its potential for anonymity and transgression overlapped with the everyday world of what was taken to be 'normal' behaviour. This ambiguity was lost, and the practice of wearing masks was transferred to spaces of its own. All in all, the practice of wearing masks was being contained; its transgressive potential was both increased and at the same time crucially limited by the introduction of masquerades. Wearing a mask ceased to be an option which was freely available on an ad hoc basis and became part of a commercialized, escapist form of entertainment.

It is a long way from the premodern face-to-face society in which masks could be used as a punishment, to the manifold uses masks and disguises were put to in the early modern, urban social context of London. The mask lost all its possible sinister connotations of a premodern shame punishment and underwent a remarkable and significant metamorphosis from a cosmetic accessory to a notional and eventually an actual disguise.

Only a society which at least began to appreciate and to cherish privacy, and in which a stranger was respected as an unknown rather than feared as an alien and an outsider, could be more or less at ease with the manifold use of both real and virtual masks and disguises. This is why, in the unique social context of London, forms of artificially created anonymity could proliferate from the late seventeenth century on.

NOTES

1 Hollar was born at Prague in 1607; he spent a significant part of his life in London where he died in 1677. The prints referred to here will be identified according to the current descriptive catalogue of his work, i.e. Pennington, 1982.)

2 Anon., *Charles II on Horse Guards Parade*. Oil on canvas, 60×105 in., painted late in the King's reign. Coll.: Duke of Roxburghe, Floors Castle. Unfortunately, I have not yet been able to obtain permission to reproduce this remarkable painting. Also Anon., *The Old Horse Guards Parade*, dimensions unknown, present whereabouts unknown. There is a photograph of this painting (file 263, British School) in the Witt Library, London.

3 Another familiar example for transgressive behaviour allowed in a controlled environment and governed by rules and rituals is 'social' and thus legitimate drinking. Ordinary patterns of behaviour may be thrown overboard from time to time if the transgression itself is sanctioned and contained by another set of rules.

ACKNOWLEDGEMENTS

The author would like to thank Penelope Corfield (Royal Holloway, London), H.R. Forsyth and Mireille Galinou (Museum of London), Ralph Houlbrooke (University of Reading), Paul Langford (Lincoln College, Oxford), Lynne MacNab (Guildhall Library, London), Diana Patterson (Mount Royal College, Calgary), Roy Porter (Wellcome Institute, London), Aileen Ribeiro (Courtauld Institute, London), Sarah Winbush and Jane Cunningham (Witt Library, London) for their manifold advice and assistance.

REFERENCES

Alberti, M.G.W. (1752) *Briefe betreffende den allerneuesten Zustand der Religion und Wißenschaften in Groß-Brittanien* [*sic*], 3 Vols, Hannover, Johann Christoph Richter.

Andrews, W. (1890) *Old-time punishments*, London, Hull, W. Andrews & Co.

Anon. (1703) (Dunton, J.) *The Athenian Oracle: Being an entire collection of all the valuable questions and answers in the old Athenian Mercuries*, London, Andrew Bell.

Anon. (1760) *The polite lady: Or, a course of female education in a series of letters from a mother to her daughter*, London, J. Newbery.

Anon. (1983), (probably Garretson, J.; ed. Whalley, J.I.), *The school of manners*, London, V & A Publications (originally published 1701).

Brewer, G. (1812) *The Juvenile Lavater; or, a familiar explanation of the passions of Le Brun, calculated for the instruction and entertainment of young persons*, London, Minerva Press.

Butler, S. (1928) *Satires and miscellaneous poetry and prose* (ed. Lamar, E.), Cambridge, Cambridge University Press.

Castle, T. (1986) *Masquerade and civilization: The carnivalesque in eighteenth-century English culture and fiction*, London, Methuen.

Cleveland, J. (1647) *The kings* [*sic*] *disguise in the character of a London-Diurnall: With several select poems: By the same author*, London, W. Shears.

Cotton, C. (1689) *Poems on several occasions*, London, T. Bassett.

Craft-Fairchild, C. (1993) *Masquerade and gender: Disguise and female identity in eighteenth-century fictions by women*, University Park, Pennsylvania State University.

Crew, A. (1933) *The Old Bailey: History, constitution, functions, notable trials*, London, Nicholson & Watson.

Emmison, F.G. (1972) *Elizabethan life: Morals and the church courts*, Chelmsford, Chelmsford Records Office.

Gordon, C. (1902) *The Old Bailey and Newgate*, London, T. Fisher Unwin.

Habermas, J. (1992) *Strukturwandel der Öffentlichkeit*, Frankfurt/M., Suhrkamp.

Hollar, W. (1643) *Theatrum Mulierum sive Varietas atq. Differentia Habituum Foeminei Sexus, diuersorum Europae Nationum hodierno tempore vulgo in usu a Wenceslao Hollar, etc. Bohemo, delineatae et acva forti aeri sculptae*, London, V.A.M.

Jackson, W. (1795) *The new and complete Newgate calendar, or, villany displayed in all its branches*, London, Alexander Hogg.

Larwood, J. (1877) *The story of the London parks*, London, Francis Harvey.

Le Brun (1713) *Conférence de Monsieur Le Brun [. . .] sur l'expression générale et particulière des passions*, Amsterdam, Bernard Picart.

London Magazine (February 1734), London, R. Baldwin.

Oxford English Dictionary (OED2) on CD-ROM, Version 1.01 (1992), Oxford, Oxford University Press.

Pennington, R. (1982) *A descriptive catalogue of the etched work of Wenceslaus Hollar, 1607–1677*, Cambridge, Cambridge University Press.

Pöllnitz, C.L.v. (1737) *The memoirs of Charles-Lewis Baron de Pollnitz* [*sic*], *being his observations he made in his late travels from Prussia thro' Germany, Italy, France, Flanders, Holland, England &c.* 2 Vols, London, Daniel Browne.

Ribeiro, A. (1984) *The dress worn at masquerades in England, 1730 to 1790, and its relation to fancy dress in portraiture*, London, Garland.

Sennett, R. (1977) *The fall of public man*, Cambridge, Cambridge University Press.

Stone, L. (1977) *The family, sex and marriage in England 1500–1800*, London, Weidenfeld & Nicolson.

Vanbrugh, J. (1698). *The relapse; or, virtue in danger*, London, R. Wellington.

Wieacker, F. (1952) *Privatrechtsgeschichte der Neuzeit*, Göttingen, Vandenhoeck & Ruprecht.

Wycherley, W. (1675) *The country wife*, London, Thomas Dering.

Wycherley, W. (1694) *Love in a wood, or St. James's park*, London, H. Herringman.

8

MASKED AND UNMASKED AT THE OPERA BALLS*

Parisian women celebrate carnival

Ann Ilan-Alter

Paris, according to Walter Benjamin, was, after 1830, the capital of the nineteenth century (Benjamin, 1989). It was a city that was continuously inventing new amusements and pleasures, whether it was shopping in the newly opened department stores, watching the great mime Deburau at the Funambules, parading the grand boulevards, dancing at popular dance halls or wildly celebrating mardi gras at the Carnival balls that mushroomed throughout Paris during the July Monarchy. Tantalized, Parisians of all classes viewed the endless possibilities of their city as though these were new tastes to be sampled and savored. Indeed, pleasure was thought to be as much a Parisian prerogative as revolution.

Only bourgeois women were singled out to be excluded from this quest for pleasure. For this was the moment when women's role within the bourgeois family was undergoing a thorough examination in an attempt to define the role of women in molding and shaping bourgeois children to be better citizens of the newly installed Citizen King (Ilan-Alter, 1981). Their devotion to family life and their fidelity to their husbands was emphasized in the belief that this was the way to create the ideal family, derived in part from Rousseau, in which the men were the politically active heads of families, while women warmed the hearth and nurtured the next generation of citizens. But women, it was argued, were not simply nurturers, for they also needed to show their seriousness of purpose by becoming the primary teachers of their children – to both the boys and girls – from birth to around the age of 11 (Pitts, 1963, p. 255).

* Research for this article was supported in part by a grant from the Swann Foundation for the Study of Caricature.

At this age the boys were sent to collège, then lycée, while the girls were sent to finishing school, and then took their place by their mother's side in the salon. As their mothers received and entertained callers, their daughters learned the ways of the social world (literally '*le monde*' in French, meaning society) they would enter once married. This remained basic to the role of bourgeois women until after World War II: it was intended to guarantee not just the proper moral education of the children and their loyalty to family and state, but also to give women a pivotal role within the domestic sphere equivalent to men's role in the public sphere. This was the bourgeois, and later republican, ideal that first gained widespread acceptance during the reign of Louis-Philippe (Ilan-Alter, 1981).

It was a role that required enormous assurance, moral rectitude and discipline. Strict manners, proper dress and artifice were only some of the props used by women to present the correct façade to the bourgeois social world. While French social intercourse was never as strict as that of Victorian England – indeed the English (Trollope, 1836) were often shocked at the behavior of French bourgeois women – none the less the responsibilities and duties of Parisian women were often at odds with the very real temptations at their doorstep. How to reconcile their bourgeois role of *mère-de-famille* (Donzelot, 1979) with the desire to enjoy the pleasures of Paris, especially during Carnival? How could they nurture, raise and educate their children, while also believing that they had the same right to enjoy the pleasures of Paris as everyone else? How could they be virtuous, yet tempt virtue? For the French bourgeoise, it was the combination of the need to uphold her identity as a *mère-de-famille* while satisfying her own yearnings to explore some of the pleasures of Paris, that provided the impetus to re-define what it meant to be a Parisian bourgeois during this period. It was her desire to attend the masked balls at Carnival, but particularly those at the Opera, that inspired her to forge a more flexible bourgeois identity within nineteenth-century French society. In choosing one mask, that of the devoted wife and mother, she created the freedom to don a second mask and enjoy the pleasures of the *bal de l'Opéra*.

The Carnival balls at the Paris Opera dated back to 1715. Originally aristocratic – Marie-Antoinette often went (Anon. 1847; Touchard-Lafosse, 1846) – the balls maintained their exclusive character into the 1830s (Faure, 1984, pp. 89–127). But by the time of the July Revolution in 1830, the heyday of the balls was long-gone, and many commentators remarked on how boring and sedate these balls had become (Girardin, 1837). Indeed, some observed that the Carnival balls in private houses were far more interesting than those at the Opera. The result was that the Opera balls, at the steep price of ten francs per head, permitted masks but prohibited both costumes and dancing, so that real intrigue, as the regulars liked to call it, was only possible at private balls (Apponyi, 1913, pp. 388–91; Sanderson, 1839, pp. 180–92). None the less, because the Opera on the rue Le Pelletier was still the bastion of the aristocracy, the aristocrats of the Faubourg St. Germain, along with some members of the haute bourgeoisie, put in an appearance at the Carnival balls at the Opera to maintain its tone and lay claim to it as their special preserve (Faure, 1984, pp. 89–127).

The government of the July Monarchy, however, was concerned that the Opera had remained a bastion of aristocratic privilege after the July Revolution while the bourgeoisie, the ostensible supporters of the new regime, preferred the more popular theaters further down the Boulevard des Italiens (Brooks, 1976, pp. 81–109). Here the bourgeoisie gleefully delighted in plays that were glorifying the sixteenth-century Huguenot revolt against the monarchy and the French Revolution at its height. And here, too, they found opera that both exalted the common people and provided the spectacle they most enjoyed. In contrast to the repertory at the Opera (Fulcher, 1987, pp. 1–25), the opera of the Théâtre des Italiens (Martin-Fugier, 1990, pp. 291–325) or the plays of the Boulevard du Crime were exciting, spectacular displays of histrionics (Brooks, 1976, pp. 89–90).

This also became true of Carnival and Carnival balls after 1830 (Faure, 1984, pp. 45–9). Prior to 1830, few dance halls and fewer celebrations of Carnival were to be found in Paris: except for three authorized balls at Parisian theaters and some private balls, the celebration of Carnival was even thought to be a thing of the past (Gasnault, 1986, pp. 29–56, 64). Yet with the July Revolution the police suddenly found that Carnival balls and dance halls in general were enjoying a new life and a new reason to exist: the political culture of Paris combined an intense opposition to Louis-Philippe with romanticism. The orgiastic celebration of Carnival and Carnival balls throughout Paris was the result (Police Générale, 1830–1848). So from about 367 *bals publics* (Gasnault, 1986, p. 31) in 1830 (in both Paris and its environs under the jurisdiction of the préfecture de la Seine), a newspaper remarked in 1842 that in 1839 the police had issued 415 permits that year to open public balls in Paris, 628 in 1840 and 650 in 1841. The result, *La Presse* noted in 1842 ('Théâtres, fêtes et concerts,' 1842), was that there would be about 700 Carnival balls taking place in the capital on that Thursday, jeudi gras, which was the first night of Carnival celebration in the week that preceded mardi gras.

Moreover, Parisian Carnival was the one time during the year when separations between classes disintegrated as authority was challenged on all fronts (Bakhtine, 1970; Burke, 1978, pp. 183–92; Davis, 1976, pp. 97–152). Political order and social control were effectively undermined as workers took off from work and employers shut their shops the Thursday preceding mardi gras through the following Ash Wednesday (Gennap, 1947, Part 1). Costumed Parisians of all classes organized parades of masked revelers through the streets on the Sunday before mardi gras and during the day of mardi gras itself. At night, they attended the hundreds of balls found around Paris, abandoning all inhibitions in anticipation of Lent when both meat and sex were proscribed as part of the religious cycle of Easter. While popular usage was never very strict, none the less the traditional lean days were observed so that Parisians felt totally justified in celebrating Carnival with the customary riot of social, political and sexual anarchy associated with this event (Gennap, 1947, pp. 3–16).

To compete with the other Carnival balls, the masked balls at the Paris Opera were transformed, by 1837, from an exclusive, sedate aristocratic preserve into a popular *bal vulgaire*, attracting as many as 6,500 to 7,000 Parisians from all social classes. These included students from the Latin Quarter, the young women who worked in the garment trades and were called *grisettes*, shop clerks, government bureaucrats and ministers, bank employees, bourgeois men and women, journalists, writers, opera dancers and courtesans. Although official policy was to try to maintain the Opera performances as a bastion of elite culture, the balls, which began at midnight after the performances were over, were seen as a means of raising money to pay for the increasingly expensive productions of grand opera. The director of the opera, a doctor, journalist and self-made man named Louis Véron, decided to lower the price of admission to the balls, which now began taking place every Saturday night from Twelfth Night (January 6) through mardi gras. Popularizing the balls was also helped by the revolution in newspaper publishing introduced in 1836 (Bellanger, Godechot, Guirnal, Terrou, 1969): cheap daily newspapers paid for by advertising instead of subscriptions (Hatin, 1861, p. 572). One result of this innovation was that the new dailies, through their gossip columns, serial novels and lithographs placed in the center of the lower half of the front page described the Opera balls as the only place to be on Saturday night.

For men of all classes, and for the women who had no position to uphold, such as the grisettes and the *lorettes* (the kept-women of bourgeois men who lived in the area of Paris dominated by the church of Notre Dame de Lorette), going to the Carnival balls at the Opera was only a question of money. For bourgeois women, however, who as *mères-de-famille* were responsible for the ideological purity of the family (Donzelot, 1979), going to the Carnival balls at the Opera meant careful planning otherwise they would be exposed to almost certain danger. The most obvious danger a woman faced was the possibility that she might meet her husband. An 1839 lithograph by Gavarni (Gavarni, 1839) (see Plate 8.1), which appeared in the popular press, caricatured one such meeting as well as the standard arguments made in etiquette books about why bourgeois women should not go to the *bal de l'Opéra*. He shows a Pierrot confronting his wife, dressed in a Hussar's uniform, at the *bal de l'Opéra*, while the properly dressed man lurking in the background seems to be the wife's lover. The husband exclaims in the borrowed language of pre-scriptive books for women: 'Ah! So this is what you mean by sleeping at your aunt's? . . . and you are not ashamed! . . . a married woman!! a proper woman, a mother of a family!! Well, Mme. Salomon, you disgust me!!'

Some commentators took this issue seriously and pointed out the tragic consequences for women who did choose to give into their temptations. In the highly moral play by the Goncourt brothers, *Henriette Maréchal* (first performed, 1865), they depicted the tragedy that ensued when a proper bourgeois mother and wife gave into her curiosity and attended the *bal de l'Opéra* just once before she died (J. A.H. de and E. L. H. de Goncourt,

Plate 8.1 'Ah! C'est comme ça que tu couches chez ta tante?'. Lithograph by Gavarni from the series *Le Carnaval*.

Source: Courtesy of the Bibliothèque Nationale, Paris.

1885). Other writers simply chose to speculate about why bourgeois women went to the balls at the Opera. One journalist said that the mask empowered these women, while some observers even suggested that this behavior continued long after Carnival was over. The question then is did masking during Carnival empower bourgeois women to turn the world upside down to seek pleasure and power in distinctly unfeminine ways; and did their experience during Carnival enable them to challenge the most conventional demands of their lives once Carnival was over?

Madame Adèle Perrotte was one Parisian whose love of the balls at the Opera led her to lead a life that verged on the improper by bourgeois standards of the day. For in February 1840 Mme Perrotte petitioned the Tribunal Civil de la Seine to grant her the closest thing to a divorce in July Monarchy France: a *separation de corps* (to live separately) from her husband. According to the *Gazette des Tribunaux*, which reported at length on this case, she demanded a *separation de corps*, after 11 years of marriage, for '. . . numerous violent actions and injuries' (Perrotte, 1840a). Both parties, as is the custom in separation and divorce cases, accused the other of outrageous behavior, but both parties cited the other's behavior at the balls at the Opera as an example of the ways in which husband and wife had transgressed the boundaries of bourgeois propriety.

Through his lawyer, M. Chaix d'Est d'Ange, the husband, M. Perrotte, argued that the marriage was generally happy for its first 11 years, from 1828 to 1839. This was not to say that M. Perrotte was not without complaints: his wife, according to his account, liked to dance, and even though she was often sickly, she managed to muster sufficient strength to go to Carnival balls either at the Opera or the Théâtre de la Renaissance so she could '. . . expose herself to being insulted while masked' (Perrotte, 1840b). In addition, the husband accused her of inviting a man friend to their house when he was out and of going out and returning home very late. After many warnings the husband finally felt compelled to ban her friend from visiting the 'marital household' because he was concerned about how this would look in the community. The wife countered by demanding to take a room on the outskirts of Paris, where she could better nurse her illness and rest. In the meantime her friend continued to visit her despite the husband's opposition. 'Think of your children and your duty', M. Perrotte allegedly wrote his wife.

Her response was to file for a *separation de corps*. She accused him of publicly behaving in ways that undermined their position as a respectable bourgeois family. For instance, the same night that his lawyer accused her of going to the Carnival ball to be insulted under the mask, her husband was dancing, without mask, face to face with his coachman on the main dance floor. This she saw from the loge from which she was watching the ball, a practice available to all women, her lawyer explained, who wanted to watch the movement of masks at the balls of mardi gras: 'saddened by this spectacle . . . she did not want her husband to know what she might have seen,' (Perrotte, 1840b). M. Perrotte accused his wife of liking to spend all her time at balls: yet, her lawyer countered, Mme. Perrotte went unmasked to the ball at the Opera with his friends. He, on the other hand, was seen one evening going into the building across the street, where two known prostitutes lived (*ibid.*).

While the stated demand of the *separation du corps* conformed to the form in which such demands were made, the particulars of this case are far from typical. In general these petitions emphasized the incompatibility of the couple and the cruelty, humiliation or, particularly in the case of the woman, her adultery. It is rare to find in these petitions, even as a means to prove public humiliation, such a lengthy discussion of the daily habits and amusements of the couple. Indeed, the very possibility that in 1840 this case included such a description of Carnival balls was an indication of the change that had taken place in Parisian life since 1830: for in 1830 the few Carnival balls that existed were either so exclusive as to exclude the Monsieur and Madame Perrottes or too popular to interest them (Gasnault, 1986, p. 31). By 1840, however, Carnival had emerged as a major celebration throughout Paris. And the ball at the Opera, where Mme. Perrotte was accused of going so she could indulge her love of pleasure, was the chicest and most popular of these balls, drawing anywhere from 2,500 to 7,000 people every Saturday night during Carnival season and the jours gras, the Thursday before mardi gras through the night of mardi gras itself.

It is these balls at the Opera which seemed to have aroused the greatest concern. Not only were bourgeois women like Mme. Perrotte going to the ball – masked as well as unmasked – but the M. Perrottes of Paris were also going and were seen dancing alongside their coachmen. While complaints about Carnival in general soared, it was the balls at the Opera that now became the focus of all that was wrong and dangerous about Carnival. Even the director of the Opera himself, Véron, remarked in his memoirs that the Opera balls had no equal for noise, scandal and vulgarity (Véron, 1856, pp. 383–4) while the Comtesse Dash, a popular novelist of the day, says that around 1835 morals perceptibly changed.

Previously, the Comtesse relates, men who had mistresses had kept this part of their lives private and separate, but during the July Monarchy men flaunted their mistresses in public, wearing them like jewels, while respectable women now developed the ardent desire to attend the balls at the Opera, to see and participate in what had been previously both unknown and prohibited. 'I can confirm however that if one had to go to the *bal de l'Opéra* without a mask, no woman would have had the audacity, no matter how curious she was. One went with trepidation that one might be recognized . . .' (Dash, 1896, pp. 246–8). The separation case of M. and Mme Perrotte, then, articulated larger concerns expressed by numerous writers about their fears that the pleasures of Paris were disruptive to the established social hierarchy (Véron, 1856, pp. 383–4), to the role of women and to the stability of the bourgeois family. Mme. Perrotte went to the Opera ball unmasked, which, according to some commentators, was not what a respectable woman should have done, while M. Perrotte mingled with the riffraff, in French, the '*canaille*' (de Forster, 1848, p. 277). The trials and tribulations of M. and Mme. Perrotte's marriage thus opens a window on this world of Parisian pleasure, providing a far more complete picture of bourgeois pleasures and anxieties than had been previously available ('Bal Musard à l'Opéra,' 1837).

The pursuit of pleasure was ostensibly the main reason to go to the *bal de l'Opéra*. Masking for women was strictly enforced after 1837, except in the foyer, where, it was said, but not necessarily believed (Huart, 1845, pp. 45, 52–3; Rozier, 1855, p. 70), that honest women such as Mme. Perrotte could go without compromising themselves: 'That's the foyer . . . it's not for us . . . It's reserved for bourgeois women who are cheating on their husbands . . .' (see Plate 8.2). Masking for men was discretionary.

The real importance of the balls at the Opera, however, was that it was generally considered the one opportunity during the year when all normal prohibitions were thrown to the winds: mothers courted their sons (Poupin, 1867), husbands deceived wives and wives, as Comtesse Dash remarked, would do anything to get to the *bal de l'Opéra* (Dash, 1896, pp. 246–8).

Other commentators concurred with the Comtesse Dash. Proper women such as Mme. Perrotte, according to the journalists who wrote these commentaries and gossip about Parisian life, risked their reputations for the intrigue they found at the *bal de l'Opéra* and managed with difficulty to be free for this one night. 'Under the mask they feel strong', one writer noted (Rozier, 1855, pp. 75–7). He also added that although these women were modest and polite at home, at the Opera they heard what they would never dare read, and after a few hours, they consented to dine with their partner of the evening. This was the moment when the women unmasked, the two revelers ate a good meal, drank lots of champagne and made love (the loges were locked and curtained). Without the safety of their masks, the Mme. Perrottes of Paris were now more intimate with this man than they had ever been with their husbands and, having chosen him, they agreed to see him the next day.

This gossip writer was not alone in presuming that truly innocent

Plate 8.2 'Ça c'est l'foyer . . .'. Lithograph by Charles Vernier from the series *Au Bal de L'Opéra.*

Source: Courtesy of the Bibliothèque Nationale, Paris.

women were fallen women after their mardi gras outing to the *bal de l'Opéra.* This was the point of the Goncourt Brothers' play *Henriette Maréchal* (1885) as well as of a popular novel by Victor Poupin, *Le bal de l'Opéra* (1867). Of course, French bourgeois women were hoping that their virtuous mask the rest of the year would permit them this transgression during Carnival. In this their transgression perfectly fits the role of gossip (Spacks, 1986, p. 10) in a community, for gossip serves, according to anthropologists (Glucksman, 1963; Haviland, 1977; Paine, 1967, 1968), to undermine the status quo as well as to uphold the values of the community. As a new breed in July Monarchy Paris, gossip writers were coming into their own as purveyors of information about the comings and goings of pleasure-seeking Parisians. But as writers for widely read daily newspapers in the most scintillating and brilliant capital city of Europe, they were also at the mercy of their editors, who paid them by the piece (Balzac, 1971). Meanwhile the numerous censorship trials of the mid-1830s further intimidated editors and writers alike. So these commentaries about the virtuous women who went to the Carnival balls at the Opera described the pleasure bourgeois women found there but also

143

reinforced the values of the community by attempting to uphold the moral order of the July Monarchy.

The other major source of gossip was found in the lithographic imagery about the balls at the Opera. Lithographs often treaded on territory that was only hinted at in the written texts by showing us what was about to happen or had just happened. They are sketches from real life, meant to capture the very moment of confusion, embarrassment or tension. But because lithographs were also part of the culture of the satirical newspaper, operating as a conscious attack on bourgeois culture, the lithographs attacked bourgeois mores and undermined bourgeois structures (Terdiman, 1985, pp. 149–97; Wechsler, 1982, pp. 104–7). They provide us with a commentary on the world of the masked ball that is both specific, portraying what is actually taking place, and global in its implication that this actuality is counter to the bourgeois discourse of domesticity and gender roles. That lithographs should thrive, then, on the marital conflicts and ambiguities engendered by Carnival is not surprising. In one 1841 lithograph by Gavarni (see Plate 8.3), the husband, M. Prudhomme, stands with arms folded across his chest, looking down at his wife while

Plate 8.3 'Allez au bal de l'Opéra avec Madame de Coquadeau'. Lithograph by Gavarni from the series *Fourberies de Femmes*.

Source: Courtesy of the Bibliothèque Nationale, Paris.

she sits, ready and dressed with her cloak thrown over the settee, disdain-fully examining her hands as she waits for him to finish: 'Go to the *bal de l'Opéra* . . . I consent. There is always a certain trust, no matter how blind it might be, that is noble . . .'

Unlike all the other Parisian women discussed so far, Mme. Prudhomme actually asked her husband's permission to go to the *bal de l'Opéra*. None the less, it is also clear that even if he forbade her to go, she was going anyway. Indeed, what is remarkable about this lithograph is the portrait of Mme. Prudhomme as a woman totally sure of her power to get her husband to consent to whatever she wants. Masked or unmasked, this wife had already found the strength to use the inverted world of Carnival to challenge her husband's authority.

Another couple (in Plate 8.4) seems to have resolved this conflict dif-ferently: this husband accompanies his wife to the *bal de l'Opéra*, but loses her every year: 'I will no longer take you to the bal de l'Opéra . . . I lose you in the middle of the crowd and after two hours of incredible anxi-ety, I see you coming with a postman from Longjumeau. Adelaide, I will not go to sleep until you tell me where the devil this postman comes from!'

Plate 8.4 'Plus souvent que je te conduirai encore au bal de l'Opéra'. Lithograph by Honoré Daumier from the series *Paris L'Hiver*.
    Source: Courtesy of the Bibliothèque Nationale, Paris.

Arms folded across his chest and dressed in the evening clothes he wore to the *bal de l'Opéra*, with the comical nose he used for a mask still intact, the husband is determined to ferret out his wife's secret which we, the audience, already understand. Moreover, the stubbornness of the cuckolded husband is pitted against the apparent calm of his wife, who, as she looks at him out of the corner of her eye from under her velvet hood, is trying to figure out what she is going to tell him that will both convince him of her innocent intentions while getting him off her back.

Bourgeois women were obviously going to the balls at the Opera, despite the generalized condemnation of such behavior. In Plate 8.5 (Gavarni, 1846a), a woman discovers her husband asleep in a loge: 'Oh! my God! It is my husband, my little, my real husband! the louse! . . . Let's get out of here!'

The real issue was how many husbands acquiesced in such behavior when they did meet their wives at the *bal de l'Opéra*. In Plate 8.1, the husband was outraged that his proper bourgeois wife went out to celebrate Carnival; in the other lithographs, as well as in M. Perrotte's separation case, the husbands were apparently willing to indulge their spouse's whim.

Plate 8.5 'Ah mon dieu! . . . c'est mon mari!' Lithograph by Gavarni from the series *Le Carnaval*.

Source: Courtesy of the Bibliothèque Nationale, Paris.

But Plate 8.6 betrays both a tolerance and a wry amusement that was probably far rarer: two husbands who could laugh about meeting their wives 'under the mask' at the Opera ball. This lithograph, again by Gavarni (Gavarni, 1846b), shows two men dressed as Pierrots. The man in the dark Pierrot costume explains to the Pierrot in white that someone introduced him to two charming dominos who were dying to have supper: '. . . I go look, and just imagine, it was my wife with . . . another domino!' The white Pierrot replies that he would have taken the other. His friend replies: 'Oh, you laugh do you? . . . ah, you would have taken the other, would you? . . . well, no, you would not have taken the other! . . . because the other was your wife . . .'

Even daughters were apparently having their fun at the *bal de l'Opéra* at the height of the Carnival season, for on 15 February 1839 a story appeared on the front page of *La Presse* entitled 'A Father Intrigued by his Daughter.' It was written by Delphine de Girardin, whose gossip about the balls at the Opera appeared on the front page of *La Presse* every two weeks under the mask of the *nom-de-plume* of the Vicomte de Launay.

She begins by observing that most fathers have never seen their daugh-

Plate 8.6 'Figure-toi mon cher que je rencontre cet animal de chose . . .' Lithograph by Gavarni from the series *Le Carnaval*.
Source: Courtesy of the Bibliothèque Nationale, Paris.

ters as 'coquettes,' flirts. The act of pleasing and flirting so transforms a woman, de Girardin tells us, that no father recognizes a flirting daughter. She continues: a member of the Académie française, or an academician, goes to the *bal de l'Opéra* and is fascinated by a young woman dressed in domino who is sensitive to his every desire and seems to share his taste in writers. She flatters him just the way he likes. Flushed with pleasure – he is, after all, used to such success with women – the academician spends the evening delighting in her company. At four in the morning he invites her to dine in a loge to continue their tête-à-tête; she accepts on the condition that she will not remove her mask, although traditionally this was the moment of revelation. After they have dined he offers to see her home. 'No, it is I,' the domino replies, 'who will see you home. I do not want to reveal my identity.' The carriage stops in front of the academician's house. He unhappily gets out, thinking he is leaving her behind; but how surprised and elated he is to see the domino follow him:

> . . . he sees her, secretive and nimble, disappear in the corridor; he tries to rejoin her and sighs very low: 'What! Madame! so much happiness! . . .' But the mask interrupts him with a loud burst of laughter, and a well-known voice cries out to him from the top of the stairs: 'Goodnight, papa, I thank you, I really amused myself. Until tomorrow!' The crestfallen academician resorted to the exclamation so frenetically applauded at that moment of recognition in a melodrama: 'My daughter!' he said hopelessly, and the echo of the vestibule replied: 'Your daughter!'
>
> (Girardin, 1839)

Here is the daughter's seduction acted out 'under the mask' on the front page of one of Paris' largest-circulation newspapers. It is a story told as the best of all *bal de l'Opéra* stories, more incredible than even those told about last year's balls. Girardin, cross-dressed as the Vicomte de Launay, addresses her readers directly: Can you really believe that a father does not recognize his own daughter? Yes, it is believable, because it's Carnival! Girardin uses the Carnival mask to give her permission to tell this story, to empower her in her transgression of the final taboo that every anthropologist agrees is basic to all societies: the incest taboo. Moreover, its placement on the front page of a major Parisian newspaper legitimized and validated what the daughter did at the *bal de l'Opéra*. The story offered permission to any daughter or Mme. Perrotte who wanted to try, who chose to act as they saw fit during Carnival. How many daughters acted out this grand seduction is, frankly, not relevant; what is relevant is that this fantasy functions as a model for the women who read it.

> Honest women, who go the *bal de l'Opéra* in disguise don't go to chase fantastic boyars: after all they have a husband, and that should suffice. But they are looking for other kinds of intrigue – a truly innocent pleasure – which that imbecile of a husband has the meanness to take in bad faith, and it is often with brutality that he pretends to bring his wife back to the road of virtue and domesticity.
>
> (Huart, 1845, pp. 52–3)

So explained yet another gossip writer in the 1840's. Perhaps it was simply curiosity, as the Comtesse Dash suggested, that prompted these bourgeois women to disguise themselves and risk going to the *bal de l'Opéra*. But it is far more likely that the taste of freedom offered by the masked balls was what motivated them to challenge their traditional roles. None the less, even during Carnival unruly and disorderly women were barely tolerated, so that the wry amusement and salacious tone of these books when they spoke of the proper bourgeois women who went to the *bal de l'Opéra* served as a way of denigrating those women who challenged male sexual entitlement. Even though these bourgeois women did not disguise themselves in pants, or put on boots and breeches, the idea of proper ladies of the bourgeoisie in one great big dance hall with the *canaille* – *grisettes*, *lorettes*, courtesans, or workers – was particularly threatening to society at large as well as to these journalists who made their living as apologists of the status quo.

Throughout the July Monarchy, from 1830 to 1848, carnival masquerade continued as part of bourgeois as well as working-class culture, mingling with the revolutionary discontent of the people until 1848, when the throne danced a can-can, to paraphrase Flaubert in *Sentimental Education* (1910). For the February Revolution took place at the height of Carnival, confirming what both the government (Police Générale, 1830–1848) and a former police chief (Gisquet, 1840, pp. 223–5) believed to be its revolutionary potential. Stallybrass and White have argued in their book about carnival, *The Politics and Poetics of Transgression*, that 'given the presence of sharpened political antagonism, it often acts as a catalyst and site of actual and symbolic struggle,' (Stallybrass and White, 1986, pp. 12–17). In the ongoing political turmoil of July Monarchy Paris, Carnival was potentially revolutionary, furthering political resistance and helping to undermine constrictive norms of behavior and propriety. Carnival and the balls at the Opera created change for bourgeois women because of their willingness to challenge the boundaries of proper behavior by participating in the pleasures of Paris. While these activities did not result in the immediate transformation of the roles of bourgeois women, none the less it is clear that under the mask many bourgeois women did feel strong. It allowed them to find ways to undermine repressive norms of behavior in their domestic routine and to create a flexible role for themselves within their families and in their daily lives.

REFERENCES

Anon. (1847) *L'Opéra: Depuis son origine jusqu'à nos jours 1645–1847*, Paris, Chez Breteau, Libraire.

Apponyi, Comte R. (1913) *Vingt-cinq ans à Paris*, vol. 2, Paris, Librairie Plon.

Bakhtine, M. (1970) *L'Oeuvre de François Rabelais et de la culture populaire au Moyen Age et sous la Renaissance* (trans. Robel, Andrée), Paris, Gallimard.

'Bal Musard à l'Opéra' (11 February 1837), *Le Corsaire*.

Balzac, H. de. (1971) *Lost Illusions* (trans. Hunt, Herbert J.), London, Penguin Books (original work published in three parts, Paris, 1837–43).

Bellanger, C., Godechot, J., Guirnal, P. and Terrou, F. (1969) *Histoire générale de la presse française*, Vols 1–2, Paris, Presses Universitaires de France.

Benjamin, W. (1989) *Paris, Capitale du XIXe siècle: Le livre des passages* (trans. Lacoste, J.), Paris, Éditions du Cerf.

Brooks, P. (1976) *The melodramatic imagination: Balzac, Henry James, melodrama and the mode of excess*, New Haven, CT, Yale University Press.

Burke, P. (1978) *Popular culture in early modern Europe*, New York, New York University Press.

Dash, Comtesse (1896) *Mémoires des autres*, vol. 3, Paris, La Librairie Illustrée.

Daumier, H. (1845) 'Paris L'Hiver,' (February 1845), *Le Charivari*, lithograph (this reproduction is from Paris: Dépot légal, Cabinet des Estampes, Bibliothèque Nationale).

Davis, N. Z. (1976) *Society and culture in early modern France*, Stanford, CA, Stanford University Press.

Donzelot, J. (1979) *The Policing of Families* (trans. Hurley, Robert), New York, Pantheon Books.

Faure, A. (1984) *Paris carême-prenant: Du carnaval à Paris au XIXe siècle 1800–1914*, Paris, Hachette.

Flaubert, Gustave (1910) *L'Éducation sentimentale: Histoire d'un jeune homme*, Paris, Louis Conrad (originally published 1869).

Forster, C. de. (1848) *Quinze ans à Paris: 1832–1848. Paris et les parisiens*, vol. 2, Paris, Firmin Didot frères.

Fulcher, J. (1987) *The nation's image: French grand opera as politics and politicized art*, Cambridge, Cambridge University Press.

Gasnault, F. (1986) *Guinguettes et lorettes: Bals publics et dance sociale à Paris entre 1830 et 1870*, Paris, Aubier.

Gavarni [Guillaume Sulpice Chavallier] (1839) *Le Carnaval*, lithograph,. Paris, Dépot légal, Cabinet des Estampes, Bibliothèque Nationale.

Gavarni (1840) 'C'est mon Débardeur! C'est mon Balochard!' *Souvenirs du Carnaval*, lithograph, Paris, Dépot légal, Cabinet des Estampes, Bibliothèque Nationale.

Gavarni (1841). 'Allez au bal de l'Opéra avec Madame Coquadeau . . .' *Fourberies de Femmes*, lithograph, Paris, Dépot légal, Cabinet des Estampes, Bibliothèque Nationale.

Gavarni (1846a) 'Ah! Mon Dieu . . . ! *Le Carnaval*, lithograph, Paris, Dépot légal, Cabinet des Estampes, Bibliothèque Nationale.

Gavarni (1846b) 'Figure-toi mon cher . . .' *Le Carnaval*, lithograph, Paris, Dépot légal, Cabinet des Estampes, Bibliothèque Nationale.

Gennap, A. van (1947) *Manuel de folklore français*, vol. 3, Paris, Éditions A. et J. Picard et cie.

Girardin, D. de (1837) *Courrier de Paris* (7 February 1837), *La Presse*.

Girardin, D. de (1839) *Courrier de Paris* (15 February 1839), *La Presse*.

Gisquet, H. (1840) *Mémoirs de M. Gisquet, ancien préfet de police*, vol. 4, Paris, Marchant.

Glucksman, M. (1963) 'Gossip and scandal', *Current Anthropology* 4, 307–16.

Goncourt, J.A.H. de and E.L.H de (1885) *Henriette Maréchal*, Paris, G. Charpentier et cie.

Hatin, L.E. (1861) *Histoire politique et littéraire de la presse en France*, vol. 8, Paris, Poulet-Malassis et de Broise.

Haviland, J.B. (1977) *Gossip, reputation, and knowledge in Zinacantan*, Chicago, University of Chicago Press.

Huart, L. (1845) *Paris au bal*, Paris, Aubier et Cic.

Ilan-Alter, A. (1981) '*Women are made not born: Making bourgeois girls into women, France 1830–1870*', unpublished Ph.D. dissertation, New Brunswick, NJ, Rutgers University.

Imbs, P. (ed.) (1973–1992) *Trésor de la Langue française 1789–1960*, vol. 4, Paris, Centre Nationale des Recherches scientifique.

Martin-Fugier, A. (1990) *La vie élégante ou la formation du tout Paris*, Paris, Fayard.

Paine, R. (1967 & 1968) 'What is gossip about?' *Man* 2, 278–85; 3, 305–8.

Perrotte, M. and Mme (1840a) 'Demande de separation du corps' (1 March 1840), *Gazette des Tribunaux*, p. 1.

Perrotte, M. and Mme (1840b) 'Demande de separation du corps' (29 March 1840), *Gazette des Tribunaux*, p. 1.

Pitts, J. R. (1963) 'Change and continuity in bourgeois France', in *In Search of France*, (ed. Hoffmann, Stanley), Cambridge, MA, Harvard University Press.

Police Générale (1830–1848) 'Rapports journaliers F7/3885–3892', unpublished archives. Paris, Archives Nationales.

Poupin, Victor (1867) *Un Bal à l'Opéra*, Paris, no publisher.

Rozier, Victor (1855) *Les Bals publics à Paris: Etudes parisiennes*, vol. 1, Paris, Gustave Havard, Éditeur.

Sanderson, J. (1839) *The American in Paris*, vol. 2, Philadelphia, Carey & Hart.

Spacks, P. M. (1986) *Gossip*, Chicago, University of Chicago Press.

Stallybrass, P. and White, A. (1986) *The politics and poetics of transgression*, Ithaca, NY, Cornell University Press.

Terdiman, R. (1985) *Discourse / counter-discourse: The theory and practice of symbolic resistance in nineteenth-century France*, Ithaca NY, Cornell University Press.

'Théâtres, fêtes, et concerts' (3 February 1842), *La Presse*, p. 4.

Touchard-Lafosse, G. (1846) *Chroniques, secrètes, et galantes de l'Opéra, 1667–1845*, vols 1–2, Paris, Gabriel Roux et Cassant, Éditeurs.

Trollope, F. (1836) *Paris and the Parisians in 1835*, 2 vols. in 1, Paris, Baudry's European Library.

Vernier, C. (1846) *Au bal de l'Opéra*, lithograph, Paris, Dépot légal, Cabinet des Estampes, Bibliothèque Nationale.

Véron, Dr L. (1856) *Mémoires d'un bourgeois de Paris*, vol. 3, Paris, Librairie Nouvelle.

Wechsler, J. (1982) *A human comedy: Physiognomy and caricature in 19th century Paris*, Chicago, University of Chicago Press.

ON WOMEN AND CLOTHES
AND CARNIVAL FOOLS

Efrat Tseëlon

Prologue

It all started with research (of a both discursive and traditionally scientific kind) on contemporary young women that I conducted over the past decade (cf. Tseëlon 1989, 1992, 1995a). It occurred to me that women use words (or avoid them) in a similar manner that they use clothes. Particularly, I was struck by the structural homology between the dialectics of disguise and disclosure that characterise Western women's use of voice and dress. Let me explain. When I talk about disguise I do not refer to an appearance which hides some essence. Rather, I refer to it in the sense that reverberates throughout this volume. I use it to mean a discursive strategy – one that indicates the degree of identification with, or distance from, certain social performances one enacts. Much like the veil that came to signify in Western texts a mask hiding the essence of the enigmatic Oriental woman (Yegenoglu, 1998) – beauty and adornment came to signify the deceptive nature of femininity in Jewish and Christian theology (Tseëlon, 1995a). In this chapter, I start off with the erotic link between body and voice as signifying feminine sexuality. A corollary of this link is the trope of silence (vocal and sartorial) as a fantastic mode of desire, and the trope of politeness as a mode of control. These I illustrate with historical examples. Further, I elaborate on three models of feminine voice: proper, provocative and mute, and illustrate them with fictive representations. Finally, I point to the affinity between the cultural spaces occupied by the woman (in the manner of using verbal and sartorial voice) and the figure of the carnival fool.

My observation regarding the similarities between contemporary verbal and sartorial strategies and a history of patriarchal definitions of appropriate feminine behaviour may strike some as bold within a context of a reflexive non-essentialist discourse. Indeed, you could say I'm asking for trouble. I run the risk of being charged with the inexcusable act of homogenising diverse groups and histories into the fictive figure of Western subject. Worse still, I might come across as using a totalising narrative in the service of a theoretical paradigm. Before we go any further I would like to clear myself of the charge of essentialising the subject. At the same time I would reserve the liberty to theorise creatively, and across disciplines – not merely reproducing the standard post-structuralist piety. I enlist Young's (1995) suggestion that setting homogenisation against historical specificity and geographical particularity in itself reproduces the very binary categories that the post-colonial discourse seeks to dismantle. Thus, I concur with Barker, Hulme and Iverson's concern about 'obsession with specificities which can become another empiricist fallacy in which all attempts to theorise are answered by the supposedly irrefutable case of a counter-example' (1994, p. 10–11).

Therefore at the outset I would like to clarify that by talking about 'Western woman' I don't refer to essence, uniformity or a simple harmonious unity. I refer to a space or position that results from the process of constitution of the (mostly) European subject. This process hinges on the fashioning of a historically specific fantasy. But while having a fictive character, this process is neither unreal nor individual. It is real in the sense of producing material effects reiterated over time. And it is external to the individual in that it is conditioned by structural processes.

If I don't use the category of woman as a category of essence, I use it as a synthesis of 'episteme' in the Foucauldian sense and 'fantasy' in the Lacanian sense. The category of woman is, then, an object which, through reiteration, guarantees desire by providing a fiction of unity in the face of contradiction and difference. This fantasy of unity is sustained by a repository of codes, images, signs and representations which serve as a regulatory principle of a discursive regime.

I draw on this arsenal of terms in order to illustrate the link between femininity, dress and voice as it figures in historical practices, theological teachings and popular culture texts. My journey through historical and contemporary modes of reification of women's voice, silence and sartorial language led me to another insight. It is about the similarity between the spaces occupied by the Western woman and the carnival fool with regard to speech and dress. The woman is to the buffoon as history is to caricature: both bearing some resemblance to a (phantasmic) fact.

The legacy of the female voice as a cultural symbol is complex. The historical dimension lends context both to the specificity of the female voice as a practice and the cultural meanings assigned to it as a symbol. In my analysis of the concept of voice three notions are fused: voice as a metaphor for social power, as a symbolic form of encoding expression, and as a material-embodied quality. And since I explore it mostly through cultural representations, I draw my examples from both history and fiction. The subtext of my analogy between words and garments is a cultural identity between body and voice, both seen as signifying sexuality. The source of the erotic (and menacing) link between voice and sexuality runs through music.

Embodied voice

That music is dangerous is a Platonic idea, or may even be older, as Dolar (1996) quotes from a text by the Chinese emperor Chun (*c.* 2200 BCE) who condemns pretentious music as 'devoid of sense and effeminate'. Music, in particular the voice beyond words, is a senseless play of sensuality. Empty and frivolous, it is none the less seductive and intoxicating, 'an access to jouissance' as Barthes (1975) put it. Its erotic power and sense of ecstasy (which achieves its most accomplished effect in opera) is feminine, in contrast to masculinity, which is aligned with 'logos', 'the voice of the Father'.

The division of labour between Sense and Reason can even be read into the musical instruments chosen by the mythical Gods. Dionysus chose the flute, while Apollo preferred the lyre. The lyre can accompany words, but playing the flute precludes such possibility. However, this division of labour is gendered. The distinction between effeminate Sense (music/voice beyond words) and virile Reason (words/text) is evident in writings from Plato to Augustine.

In Plato's words, in good measure music is elevation to the spirit. In excess it is a source of threat and decay to the mental faculties 'when he continues the practice without remission and is spellbound, the effect begins to be that he melts . . . till he completely dissolves away his spirit . . . and makes of himself a "feeble warrior"' (*Republic* 3, 411a–b). And weren't the sirens with their alluring sweet singing the dread of abandoned seamen and brave warriors?

Fear of the female voice, and its link to the fear of female flesh and desire, has been reinforced by religious perceptions of a Jewish, Christian and Moslem kind. Eroticisation of the mouth in ancient Judaism is expressed, for example, in Rabbinic literature (between the third and fifth centuries) through such a statement as 'a woman's voice is nakedness' (*Babylonian Talmud*, Berachot 24a). This statement is part of a larger discussion of what constitutes indecent exposure in a woman in a context in which a man is reciting the *Shema* (one of the most important Jewish prayers) (Eilberg-Schwartz, 1995). Actually, it all begins with Eve. Having sinned through speech, goes the interpretation of the Biblical story, woman has made her own destiny (Régnier-Bohler, 1992, p. 429). The connection between Eve's seduction, the Fall from Grace and sexual union is an archetypal projection of the male fear of female irresistible powers (like the siren song). In the Jewish Bible there are some references to this fear, such as the following advice from *Proverbs* 5: 1–3: 'My son, listen to my wisdom: incline your ear to my insight . . . while your lips hold fast to knowledge. For the lips of a forbidden woman drip honey; her mouth is smoother than oil.' Similar concern at the dangers that lie in the carnal pleasures of the unbounded voice echoes through Augustine's *Confessions* (1992). In a meditation on 'sinning by the ear' he writes:

> Now in those melodies which thy words breathe soul into, when sung with a sweet and attuned voice, I do little repose . . . But with the words which are their life and whereby find admission into me . . . But this contentment of the flesh, to which the soul must not be given over to be enervated, doth oft beguile me, the sense not so waiting upon reason, as patiently to follow her; but having been admitted merely for her sake, it strives even to run before her, and lead her.
>
> (book 10, 33)

The Venetian Senator Barbaro advised that

> Speech in public, especially with strangers, is not suitable to women, whose voice is not less to be dreaded than their nakedness, since habits and emotions are easily betrayed in speech . . . By silence indeed women achieve the fame of eloquence.
>
> (1677, p. 101)

The carnality and materiality of the feminine singing voice underlies the use of castrati in the opera to substitute for female voices. The first opera stars were castrated men whose high voices lent them angelic androgyny and sexual purity (Poizat, 1992). Women were excluded on account of St Paul's injunction (*I Cor.* 13: 34). The castrati rose within the Catholic Church in the sixteenth century; and the vogue for them lasted until their decline in late eighteenth century, which finally opened up operatic opportunities for women. In the same way that sartorial self-expression was almost exclusively a feminine sphere of power at the time, the nineteenth-century opera became a feminine sphere of vocal power. Robinson (1989) suggests that, contrary to the discursive impotence of the female voice, women in opera sing with an authority and voice quality equal to that of men: 'they seem subversive presences in a patriarchal culture; since they so manifestly contain the promise – or rather the threat – of women's equality.' Yet, as Clément (1989) and Locke (1995) argue, neither the presence of the 'strong woman' of the opera, the Prima Donna, nor the subversive manipulation of feminine traits in comic opera undermine the masculinist fantasies of the desirable woman depicted through a rather limited range of female characters and plots. Whether active or passive, coquette or femme fatale, the opera diva inspires adulation and desire but ultimately is tortured and destroyed for herself daring to desire or for refusing a masculine desire. She dies singing the aria of her death dictated by her score or script, only to be endlessly resurrected to enact a dialectic of undoing and victory.

Clément compares two tropes of nineteenth-century cultural representations of femininity: opera divas and hysterics. Both the diva and the hysteric perform masculinist fantasies and images of femininity to a public audience. Like Jean Martin Charcot's famous patients in his Paris clinic performing public gestures of feminine madness (Showalter, 1987), the diva enacts her own undoing, only to rise after her aria unaffected. What these two archetypes of womanhood share is a denial of their voice through practices that either constrain it or streamline it.

Contemporary additions to the list of conflations between feminine body and voice come from psychoanalysis and popular culture. For Lacan the maternal voice constitutes a lost object of desire in the category he designates as the '*objet petit (a)*'. These are objects once experienced as part of oneself, but which have been severed as part of the child's realisation of the bounds of the self. From first being seen as examples of plenitude, they become symbols of lack and yearning; the prototype of unattainable desire modelled on a lost primary maternal fusion. The status of the maternal voice as an object (a) helps to explain the vocal/corporeal link in Hollywood cinema, obsessed as it is with representations of fetish and lack. Like the female body, female voice 'functions as a fetish . . . filling in for and covering over what is unspeakable within male subjectivity' (Silverman, 1988, p. 88) which maintains phantasmic unity in the face of (sexual) difference. Functioning like the sartorial fetish, the vocal masquerade of 'proper' femininity veils the fantasy of strong (phallic) femininity. Similarly, polite and soft speech is non-threatening. Swearing, however, is a male register because it conveys an illusion of phallic strength (Hughes, 1991). It was Freud who first discovered that, for women, voice and sexuality were interlinked. When women could not speak with their voice, they spoke with their body, manifesting hysteric symptoms such as paralysis or speech disorders.

The historical trajectory of the female voice is overlaid with its relationship (both as metonymy and metaphor) to sexuality. Exposure of female voice produced cultural anxieties and suppressive mechanisms equalled only by the suppression of the display of naked female flesh.

Silence and politeness

The female predicament of having to articulate thoughts and experiences through male-monitored codes exists cross-culturally as demonstrated by Ardener (1975) and Kramarae (1981) in 'the muted group theory'. This theory states that where men define reality in ways that correspond to *their* needs, women are muted by exclusion from prestigious cultural discourses. Social silencing need not operate through force or threat. But power, as Foucault (1980) compellingly illustrated, can operate through social control and surveillance. Feminist linguists (Cameron, 1998; Coates, 1993; Crawford, 1995; Spender, 1980; Tannen, 1996; Wodak, 1998) have argued for and demonstrated the subtle ways and means by which patriarchal culture includes and excludes, legitimates and sanctions certain codes and forms. Like the nymph Echo, the female voice is all too often condemned to repeat the words of others metaphorically or literally. This is not to say that the woman does not speak. On the contrary. But her 'speech' is often problematised (as emotional, or illogical) or trivialised (as in soap operas, romantic novels and women's magazines).

In medieval culture, 'the voices of women were stifled by an ethic that treated sins of the tongue as gluttony and as harbingers of lust and pride. Women who presumed to speak out publicly only compounded the sin' (Klapisch-Zuber, 1992, p. 425). In order to speak they had to defy hostility, suspicion and derision. When their speech exceeded the bounds of propriety it became 'bad language'. In order to speak they had to go beyond the limits of femininity, and could only do so if they were women of letters and rank (privately educated like Christine de Pissan) in possession of the cultural code. The female voice made itself heard persistently but it was measured relative to a male norm, against which it was seen as defective or deviant. Excluded from university education, women had only ecclesiastical education available to them. The common view, expressed, for example, by the moralist Philippe of Novare, held that it was dangerous to teach women to read and write. Literacy in women aroused men's fears of both female imprudence and male impotence. Women were expected to engage in temperate speech and not 'wildly abandon themselves to harmful speech or wicked arts' (Régnier-Bohler, 1992, p. 453).

Religious training thus provided another means of self-expression, one that was exercised by the female mystics who could invent their own tongue, using body and silence as well as words in the creation of a 'total' language (Régnier-Bohler, 1992, p. 432).

More than half a century later, in the nineteenth century, women would be using the body in a different way to articulate narratives of desire and sexuality that the tongue was not allowed to express. In an age which saw hysteria reach epidemic proportions (Gordon, 1990), symptoms like aphonia, the loss of control over one's voice, the sudden inability to use one's voice, epitomised muteness as a form of language. Breuer's famous patient Anna O exhibited a catalogue of discursive disorders. Breuer observed that what triggered her loss of speech was mortifying fear, suppression of a remark or being unjustly accused of something (Freud and Breuer, 1895).

The status of the woman during the Renaissance was largely a continuation of the situation during the Middle Ages. Apart from a small number of books describing the special qualities and pursuits of the 'lady', there was no distinctive ideal of the lady in the Renaissance courtesy literature (Kelso, 1978). The principal handbook of aristocratic values of the period prescribing proper behaviour for both sexes was Castiglione's *The Book of the Courtier* (published in sixteenth-century Italy in 60 different editions, cf. Burke, 1995). While the courtly model defined virtues of grace, good manners, cleverness and prudence as principles of behaviour for both sexes, it did define some requirements specific to the lady. Unlike the gentleman she is required to be delightful and charming. Castiglione writes: 'just as he must show a certain solid and sturdy manliness, so it is seemly for a woman to have a soft and delicate tenderness, with an air of womanly sweetness' (King, 1991, p. 164). Here lay the foundation stone of defining feminine beauty as a necessity, not as an added bonus. The standards of manners and graces set for the woman in the Renaissance courtesy book included modesty, sensibility and courtesy, while wit, learning and knowledge were considered manly embellishments. As for the art of speech, the most common advice was simply to remain silent.

The Spanish humanist Juan Luis Vives, a firm advocate of the schooling of women (whose 1523 instruction manual was published in 40 editions, and translated into six languages) none the less recommended that the woman should not be concerned with rhetoric because

> that which a woman needs is probity and prudence; it is not unbecoming for a woman to be silent . . . most of the vices of women in our age and ages past . . . are the products of ignorance, since they never read nor heard those excellent sayings

and monitions of the Holy Fathers about chastity, about obedience, about silence.

(Vives, 1996, pp. 79, 83)

Thomas Becon observed that 'there is nothing that doth so commend,
avaunce, set forthe, adorne, decke, trim, and garnish a maid, as silence.
And this noble vertue may the virgins learne of that most holy, pure and
glorious virgin Mary' (1543, p. 532). Indeed, in the recommendations of
Barbaro writing in 1513, impeded speech becomes the model of ideal
speech 'by silence . . . women achieve the fame of eloquence' (1677 cited
in Kelso, 1978, p. 101).

Similar notes are echoed in much writing of the age. An Italian advises
that the speech of a girl be rare, slow and low, and that her lips remain
closed when she is silent. An Englishman declares

> my nature so much abhorreth a Woman of much tongue as I
> had rather have her infected with any of the seaven deadly
> sinnes . . . after all what has a woman to say that can delight a
> man? she can only complain, weep, threaten, or tell empty sto-
> ries . . . no pleasure but torment.

A Frenchman writing matrimonial guidance advises girls who want to
marry to reply humbly and in sweetness mixed with gravity and adorned
with prudence, weighing their words that nothing may be superfluous,
ambiguous, ill-intended, crude or derogatory (cited in Kelso, 1978, p.
287). And it is not just young girls who are advised on the virtues of
silence. The wise wife, wrote Bernardo Trotto (1578)

> never contradicts, even if right, never opposes, disputes, blames,
> interrupts, or answers back if chided. Silence is a great pre-
> server of love in husbands, who are thus not plagued by idle
> words but are listened to reverently when they wish to speak.
>
> (Trotto, 1578, p. 100; cited in Kelso, 1978, p. 417)

The recommendations for silence and temperance were extended to what
the woman is allowed to listen to, as well as to utter. She was prescribed
to 'listen to no vulgar tales . . . worldly follies, salacious suggestions . . . and
anything that might cause carnal desire' (Kelso, 1978, p. 52). Her purity
was to be guarded by men who are obliged to observe a measure of decorum in her company, in order not to offend her gentle constitution. In her
'essay in defense of the female sex', Mary Astell wrote how men modify
their speech in the presence of a lady to accommodate her delicate

nature: 'They . . . are very careful of the expression, that nothing harsh or obscene can escape 'em, that may shock a tender mind, or offend a modest ear' (cited in Curtin, 1987, p. 207). That these tenderness and delicacy were manufactured through a careful induction process was beside the point. Centuries of social habit create a well-rehearsed performance that becomes ingrained.

Furthermore, the Renaissance ideal of the lady as a locus of gentility and virtue (domestic idealism) was supplemented in the late eighteenth and nineteenth centuries as women were assigned the task of binding the family together (Gorham, 1982). This 'cult of domesticity' waned by the third quarter of the nineteenth century when models of femininity emerged which emphasised fashion and sociability. This change was facilitated by the growth of middle-class incomes which freed wives from domestic labour by allowing increased employment of servants. The extra time and money enabled the middle-class wife to pursue other domestic activities. It has also channelled her awakening desires for power into the innocuous spheres of fashion and leisure, where an illusion of power can substitute for real worldly power. Ladies constructed hierarchies of power, prestige and accomplishment out of the spheres of life available to them. Leisure was one of these (Curtin, 1987, p. 212).

An index of this change is the shift from the Renaissance courtesy book (which was mostly a masculine genre) to the genre of etiquette book. The etiquette book (detailing rules of conduct in the extra-domestic world) which flourished in this era, was largely a feminine genre (Curtin, 1987, chapter 8). The transition from courtesy to etiquette reflected the trivialisation of the genre of instruction books from a concern with morality to gentility, or from fundamental values to surface appearances; a dualism, alas, all too gendered.

Thus, the model for the lady contained the conflicting images of the domestic and the worldly. The conflict between the image of the fashionable lady and the domestic wife runs through ideals of femininity since Roman times. The Renaissance concept of the wife's role came intact from St Paul and the Church Fathers, and included a list of such virtues as obedience, patience, humility, modesty, chastity and temperance (Kelso, 1978, chapter 3). This was contrasted with the aristocratic model of a lady which blossomed in the Parisian salons. The salonière was a woman of letters, educated in the arts and dance, modest and graceful. She was an agent of morality and decorum, propriety and good manners. But she could also begin to command some of the advantages of her wealth and rank by occupying an active and public role as a leader of fashion and manners. Here she ran into another paradox, an inbuilt design law: what she was required to be was also that which she was condemned for being (Tseëlon, 1995a). The fashionable lady was praised for her elegance, gentility and natural beauty, yet engaging in fashion, artifice and sociability she constructed herself as an object of moral triviality, satire, and criticism.

Juan Luis Vives put it thus:

> Since extravagance in personal adornment is the particular fault of women, the good mother retrains her daughter and teaches how ugly it is for a chaste gentlewoman to dress like a prostitute who learns a different way every day of tricking herself out after the latest fashion to set off her beauty when the true adornments of a wife will be chastity, modesty, truth, silence, sobriety, love of husband and children, knowledge of how to conserve goods, spend wisely, and the like.
>
> (Vives, 1523/1783; cited in King, 1991, p. 47)

As is apparent from this sketchy account, feminine fashion, as one of the few outlets for feminine expression, had grown into a sort of language substitute. It came to occupy a space where the woman could exercise non-threatening forms of power and voice.

There is an interesting parallel between the prescriptions given to the woman with regard to words and to garments. In both cases she is advised to steer towards modesty and away from extravagance, as well as to economise on using words and exposing her flesh. Both words and garments are constructed as mirrors of the soul, and therefore as a measure of virtue and purity of mind. Identity of speech and clothes maps onto the identity of voice and body, since clothes, by their nature, index the body and gain meaning through association with bodily virtues and vices. Throughout the ages voice, particularly female voice, has been similarly embodied and eroticised. And if silence is invoked to counteract sexuality, politeness indexes submission to a social superior. That the female voice has been strait-jacketed or tight-laced is not only on account of its carnal, material qualities. Polite speech, one of the requirements of a lady, was not merely a feature of a Renaissance feminine ideal; it was (and widely is) also a recognised form of deference of the powerless towards the powerful, and as such reflects the power differential inherent in the phallocentric system (Holmes, 1995). 'Superiors', observed Curtin, 'commanded deference by their power, ladies were granted [chivalric] deference in their weakness' (1987, p. 270).

In their landmark socio-linguistic research on politeness, Brown and Levinson (1987) accounted for some systematic aspects of language usage. Relying on extensive ethnographic data from three disparate cultures and languages – English, Tzeltal (a Mayan language from a Mexican community) and south Indian Tamil – they were able to substantiate their predictions about cross-cultural universals. Their model posits a rational agent who would seek to achieve ends using appropriate means while saving face (of self and other). Brown and Levinson identify a number of variables which influence the choice of strategies, especially those involving potential loss of face. Those variables are: social distance, relative power and absolute ranking. From this perspective it is easy to see that the structural asymmetry inherent in gender relationships in patriarchy is such that women, as a group (although perhaps not always as individuals), occupy a subordinate position *vis-à-vis* men. Hence, their greater tendency to use prestige speech (Trudgill, 1972), or standard speech (Deuchar, 1988; Larson, 1982) or to acquire other status markers (Eckert, 1989) is part of a broader attempt by the socially marginalised (or aspiring) to symbolically attain respect *vis-à-vis* the socially dominant (or established). This goes beyond gender to class and ethnic relations, and the relationship with any type of Otherness.

I can summarise my survey so far by positing three models of female voice: proper, provocative and mute. Out of the vast range of cultural representations of femininity that exist, I have chosen, for each model, to elaborate a paradigmatic example.

Literal voices

Proper voice

The easiest voice to use as a guise is the least marked: that which is expected of a lady. It is the polite, gentle, non-challenging voice. It is described in the Renaissance courtesy manuals, and the religious and moralistic teachings from the Early Church through the Middle Ages. It also features in stories that build on the motif of the woman who is rewarded for her gentility and command of good manners. The handful of literary examples that come to mind are indicative of some representational strategies to impart the proper voice: bullying (as in George Bernard Shaw's *Pygmalion* and the film *My Fair Lady*), stigmatising (as in Leland's film *Wish You Were Here*), correcting (as in the film *Educating Rita*), blackmailing (as in Andersen's tale *The Little Mermaid*), patronising (as in Ibsen's play *A Doll's House*), ridiculing (as in cross-dressing films such as *Tootsie*, or *Some Like it Hot*).

Two screen adaptations of Shaw's *Pygmalion* where socially powerless women learn to speak from prestigious men will serve me as illustrations of the dynamics of the proper voice. In the first version of *Pygmalion*, *My*

Fair Lady, a flower girl becomes party to a professional competition between two linguistic experts, one of whom, Professor Higgins, stakes his reputation on his ability to teach her to 'talk like a lady' and to pass her off as one without being detected. Professor Higgins's interest in the common flower girl is initially purely professional. She is the raw material for a linguistic game. His treatment of her is dismissive and patronising. In his politically incorrect mind, Eliza's use of the language amounts to a criminal perversion. Eliza recognises with a basic instinct that, in a society whose values he represents, she would do better if she sang his tune. And she comes to him for elocution lessons. She comes to learn to exchange her native tongue for the kind of social mask that opens doors and influences people. And yet, in her puritanic persona she possesses more gentility than he possesses in his irreverent persona. Except that his mask is the one that commands social power. A similar, but more subtle version is contained in the second version of *Pygmalion*, the film *Educating Rita*, where a Cambridge don who drowns his feelings of personal inadequacy (as a husband and a poet) in drinking, is confronted with an eager Open University student.

She is a hairdresser who desires to move up socially, and comes to the Open University to study literature, expecting her troubled tutor, who she looks up to, to deliver the goods. Here it is the protagonist herself who derides her own voice as 'worthless'. Aware of her own inadequacy as far as the academic genre is concerned, she works hard and takes devastating criticism. Her tutor is more ambivalent, though. On the one hand, he knows what she lacks in order to communicate in an articulate fashion (one that would get her through her exams). On the other hand, he is charmed by her direct and original ways of looking at things. He knows that educating her means replacing her spontaneous mask with a more predictable one. Yet she insists. Like Eliza she craves the power and privilege that come with the currency of correct speech.

Provocative voice

This is daring speech which is manifested in erotic and sensual forms of feminine expression. It is found, for example, in the mythological sirens whose enchanted voices lure sailors to their ruin, or in the mythical Eve whose alluring voice is held responsible for Adam's Fall. Its contemporary archetypal example is probably the larger-than-life Diva whose voice is a source of erotic attraction for straight and queer desire (e.g. Abel, 1992). Daring voice can also refer to bad language. Bad language is the voice which is marked in the woman. Functioning like fetishism, it defends against the fantasy of castration with the fantasy of the phallic mother, which is usually maintained through items of clothing or in rare cases by female voice (Bunker, 1934). Dirty words are an aspect of what Michelson calls 'the myth of animality', naked power which, 'in the case of dirty words, it means the power to dare defy social conventions' (1993, p. 49). This explains the excitement produced by Lynda in the film *Wish You Were Here* (Leland, 1988), which depicts the struggles of a young girl growing up in the 1950s in a conservative British small town. It is about her struggle to find her own voice. Lynda (who is brought up by her father) shocks everybody by constantly using swear words. Her favourite expression, 'up your bum', sends out electric shock-waves. It leads to abuse by her father, and disgust/ desire by others. At one point her father is so outraged that he takes her to a psychiatrist in the hope of curing her. In a farcical scene the psychiatrist wants her to generate all the swearwords she knows in an alphabetical order. Her playful attitude contrasts sharply with his desperate attempts to get her to utter certain words she does not spontaneously volunteer, or to superimpose guilt upon her for uttering the words she does. This scene caricatures and captures the woman caught up in a double bind: disciplined to avoid the use of certain genres, while at the same time encouraged to use them to satisfy a perverse desire of those who appoint themselves custodians of 'proper ladyspeak' in the first place.

Mute voice

From the limited repertoire of choices of voices available silence emerges as a potent alternative. It is a complex speech containing contrary meanings. It is an exercise of power but also a charade of power. Lacking the edge of an open confrontation it causes tension, creating a foil on which the other's reactive response can be projected. Dumbness (as King Lear perceives it in Cordelia) can be seen as aggression. Recounting an incident where Ted Hughes's sister, Olwyn Hughes, made a critical comment towards Sylvia Plath to which Plath made no response but an unnerving stare, Janet Malcolm notes: 'Olwyn verbally attacks Plath, but Olwyn's words are only words; it is Plath's (Medusan) speechlessness that is the deadly, punishing weapon' (Malcolm, 1993, p. 49). Mute voice is marked as a feminine register in nineteenth-century folk-tales and contemporary fiction. The figure of the woman who surrenders her voice is a common motif in The Grimm Brothers' tales and also appears in Hans Christian Andersen's 'The Wild Swans' (about a princess who takes an oath to keep silent in order to avert a magic spell, or for fear of retribution). She also appears in Andersen's tale of 'The Little Mermaid' who sacrificed her voice in exchange for love and eternal soul. She features in Offenbach's *Tales of Hoffman* as Antonia, Hoffman's third love whose illness prevents her from singing; when she chooses to sing (despite her lover's and father's objections) she loses her life. She is encoded in many of Isak Dinesen's tales, the author (herself a woman – Karen Blixen) – who has chosen to sound her own voice under a male mask. In her story 'The Dreamers' (1963) the heroine, an opera singer who lost her voice in the middle of a performance spends her life living incognito and becomes the elusive object of desire for three storytellers: a mythical image that also contains, as Walter Benjamin suggests such images always do, something of both the utopian and the cynical (Horton, 1995, p. 126). The silent woman is also encoded in the Hollywood icon of the dumb blonde as the cultural fantasy of what Magritte depicted in his painting 'collective invention', an inverted mermaid.

Figurative voices

In my book (Tseëlon, 1995a) I argue that core cultural prescriptions which defined the Western woman through the centuries are echoed in the contemporary discourse of the role of body, beauty and clothes in 'the feminine'. On the basis of my own research as well as my observations of media and everyday life I want to suggest that the same models I identified with regard to voice (proper, provocative, mute) apply to sartorial strategies.

Proper voice, like dressing the part, carries very little personal information. It is 'dressed for the occasion' and subdues personal expression behind a 'front' of some form of (formal or informal) uniform, a business suit or other conventional and 'safe' solution. By blending in with the background it avoids calling attention to the wearer, it plays up belonging over individuality, and social awareness over creativity. By following the script of social expectations one's own position is masked. The photographs of Sylvia Plath in various biographies show how, with her 'shining blond hair and her soft, round face, she evokes the soap and deodorant advertisements of the 1940s and 1950s in which the words "dainty" and "fresh" never failed to appear' (Malcolm, 1993, p. 34). Yet, it was only through shedding this American suburban image of neatness and freshness observes Janel Malcolm, that 'her wicked wit could flourish and her writing could break out of the caul of obedient mannerism that encased its early examples'. Safely away in 'harsh England' she wrote *The Bell Jar*. 'She could not have written it in her native Massachusetts. The pitiless voice of the *Ariel* poet was a voice that had rid itself of its American accent' (*ibid.*, p. 53).

It is through deviance not conformity that personal information can be revealed. Provocative voice relates to sexy dressing but also to subversion and outrage (from punk and grunge to piercing and tattooing). It is designed to shock, to stir, to antagonise, to draw a smile – or simply to provoke a reaction, any reaction. If appearing gauche is the dread of the proper voice, being unnoticed is the dread of the provocative one. The provocative voice may just be following a trend, but its mode of deviance still indicates a form of role distance from a social performance.

Mute voice signals the desire to be present and absent at the same time; the wish to suppress a desire the wearer dare not display. It wears baggy shapeless clothes that do not define the body contours (and in some societies these include veils) and do not call attention to bodily presence either because of embarrassment (as is the case with adolescent girls) or shame (as is the case with the grotesque body) or 'civil disobedience', which has neither the desire to go along with prescribed codes nor the power or courage of defiance.

Epilogue: from the woman to the fool

Closer examination reveals that underlying the representations of those feminine discursive strategies is a specific feminine anxiety. The fear of the unruly, uncontainable and disorderly feminine body. This is evident through a range of cultural institutions (providing such services as working out, slimming diets and surgical make-overs) representing a (Western) cultural obsession with defeating ageing (Bauman, 1992) and controlling the body. The feminine perspective on this trend echoes a particular sort of feminine anxiety (about falling short of a model of perfection, see Tseëlon, 1989; Tseëlon, 1995a, p. 61) of 'letting oneself go' thus revealing the grotesque body (Russo, 1986).

According to Bakhtin's reading of Rabelais' satire as a carnivalesque text, the grotesque body is a body in a process of becoming: 'it is never finished, never completed; it is continually built, created and builds and creates another body' (1984, p. 317). The logic of the grotesque, according to Bakhtin, is not concerned with the closed and smooth surface of the body. It is interested only is those parts of the body which protrude beyond the body's surface and limits. The grotesque body is unruly, protruding, excessive. It deviates from the norm, as Russo argues, by creating a space of risk and abjection (1995). As a quintessential site of transgression and disorder, the female body shares a pedigree with another marginal carnivalesque figure, that of the carnival fool. The fool's body represents the spectre of the grotesque body that the female body dreads. Just like the female body, the fool's body violates the image of the classical body.

The fool is mentally and physically deformed, his dress is lumpish and motley. His manner is inappropriate, uncoordinated, clumsy, chaotic. He transgresses boundaries unawares. He represents the extreme end of the strategies of self-expression. Because of his mental inadequacy his speech is regarded as nonsense, as close to meaning as silence 'Many fools babble as though speaking in tongues, others, like mimes are mute' (Willeford, 1969, p. 29). The fool's costume is made of patches of cloth in incongruous colours, and is shapeless in form. His disproportionate appearance creates a shapeless comic effect. It signifies the 'spirit of disorder' and the 'principle of motley'. When a garment is perceived as separate from the body it is no longer regarded as an expression of the person, but acquires a mechanico-grotesque effect 'the fool is "pure transgression" . . . because he appears to lack a body', says Terry Eagelton (1986). Indeed, the fool's disguise, however baggy, is meant to draw attention to his deformity, not to mask it behind an illusion of 'normality'. His costume has an affinity with chaos, achieved through the breaking of forms and conventions and by choosing from contemporary fashions those exaggerated elements that match his character. His emblematic costume borrows from Middle Ages' fashion: it consists of multi-coloured tunic and leggings, cloak, and a cap with ass's ears decorated with bells. By his breach of conventions, his dress (like that of servants' cast-offs), stands outside fashion (Laver, 1969). This style of dress started off as a courtly hunting fashion, moved to hunters and foresters, then to craftsmen and common soldiers, and finally to lunatics and fools. The bells which characterise the fool's cap belonged initially to men's extravagant fashion, perhaps originating from Persian kings, coming to Europe through bishops, becoming a common aristocratic and royal accessory. They were attached to necklaces, belts, arms and shoe tips. The ruff began as an extravagant courtly fashion, and ended as part of the emblematic costume of Pierrot. Unlike servants, whose outdated style affirms fashion's rule, the fool's is an anarchic comment, an outmoded anachronistic space in the midst of a dynamic fashion system (Belkin, 1975; 1982).

As borderline figures the woman and the buffoon share other characteristics as well. Both are themselves objects of ridicule. The comic actor and the drag comedian use comic elements as raw materials in their performance, but the real buffoon or the real woman they allude to *are* the real joke. Barbieri, writing in the seventeenth century about improvised comic performance defines the difference thus:

> In both comedy and buffoonery laughter is laughter, but in comedy it is provoked by a misunderstanding or a witty remark, while in buffoonery it is produced more by excessive nimbleness: the one has as its goal instruction to virtuous conduct, the other is concerned more to ridicule human beings . . . The buffoon is

himself actually a buffoon; but the actor who plays a comic role only pretends to be a buffoon, and for that reason wears a mask, or false beard, or make-up that he may appear to be another.

(in Richards and Richards, 1990, p. 205)

Both embody a paradox: a synthesis of irreconcilable opposites; the impossibility of existing as one thing and its opposite (Handelman, 1981; Tseëlon, 1995b). Both are hideously attractive: they induce horror and fascination, approach and avoidance. Their intermediary position between order and chaos (like that of monsters, mermaids etc.) – nonsense and wisdom – is expressed in the woman in the dynamic oscillation between contrasting modes of appearance and voice (Madonna/whore). They both play with fantasy. In addition to being figures of fun, the woman and the fool inhabit a position that anyone can fall into if caught off guarded. What is so threatening about them is that we all recognise ourselves in them. We can all 'make a fool of ourselves' or 'let ourselves go'. Are they threatening because we feel that we could easily and comfortably look like them if we did not consciously cultivate a front with powerful, rational and realistic components?

The fool combines elements of all three voices I identified with regard to speaking and dressing. Like the proper voice, he is funny in the expected manner of the buffoon. Like the provocative voice, his speech is subversive. Being on the darker side of consciousness, where intuition and magical thought are active, sometimes fools are attributed with divine or demonic inspiration – the wisdom of the sage.

His ambivalence is expressed in his mute voice, signified literally in the quality of the double. Sometimes he appears in pairs (like Papageno and Papagena in *The Magic Flute*, Tweedledum and Tweedledee in *Through the Looking Glass*, and Arlecchino and Brighella in the *Commedia dell'arte*, where one is the fool, the other is the wit). This duality is also expressed in his costume, with symmetrical mirroring of contrasting elements (Willeford, 1969).

As archetypal 'Others', both the woman and the fool provide a unique point of view of the society on which they depend but to which they don't quite belong.

The analogy I have drawn between the woman and the fool reinforces their identity as society's quintessential 'Others'. Their ambivalent quality is inherent in this position of 'Other', the outsider within, whose observations, by their very being, offer an insight and a discomfort. In this, they share some fundamental features with the mask whose otherness is part of its unending charm. In their bodies and in their perspectives, the woman and the fool threaten to reveal the secrets of social performance: to reveal that the emperor actually wears no clothes.

169

REFERENCES

Abel, Sam (1997) *Opera in the flesh: Sexuality in operatic performance*, Boulder, CO, Westview Press.

Andersen, Hans-Christian (1976) 'The little mermaid', in *80 Fairy-Tales*, Odense, Denmark, Hans Reitzels (originally published 1846).

Ardener, Edwin (1975) 'Belief and the problem of women', in *Perceiving women* (ed. Ardener, S.), London, Malaby Press.

Augustine, Saint (1992) *Confessions*, 3 vols (ed. O'Donnell James J.), Oxford, Clarendon Press.

Bakhtin, Mikhail (1984) *Rabelais and his world* (trans. Iswolsky, H.), Bloomington, Indiana University Press (originally published 1965).

Barbaro, Francesco (1677) *Directions for love and marriage*, 2 vols, London, John Leigh (originally published 1513).

Barbieri, Niccolò (1971) *La Supplica, discorso famigliare di Niccolo Barbieri detto Beltrame diretto a coloro che scrivendo o parlando trattano de' comici trascurando i meriti delle azzioni virtuose* (trans. Richards, Kenneth and Richards, Laura), Milan, F. Taviani (originally published in Venice, 1634).

Barker, Francis, Hulme, Peter and Iverson, Margaret (ed.) (1994) *Colonial discourse/postcolonial theory*, Manchester, Manchester University Press.

Barthes, Roland (1975) *The pleasure of the text* (trans. Miller Richard), New York, Hill & Wang.

Bauman, Zygmunt (1992) *Mortality, immortality, and other life strategies*, Cambridge, Polity.

Becon, Thomas (1543 [0r 1546]) *The christen state of matrimonye*, (trans, Bullinger, Heinrich), London, John Gough.

Belkin, Ahuva (1975) *'Aspects of the fool's appearance'*, unpublished MA thesis, Department of Theatre, Tel Aviv University.

Belkin, Ahuva (1982) *'A study in the iconographical Non Est Deus development of the historiated initial to Psalm 52'*, unpublished Ph.D. thesis, Department of Theatre, Tel-Aviv University.

Bergler, Edmund (1936) 'Obscene words', *Psychoanalytic Quarterly* 5, 226–48.

Brown, Penelope and Levinson, Stephen (1987) *Politeness: Some universals in language usage*, Cambridge, Cambridge University Press.

Bunker, Henry Alden, Jr. (1934) 'The voice as (female) phallus', *Psychoanalytic Quarterly* 3, 391–429.

Burke, Peter (1995) *Fortunes of the courtier: European reception of Castiglione's 'Cortegiano'*, Cambridge, Polity.

Cameron, Deborah (ed.) (1998) *The feminist critique of language: A reader*, 2nd edn, London, Routledge.

Clément, Catherine (1989) *Opera, or the undoing of women* (trans. Wing, Betsy), London: Virago.

Coates, Jennifer (1993) *Women, men and language: A sociolinguistic account of gender differences*, 2nd edn, London, Longman.

Crawford, Mary (1995) *Talking difference: On gender and language*, London, Sage.

Curtin, Michael, (1987) *Propriety and position: A study of Victorian manners*, New York, Garland.

170

Deuchar, Margaret (1988) 'A pragmatic account of women's use of standard speech', in *Women in their speech communities* (ed. Coates, Jennifer and Cameron, Deborah) London, Longman.

Dinesen, Isak (1963) *Seven Gothic tales*, London, Penguin (originally published 1934).

Disher, M. Willson (1968) *Clowns and pantomimes*, New York, Benjamin Blom (originally published 1923).

Dolar, Mladen (1996) 'The object voice', in *Gaze and voice as love objects* (ed. Salecl, Renata and Žižek, Slavoj) Durham, NC, Duke University Press.

Eagelton, Terry (1986) *William Shakespeare*, Oxford, Blackwell.

Eckert, Penelope (1989) 'The whole woman: Sex and gender differences in variation', *Language variation and change* 1, 245–68.

Eilberg-Schwartz, Howard (1995) 'The nakedness of a woman's voice, the pleasure in a man's mouth: an oral history of ancient Judaism', in *Off with her head: The denial of women's identity in myth, religion, and culture* (ed. Eilberg-Schwartz, Howard and Doniger, Wendy), Berkeley, California University Press.

Foucault, Michel (1980) *The history of sexuality, vol. 1: An introduction* (trans. Hurley, Robert), New York, Vintage.

Freud, Sigmund and Breuer, Joseph (1895) *Studies on hysteria*, vol. 2, in *The standard edition of the complete psychological works of Sigmund Freud* (ed. and trans. Strachey, James), London, Hogarth Press, 1953–86.

Gordon, Richard A. (1990) *Anorexia and bulimia: Anatomy of a social epidemic*, Oxford, Blackwell.

Gorham, Deborah (1982) *The Victorian girl and the feminine ideal*, London, Croom Helm.

Handelman, Don (1981) 'The ritual clown: Attributes and affinities', *Anthropos* 76, 321–70.

Holmes, Janet (1995) *Women, men and politeness*, London, Longman.

Horton, Susan (1995) *Difficult women, artful lives: Olive Schreiner and Isak Dinesen, in and out of Africa*, Baltimore, MD, John Hopkins University Press.

Hughes, Geoffrey (1991) *Swearing: A social history of foul language, oaths and profanity in English*, Oxford, Blackwell.

Kelso, Ruth (1978) *Doctrine for the lady of the Renaissance*, Urbana, IL, Illinois University Press (originally published 1956).

King, Margaret L. (1991) *Women of the Renaissance*, Chicago, Chicago University Press.

Klapisch-Zuber, Christiane (1992) 'Silences of the Middle Ages', in *A history of women in the West*, London, The Belknap Press of Harvard University Press.

Kramarae, Cheris (1981) *Women and men speaking*, Rowley, MA, Newbury House.

Kristeva, Julia (1980) *Desire in language: A semiotic approach to literature and art*, (trans. Gora, Thomas, Jardine, Alice and Roudiez, Leon S.), New York, Columbia University Press.

Larson (1982) 'Role playing and the real thing: socialisation and standard speech in Norway', *Journal of Anthropological Research* 38, 401–10.

Laver, James (1969) *Modesty in dress: An inquiry into the fundamentals of fashion*, London, Heinemann.

Leland, David (1988) *Wish you were here*, London, Faber & Faber.

Locke, Ralph P. (1995) 'What are these women doing in opera?', in *En travesti: Women, gender subversion, opera* (ed. Blackmer, Corrinne E. and Smith, Patricia Juliana), New York, Columbia University Press.

Malcolm, Janet (1993) *The silent woman: Sylvia Plath & Ted Hughes*, London, Vintage.

Michelson, Peter (1993) *A poetics of obscenity*, Albany, State University of New York Press.

Nietzsche, Freidrich (1987) *Beyond good and evil*, Harmondsworth, Penguin (originally published 1886).

Poizat, Michel (1992) *The angel's cry: Beyond the pleasure principle in opera* (trans. Denner, Arthur), Ithaca, NY, Cornell University Press.

Régnier-Bohler, Danielle (1992) 'Literary and mystical voices', in *A history of women in the West, vol. II: Silences of the Middle Ages* (ed. Klapisch-Zuber, Christiane), Cambridge, MA, Harvard University Press.

Richards, Kenneth and Richards, Laura (1990) *The Commedia dell'Arte: A documentary history*, Oxford, Blackwell for the Shakespeare Head Press.

Robinson, Paul (1989) 'It's not over till the soprano dies', *NY Times Book Review*, January 1, p. 3.

Russo, Mary (1986) 'Female grotesque: Carnival and theory', in *Feminist studies critical studies* (ed. de Lauretis, Teresa), Bloomington, Indiana University Press

Russo, Mary (1995) *The female grotesque: Risk, excess and modernity*, London, Routledge.

Shaw, George Bernard (1965) *Pygmalion*, Harmondsworth, Penguin (originally published, 1916).

Showalter, Elaine (1987) *The female malady*, London, Virago.

Silverman, Kaja (1988), *The acoustic mirror: The female voice in psychoanalysis and cinema*, Bloomington and Indianapolis, Indiana University Press.

Spender, Dale (1980) *Man-made language*, London, Routledge & Kegan Paul.

Tannen, Deborah (1996) *Gender and discourse*, Oxford, Oxford University Press.

Trotto, Bernardo (1578) *Dialoghi de matrimonio, e vita vedovile del signor C. A. Bernardo Trotto*, Turino, Francesco Dolce.

Trudgill, Peter (1972) 'Sex, covert prestige, and linguistic change in urban British English of Norwich', *Language in Society* 1, 179–95.

Tseëlon, Efrat (1989) '*Communicating via clothes*', unpublished Ph.D. thesis, University of Oxford.

Tseëlon, Efrat (1992) 'Self presentation through appearance: A manipulative vs. a dramaturgical approach', *Symbolic Interaction* 15, 501–14.

Tseëlon, Efrat (1995a) *The masque of femininity: The presentation of woman in everyday life*, London, Sage.

Tseëlon, Efrat (1995b) 'The little mermaid: An icon of the woman condition in patriarchy, and the human condition of castration', *The International Journal of Psycho-Analysis* 7, 76, 1017–30.

Vives, Juan Luis (1996) *The Education of a Christian Woman*, (trans. Fantazzi, C.), Leiden, Brill (originally published, 1523).

Weich, Martin (1989) 'The fetishistic use of speech', *International Journal of Psycho-Analysis* 70, 245–53.

Welsford, Enid (1968) *The fool: His social and literary history*, London, Faber & Faber (originally published 1935).

Willeford, William (1969) *The fool and his sceptre*, London, Edward Arnold.

Wodak, Ruth (1998) *Gender and discourse*, London, Sage.

Yegenoglu, Meyda (1998) *Colonial fantasies: Towards a feminist reading of orientalism*, Cambridge, Cambridge University Press.

Young, Robert (1995) *Hybridity in theory, culture and race*, London, Routledge.

INDEX